Fools & Babies

Tee Madden

For Africa to me... is more than a glamorous fact. It is a historical truth. No man can know where he is going unless he knows exactly where he has been and exactly how he arrived at his present place.

— Maya Angelou, 1972

I dedicate this book to my family and friends of Western North Carolina during my youth.

To my five children, nine grandchildren, and six great-grandchildren.

To the Stephens-Lee High School Class of 1965, and all the praise to GOD for blessing me with the people involved in raising me to become who I am today.

Asheville, you ROCKED!

My great-grandmama told my grandmama the part she lived through that my grandmama didn't live through and my grandmama told my mama what they both lived through and my mama told me what they all lived through and we were suppose to pass it down like that from generation to generation so we'd never forget.

Gayl Jones, 1975

CONTENTS

CHAPTER I

MOMMA, I MADE IT! RIGHT?

Jesse Ray Jr.
"Butch"

Tierron LaVon Madden
"Tee"

Robert Foster Jr.
"Robert Jr"

" **A**s you travel the highway of life, there will be obstacles too wide—you can't go around them; too high—you can't go over them; and too big—you can't move them. These are the times that try a man's soul."

The words of Mr. Belton, the Principal of Stephens-Lee High School, reached out to me as I sat with my cap and gown on, waiting for the piece of paper that said I had successfully completed my learning requirements.

This should have been the happiest day of my life. So why was I feeling so confused and filled with doubt?

I had achieved my grandparents' dream of graduating from Stephens-Lee High School. I was the first Madden to graduate from her walls. Momma dropped out of school in the twelfth grade to have me. Uncle June, my mother's younger brother, dropped out of high school to join the Navy. My father, C. Ray, a World War II veteran and the city playboy, graduated from Stephens-Lee High School—but he wasn't a Madden.

This was a very auspicious occasion, indeed, and I couldn't help but wonder how Momma would have felt to achieve this milestone. My mother, Delores, was a majorette at Stephens-Lee. I would always look at her majorette pictures with pride. Momma was so beautiful and seemed so happy with her snow-white teeth, which appeared even whiter than her uniform. She wore white knee-high boots that enhanced her long, superbly shaped legs. She looked so young, innocent, and filled with the youthfulness of a high school teenager.

Delores Costella Madden (in the middle)

My favorite picture is the one where she is standing on one leg, leaning back with her other leg arched high in the air, with her baton nestled in her long, slender arms.

She was poised for greatness.

Then I came along and messed everything up for her.

I was born on August 6, 1947, exactly two years after the atomic bomb was dropped on Hiroshima, Japan, on August 6, 1945.

I was raised by my grandparents—the Reverend Arthur Robert Madden and Liler Brite Madden. My grandmother, who we called Nannie, would say, "Tierron, you can be the President of the United States with a high school diploma."

But getting a diploma was not a problem for me. I passed all of my courses with a seventy percent average or higher, yet I didn't feel equipped in the slightest to become the President of the United States after receiving my high school diploma. I'm not taking anything away from my teachers, but I felt as if I graduated from high school with only a ninth-grade level of education.

Everyone called the Reverend "Lil Daddy" because he was about five foot two. I called him Daddy because he was my daddy. He wanted me to become a minister and continue in his steps. I wanted no part of leading the flock; I wanted to be a free spirit like my father, as Nannie often said he was.

As Mr. Belton finished his speech, I could see tears of joy and sorrow from my classmates. Most of us had been together since the first grade and had known each other most of our lives.

When my name was called—Tierron LaVon Madden—I stood up like a toy soldier and marched to the stage. I walked with the pride of a conqueror, and, in that moment, Alexander the Great didn't have anything on me.

As I approached Mr. Belton, he smiled. He handed me the diploma with one hand and shook my hand with the other. I returned his smile as I received my document of accomplishment, or should I say completion. I favored the latter.

I continued my victory march to my seat, and I could see Daddy, Nannie, and Momma with tears of joy in their eyes. How good it felt to see them happy!

I always thought I was a burden and that the best thing for me to do was to get out of Dodge City after graduation. Yet, I was at a crossroads. I did not know which highway to take, let alone how to move the obstacles in my way.

When I looked at my classmates receiving their diplomas, I saw young adults instead of teenagers. I was looking at my classmates growing up right in front of me. I saw the same pride in their walk as I felt in mine.

When the last recipient sat down, Mr. Belton said, in his most masculine voice, "I present the 1965 graduating class of Stephens-Lee High School. May God be with you."

After the applause and cheers subsided, the pianist pressed the keys, and we stood in unison. She pressed the keys again, and the students from the even rows turned right while those of us in the odd rows made a left face. The final key was pressed, and we started marching into the aisles, exiting the Asheville City Auditorium. We could have beaten the United States Army drill team that day when the pianist began playing "Pomp and Circumstance." We moved to the beat of the music, and I knew this was the ending of one life and the beginning of another. As I reached the exit, I felt tears rolling down my face. I didn't know if they were tears of joy or tears of sorrow.

CHAPTER 2

SOUTHSIDE

Grandpa Reese, Grandma Mary, Nannie, and Nannie's brothers

Asheville is situated on a plateau in Western North Carolina, nestled within the Blue Ridge Mountains. The French Broad River flows directly through the center of the city.

My family, paternal and maternal, comes from Northeastern South Carolina.

(Paternal family) Bertha Lee, Bertha, Inez, Queen, Dan, Jessie, Lemont, Howard, C. Ray, Will Ray

(Maternal family) Daddy Bill, Momma, Nannie, Daddy

I was born and raised on Congress Street, right off Southside Avenue. That entire section of Asheville was known as "Southside." There was a branch of water that bordered most of Southside and emptied into the French Broad River. We called it the "Nasty Branch" because it was the neighborhood dump.

As a child growing up, this was one of our playgrounds. I would always wear Momma's old white majorette boots while wading through the water. Most of the time, we walked on our hands through about three feet of water—that was what we called swimming. Believe it or not, none of us got any illnesses or diseases from playing in the polluted water.

Sometimes, when it rained, the water would crest to the top of the sidewalls. This was the part of the branch that bordered Congress Street. It had brick walls and a solid cement bridge.

The walls were about ten to thirteen feet high, and the branch was about thirty-five feet wide, give or take.

Southside had a reputation for being the bad section of town. It had its share of killings, shootings, and stabbings. There were plenty of black-owned businesses—nightclubs, restaurants, pool halls, and grocery stores. There were also many illegal enterprises, such as number rackets, bootlegger houses, and after-hour joints. You could do yourself some damage if you were in the wrong place at the wrong time.

There seemed to be a church on every street corner on Southside. Every Sunday after church, herds of pretty girls would walk the streets showing off their dresses and freshly made hairdos.

Momma was a beautician and owned an eight-booth beauty salon called Venus House of Beauty until she got sick. She had a nervous breakdown from which she never fully recovered.

I can remember my mother talking to herself. When I asked her about it, she said she was talking to God, so I started talking to Him myself. He is a great listener.

Momma married William Collette, who I called Daddy Bill. He was tall, dark, and handsome. Daddy Bill wore a Clark Gable mustache and was a sharp dresser. He had a wardrobe that would put most movie stars to shame. I remember he used to wear this brown silk chalk-stripe double-breasted suit, giving him the appearance of a chocolate Clark Gable. Daddy Bill stood about six foot one and had the body of a Greek god. He was a superb swimmer and was one of the few swimming instructors at Walton Street Park. My mother had good taste in men.

Cookie, Momma, Connie

Momma and Daddy Bill had two girls, Connie and Cookie. I was two and five years their senior. Nannie and Daddy Bill did not get along because Nannie blamed Momma's condition on him. I couldn't show him too much affection because Nannie still ran the show. Still, Daddy Bill would introduce me as his son. Every now and then, he would drop me a couple of dollars, which helped secure our relationship. I always thought that Daddy Bill and Momma made a good couple, but I also believed that C. Ray and Momma were the ideal couple, even though he was on his second marriage.

Daddy and Nannie

My grandparents, the Reverend and Mrs. Madden, were devout Christians. There was no rock 'n' roll played in the house and, of course, no dancing allowed. I sometimes used my friend's record player in my room and listened to the Motown sound, especially Little Stevie Wonder, The Temptations, and The Supremes. I loved to dance and sing along with the artists on my twelve-transistor radio under the bed covers. I would just imagine that I was a Mandingo Warrior because Grandpa, Nannie's daddy, said that his family came from the Ivory Coast. He was Mandingo, and that makes me Mandingo.

Sometimes, I would swing dance with a doorknob and show Bill Robinson a thing or two. For the slow records, I would dance with the broom while thinking about Annette Funicello (a Disney Musketeer), Florence Ballard (one of The Supremes), or Mae (my aunt's sister).

Annette Funicello was the only Musketeer I really liked. She was a living doll and my slow-drag partner. I'll bet if she knew how close we were, she would have forgotten about Frankie Avalon. Sometimes, while listening to Jackie Wilson or Little Anthony and The Imperials, I imagined I was holding one of the many pretty girls I had a crush on but was too shy and bashful to tell them. I had a wild and wonderful imagination.

CHAPTER 3

SECRETS IN
THE SHEETS

1 0 Congress Street was God's second home. There were no cards or card playing. "Lie" was a bad word. Nannie was always 99.9% right, and only God was 100% right. Nannie was the strong arm of the law. She could whip with one hand and cook dinner with the other. She was a professional ass-whipper.

The first verse I learned from the Good Book was, "Spare the rod and spoil the child."

And believe me, there were no spoiled kids in our house. I should know because I averaged about three whippings a week, give or take a whipping.

You see, Nannie whipped and talked and whipped and talked until she got tired, and she was long-winded.

I remember one particular time when Nannie and Daddy came back from a week-long revival meeting in Jacksonville, Florida. That was before Momma and the girls moved in with us, and I had the whole house to myself.

I had my girlfriend, Sissy, and my friend, Bobby, over. We were messing around on the piano. Bobby could play Gospel as well as jazz songs. Every now and then, Bobby would kick in a little jazz and hope Nannie wouldn't catch on.

I was especially proud of the house because I cleaned it from top to bottom, especially Nannie and Daddy's bedroom. Or so I thought.

Bobby was mixing the Gospel and jazz songs up, Sissy was under my arm, and we were swaying to the rhythm of the beat. The music was hypnotizing and had us in a trance. Then came this loud, belligerent war cry from my grandparents' bedroom.

"TIERRON!!!!"

I had never heard Nannie use that tone of voice before.

We all jumped back a couple of feet when she marched in, ready to spring at me. Her eyes were dark and cold, turning devil red. The first thing that came to my mind was to run because it looked like Nannie was about to kill me.

I had no idea what was going on.

By this time, my friends were about five feet away from the piano. I was leaning on the side of the high-back piano, trying to be cool, but I was as terrified as a fly caught in a spider web awaiting death.

"Tierron, what is this?"

Nannie stood by the opposite end of the piano. Her voice had lowered but was still menacing.

"What, Nannie?"

I tried not to show my fear of this five-foot Goliath.

"Tierron, do you think I'm a fool?"

"No, ma'am, you're not a fool. I just don't know what you're talking about,"

I used my most boyish voice, still leaning against the piano with my right arm resting on the top.

Nannie held a condom in full view. It was partially wrapped in a piece of newspaper. She was holding it with her thumb and index finger; her arm was fully extended as she moved toward me with her nose high in the air like she was carrying dog shit.

Nannie screamed, "What the devil is this thing doing in my and your grandfather's bed?"

She narrowed her eyes in disgust. Nannie was so close I could smell what she ate for breakfast.

"I'm sorry, Nannie! It won't happen again."

I couldn't look her in the eye. I knew I had messed up and I was ashamed of what I had done. When I looked at Bobby, who was trying to hide his amusement, I could see his initial fear had subsided; he was enjoying this.

Sissy had sat down on the couch and was obviously mad.

Now why is she so mad?

Then it dawned on me. Sissy was not involved in this.

I was up the creek without a paddle. I couldn't come up with a good answer, but I knew Nannie was going upside my head if I didn't come up with an answer soon. The only thing that came out of my mouth was a repeat of what I had just said.

"I am so sorry, Nannie. It won't happen again."

Well, I shouldn't have said that because all hell broke loose. Bobby burst out laughing, Sissy started crying, and Nannie started swinging. I wanted to save face in front of my girl, if I still had either after this.

I braced myself for the inevitable. Nannie began raining blows on me as God rained on Noah's ark. I was getting hit upside the head and shoulders, and the more I ducked her punches, the more accurate she got.

Then the pain started, but I refused to run. I had to be a man and take this ass-whipping. So, I gritted my teeth and balled my fists. Then I closed my eyes in anticipation of more pain. Well, I shouldn't have done that either.

"Oh, you are a man now? You're going to hit me?" Nannie asked, raising her voice in anger.

Before I could correct the situation, she gave me a blow that could have knocked out Joe Louis. It was getting too hot for me. I saw my pride run first, then my honor took off in hot pursuit. Finally, that manhood I thought I possessed was running down the steps to the front yard. I could hear Bobby laughing his ass off and Sissy telling Nannie to hit me again.

Nannie made me clean up her room for about a week after that, which also included mopping and waxing the floors in her room, the living room, and the hallway.

That was just one of the many whippings I received from Nannie, but regardless of how many whippings I got from her, I always knew she loved me.

Daddy, on the other hand, was totally different. He was a lecturer and could talk to you about the do's and don'ts of life for hours. Daddy never looked you in the eye. His eyes were always focused on the ceiling or the floor. Most of the time, I preferred the whippings over the lectures. I never got a whipping from Daddy. In fact, I never even remember him getting mad or angry.

I do remember another one of the many whippings I received from Nannie though.

On this occasion, I left the yard to play football with my friends on Southside, down below Southside Apartments—something I was forbidden to do. As we were playing, I heard Nannie's voice.

"Tierron!"

My friends laughed and mocked Nannie as her voice got louder. She was coming up Southside with a leather belt in her hand, wearing an apron and headscarf. Seeing her crossing the street, about eighty yards away, I immediately dropped the football and went to the opposite side of the street. Although I was moving in her direction, I still needed some distance between us.

"Nannie, I'm coming, I'm coming!"

I was pleading for her to go home as I didn't want to be embarrassed and whipped in front of my friends. When she heard me, she crossed back over Southside marching like a Roman gladiator ready to slay some Christians. I was still pleading with her as I crossed to the opposite side again.

There were two cars coming, one on the left side of the street and one on the right side of the street. An approaching car was coming up, and that is when I took the opportunity to run, knowing Nannie was blocked both ways.

I got home about two to three minutes before she walked in the door. I was hoping she was tired after climbing the steps, but she wasn't. I started pleading my case and begging for forgiveness, but with one Bruce Lee move, she reached down, picked up a tree limb from the couch, and made a 180-degree spin that caught me across the upper chest and shoulder down my back.

The sound that came from my body, and the pain!

"Shit! That hurt, Nannie!"

Daddy said, "Watch your mouth, young man!"

"Daddy! Nannie hit me in the eye." I cried.

Nannie just kept swinging as she shouted, "Tierron, I didn't hit you in the eye!"

I ran to Daddy, who was at his desk in the bedroom preparing for Sunday's sermon. I was holding my eye with one hand and grabbing Daddy's arm with the other. Nannie hadn't lost a step because she was still swinging.

"Oh! Daddy, Nannie hit me in the eye and it hurts so bad!"

Daddy got up and stood between us, slowing down Nannie's assault on my ass.

"Now Liler, you done hit him in the eye. Don't you think he's had enough?"

"Rev, I didn't hit him in the eye," she snapped back.

"Yes, you did, Nannie! I can't see. I think it's bleeding! Daddy, make her stop!" I cried.

With one hand, Nannie jerked me from my protection. Then she really started her mission of pain. I was still holding my eye and pleading with Daddy.

Daddy grabbed Nannie's arm. "Now Liler," he said, putting more bass in his voice. "Enough is…"

He was not even able to complete his sentence. Nannie turned me loose and with one quick move, turned around and hit Daddy across the upper arm and back. Daddy went one way, and I went the other. Needless to say, that was the last time Daddy interfered with Nannie's disciplinary practices.

Nannie was tough, but I wouldn't have traded her or Daddy for the world.

My high school diploma meant everything to Nannie. She framed and hung it in her bedroom. When I graduated, Nannie and Daddy threw a party for me. The dinner was a feast befitting a king, or should I go one step further and say a dinner for the gods. We had four different meats: stuffed pork chops, southern fried chicken, a shoulder roast, and a ten-pound ham. They served fresh green beans, potato salad, candied yams, along with lettuce, tomatoes, and onions from Nannie's garden. There was also rice and gravy with hot rolls and ice-cold lemonade. For dessert, Daddy made two sweet potato pies. Nannie made a banana pudding, a German chocolate cake, and her prize-winning pound cake.

Liler Brite Chriswell Madden "Nannie"

I invited a couple of my friends. Johnny "Slab" Bailey (my best friend) and I brought dates, and they had a great time. Nannie even suggested that my date was marriage material.

Everyone had a ball!

We sang Gospel songs. Connie and her beau, Cornell, played the piano. Nannie and I sang "Nearer My God to Thee," which got a round of applause from everyone.

After dinner, I hugged and kissed Nannie and Daddy. I loved them so much, but I knew it was time to go. When and where were the big questions.

I really didn't have any plans for after high school. I knew college was out of the question because of the money situation. My grades didn't help matters either. I remember a doctor complimented me on how long and graceful my hands looked and that I should consider becoming a surgeon. Well, he shouldn't have told me that because the next day, I went to see my school counselor and told her what the good doctor had said. After briefly looking over my transcript, she quickly informed me of my academic status and that I should look for something less demanding.

Momma wanted me to become a barber. In fact, that is what I put down on my dream sheet for the school's yearbook. She said she was an artist and could transform anyone into a masterpiece. Well, after further consideration, I couldn't see myself standing all day cutting hair. I did not have the passion for it.

My father was a rolling stone in the highest sense. He had a reputation for being a womanizer, but that's about all I knew about my father. I knew more about his brother than I knew about him. Uncle Jesse was one of Asheville's most prominent Black business and community leaders. He was a graduate of Stephens-Lee High School. He later attended North Carolina A&T University. He owned and operated Ray's Funeral Home. Uncle Jesse smoked a cigar and was always clean. His wife, Aunt Julia, was a picture of pure class and beauty.

Uncle Jesse & Aunt Julia

23

I remember when Uncle Jesse used to take me to town and buy me clothes and shoes. Oh, how proud I was, just to be in his presence. Sometimes he would see me while he was sitting in his car on the street and call me over to give me a couple of dollars. I would stick my bird chest out, and you couldn't hit me in the ass with a red apple. Then there were times I was in places I shouldn't have been, and if Uncle Jesse saw me, he would jump on my case.

Uncle Jesse and Aunt Julia had four children: one girl and three boys. Jesse Jr., "Butch," was the oldest of the boys and my classmate. We grew up together, and I always thought he was the prince, and I, the pauper. He was going up north to college in September and would probably take over his father's business.

I remember once when Butch and I were passing out annual calendars for the funeral home, one of the neighborhood drunks, Gail Sanders, grabbed me. Now she was the type that patted her naked behind at you if you said something she didn't like. Sometimes she would walk in the middle of Southside Avenue, talking trash and cursing every step of the way. If you blew your car horn at her, she would flip a moon shot. Yes, she was a character.

Well anyway, she told me she knew I was C. Ray's son and that she had two of his kids. I was so embarrassed that I just dropped the calendars and ran home. I could not believe my father would go to bed with someone like her. I told Daddy what had happened, and he said,

"That Gail used to be a nice-looking woman."

It was hard for me to believe that this woman ever looked good.

For a long time, I had this love/hate relationship with my father. I never heard anything bad about him. Even in the household, Nannie would say that C. Ray was "free-spirited." Nannie thought Daddy Bill was no good and C. Ray was good. I could never understand it. Daddy Bill was around, and C. Ray was never around.

I wanted to be free-spirited like my father.

CHAPTER 4

CHRISTMAS MEMORIES

Christmas holidays were the best time of year for me. Every Christmas, after opening up my presents and gifts from Santa, I had to write a thank you letter to him and a list for next Christmas. Momma would check my spelling and put my letter in a stamped envelope, addressed to the North Pole. I would seal it and drop it into the mailbox. I got almost everything I asked for, including cap pistols complete with cowboy outfits and skates, but I never got that pony that I asked for every year. I started off with training skates, then Union 5, and finally, Speedway skates—that's what the big boys skated with.

Sometimes I would wait for Santa to come down the chimney. I could never understand how fat Santa could fit down the chimney and into the fireplace. Momma said he was magical and could fit down a milkshake straw if he wanted to. She told me if I didn't go to sleep, Santa would put pepper in my eyes and would not leave any gifts, even though I left him some Oreos and a glass of milk.

Christmas morning, I was the first up and rambling through my presents. Then I grabbed my skates and headed next door to Robert Jr.'s house. We then headed over to the Saxton Apartments to meet up with our good friend Roach. Soon, we were skating on Southside. There would be fifteen to twenty of us skating in a train with our transistor radios moving to the beat. We would then head to Ashland Avenue because it was steep and perfect for street skating. Skating backward, then eagle spread, then backward again. By the time we got to the bottom, we had to watch out for six-way traffic because we were really moving fast.

Another hot spot was the Firestone Tire Company located on the corner of Biltmore and Choctaw, across the street from St. Joseph's Hospital. Its parking lot was indoor, which was about fifty yards of smooth cement perfect for my Speedways. The ride down Choctaw required real skill because it ran into McDowell, and most of the time, you had to stop because of traffic.

We also celebrated the birth of Jesus at one of Daddy's churches, St. John Baptist Church in Fletcher, North Carolina. Every year for as long as I could remember, we gave a reenactment of the birth of Baby Jesus. I enjoyed playing Joseph when Alice was playing Mary; I also played one of the Three Wise Men a couple of times.

Every gift was perfectly wrapped in preparation for the Christmas program. Daddy would locate one of the biggest Christmas trees he could find, and the church would decorate it. Between fifteen and twenty presents were given out, and there were big bags of fruit and candy for everyone as well.

Nannie would be on the piano, and the congregation sang "Silent Night," "Joy to the World," "It Came Upon the Midnight Clear," and "The First Noel." I knew them all by heart. Plus, there were Christmas programs for Daddy's other two churches: one in Brevard, North Carolina, and the other in Saluda, North Carolina.

Rev. Perkins, another local pastor, had a church on the corner of Southside and Gaston Street, right across from Charlie's Market. He gave out bags of fruit, candy, and toys for the little ones, and turkeys and boxes of food for the needy. I helped deliver some of those packages. We would sing Christmas carols in front of his church, and there had to be at least ten to twenty people singing.

We gathered right across the street from Mr. Charlie's market but he never participated in the festivities.

I once asked Mr. Charlie why he didn't celebrate Christmas. He said he was Jewish and did not believe in Christmas.

I said, "Mr. Charlie, you know that Jesus is a Jew, so were His parents."

He just smiled and said, "Happy Holiday."

I shook my head in amusement and returned his smile.

"Thank you, Mr. Charlie, and you have a wonderful day."

Another local pastor, Rev. Posey, had a church at the top of Congress and Livingston Street. His church was where I was baptized at eight years old. Before the baptism, we had dinner, and Sister Walker made her delicious cracklin' cornbread. I must have eaten three to four pieces, and I wrapped one piece and put it in my pocket. When it was time for my baptism, I stepped in the pool.

Daddy said, "I baptize you in the name of the Father."

I went down and up.

"In the name of the Son."

I went down and up again.

"And in the name of the Holy Ghost."

When I came up the final time, the cracklin' bread was floating on top of the water.

Nannie yelled out, "Dump him again, Rev, sin is coming out in chunks!"

I thought, if Sister Walker's cracklin' bread is a sin, I'm going straight to hell because as soon as I dry off, I'm looking for its replacement.

Rev. Posey's church celebrated Christmas the same as Daddy and Rev. Perkins. I always got my Christmas joy from all three churches.

Now how could you not like Christmas, Mr. Charlie, I thought.

I remember every Christmas, Nannie sold cakes for extra money. Sometimes she would get twenty dollars or more depending on what you ordered. Now if it was a rum cake, you paid for it. She baked about two to three cakes a day and made up to ten to fifteen during the Christmas season, not counting the ones she made for the family. Just getting the batter was a treat. Sometimes there would be six to eight cakes ready for pickup on the dining room table. I would get up while everyone was asleep and, with my index and middle finger curled like a claw, nick the base of the cakes of choice.

When Nannie discovered the cakes had been tampered with, the first thing out of her mouth was, "RATS! RATS!"

Nannie would then cut the cakes in half and give the house the bitten half. I got away with this for about a couple of years, until she caught me red-handed. Need I tell you what happened?

CHAPTER 5

UNINTENDED CONNECTIONS

I remember when I was in the seventh grade; we were tracing the family tree. There were three sections to the chalkboard and three students diligently working on their family trees. When one student put my father's name down as her father, I was devastated, to say the least. Yes, my father was a rolling stone. Needless to say, that little crush I had on her just melted away. I refused to put my father's name down when it was my turn. I was too embarrassed.

Fact or fiction about my father, I wanted to be like him or what I thought he was. I was so caught up with being like him that I started dating a girl named Dolores. When she got pregnant, I knew I was following in my father's footsteps. I was one happy dude. Some of my friends had one or two babies. They seemed to be the most popular boys in school, and Lord knows I could use all the popularity I could get.

Dolores' mother called Nannie. After the phone call, Nannie called me into her bedroom and said, "Tierron, I just received a call from a Mrs. Chapal. She tells me her daughter Dolores is with child, and you're the father."

With sadness in her voice, she asked, "Are you the father?"

In a tone that was pleading for it not to be true, she continued, "Tell your Nannie this isn't true."

I was very proud at first. Now I was scared stiff. I could tell that Nannie was upset. I had no idea that I was bringing back the pain she felt when she found out about Momma's pregnancy. This was déjà vu, and I had recreated a nightmare for her. I could see the hurt and tears in her eyes, which were welling up and rolling down her face.

"I might be, Nannie."

I had messed up again and had hurt the very one I loved so much. I was full of remorse as I watched as a teardrop finally dislodged itself from her chin.

"What do you mean, young man?"

Nannie's voice held a note of contempt. Now she was totally different. Her eyes were like hot coals, and I could feel the fire.

"I mean I think I'm the father."

As I stumbled through that line of bullshit, I could not look her in the eye.

"What are your intentions?" she asked as if I hadn't said a thing.

"Nannie, I'm not marrying her."

I put a little more bass in my voice while making eye contact for the first time.

Well, I shouldn't have said that because pain shot through the right side of my face. Now Nannie was crying and swinging.

The more she swung, the less bite she had in her swing, and the more the tears flowed. She was hysterical and mumbling words about Momma and C. Ray.

I grabbed her arms and tried to console her.

By this time, her head was resting on my chest, and I had both of my arms around her. She was like a baby, still saying incomprehensible things.

"You are just like your father. You take but you never give. Why, Tierron? Why, baby? We didn't teach you this. Where did I go wrong? Talk to me, Tierron, where did I go wrong?"

"Nannie, everything is going to be all right. I'll take care of the baby," I said, not even knowing where that came from.

I hadn't thought about the kid. I'd known about Dolores' pregnancy for about two weeks, but I never once thought about the welfare of the child. My child, to be exact. I wanted to be so much like my father that I had overlooked the small details, like feeding and clothing them, medical expenses, plus this and plus that. This could be disastrous when money was a major issue in this household, I thought as Nannie was pulling away from me.

"Tierron…"

I could hear the pain and disappointment in her voice. Nannie's eyes were so swollen that she was having difficulty opening them.

"What about Dolores? Don't you think she needs you too? What about her life? She deserves more than just taking care of the baby. She really needs you now. Don't do me this way. I mean, don't do Dolores this way."

She was pleading with me, and I knew what she was getting at. "Nannie, I don't love her."

"What do you mean you don't love her? You should've thought about that before you slept with her. Where do you men get off thinking that all is well by giving up a little money? The baby needs more than money. He needs the love of both his parents, and Dolores needs you, too. You need to marry her, Tierron. Can't you see the importance of it all?"

She searched my eyes for understanding.

"Nannie, I am not marrying nobody," I said without hesitation.

Reaching for a Kleenex, Nannie said, "Well, young man. So that's the way it's going to be."

After blowing her nose, she continued, "Your grandfather and I didn't raise you that way. I believe in the sanctity of marriage. You have committed fornication, which is a sin. You should fall on your knees right now and ask the Almighty to forgive you."

I dropped to my knees.

"Nannie, I'll pray every night until God forgives me, but I will not get married to someone I don't love."

I looked up at her while silently praying to God.

Nannie bent down and held my face with both hands, and said in almost a whisper but definitely comprehensible, "Then you need to find another home."

She released my face and walked out the door. I felt like someone had hit me with a sledgehammer. I opened my mouth to scream, but nothing came out. I knew marriage was out. I had seen Uncle June work from sunup to sundown, sometimes working two or three jobs. He always had a smile on his face and never complained. I knew that he loved his wife, Aunt Sue— that was the kind of love I was looking for.

Uncle June and Aunt Sue

I was too young to get married. I would support my child financially, but marriage was not an option. I believed in marriage, and maybe one day I'd meet the girl of my dreams. But Dolores was not the girl of my dreams, and, of course, I didn't love her.

I asked God to forgive me for getting Dolores pregnant, and I also prayed for a way to be able to support myself and the baby.

I knew Nannie meant every word she said.

As it turned out, Dolores had a miscarriage about two months into her pregnancy, which was about three months before graduation.

God does work in mysterious ways.

CHAPTER 6

BONDS OF
BROTHERHOOD

I started working for Saint Joseph's Hospital when I was fifteen years old. I began in the dietary department, washing pots and pans and delivering and retrieving food for the patients. When I turned sixteen, Robert Jr. and I trained at Memorial Mission Hospital as male nurse attendants. In other words, orderlies or bedpan retrievers. I worked on the second and third floors, and in the operating room.

Cousin Robert   Cousin Betty

We both grew up on Southside, living next door to each other all our lives. In fact, I did a lot of my growing up at Robert Jr.'s house. Cousin Robert and Cousin Betty were my semi-adopted parents. Cousin Robert was a male nurse attendant at the VA Hospital in Oteen. He would take Robert Jr. and me on fishing trips, and sometimes just mess around with us.

Cousin Robert was a World War II veteran who was awarded the EAME Campaign Medal with three Bronze Service Stars, the Good Conduct Medal, and the World War II Victory Medal. I'm pretty sure he was in the invasion of Normandy on June 6, 1944. He held the rank of Tech 5. He kicked ass and took names. When Cousin Robert spoke, we all listened.

Cousin Betty was a housewife, the Queen of the castle.

Cousin Betty loved to play cards, and I was fascinated by card games. Sometimes when she needed a fourth player to play Bid Whist, she'd let me play. Cousin Betty taught me all about cards, and sometimes we would play till dawn. Of course, that was only on Friday nights because everyone in the Madden household slept late on Saturday morning.

Cousin Betty taught me how to play Pinochle, Poker, Tonk, Skin, Bid Whist, Blackjack, Spades, and Dirty Hearts. The first time we played card games, it would cost me about two weeks of lunch money. I learned quickly and began to get a little respect at the card table. She told me no card tricks because she said that was a sure enough reason to make enemies or a quicker way to meet the Almighty.

Sometimes, Cousin Betty and I would just sit on her front porch and talk. I could talk to her about things I felt I couldn't talk to Nannie or Momma about.

Robert Jr. and I used to dance with each other and practice the latest steps. Yes, we were good dancers, sometimes comparing ourselves to Sammy Davis Jr., Fred Astaire, or Gene Kelly. We knew we were at least the best in Asheville. Every time a Motown record came out, one of us would purchase it. We would listen to every word until we knew the song backward and forward. Of course, this was all done at Cousin Betty's house.

I spent so much time at Cousin Robert's house, I should have packed my clothes and moved right in.

Robert Jr. dated older women. He was a bodybuilder and should have had his body chiseled in stone. He looked twenty-one or older, and I, on the other hand, looked like I was twelve. He dated older women and sometimes white women, and although it was never stated as being forbidden fruit, we knew it was. He would tell me stories about his escapades. I would listen like there was no tomorrow. Then I would tell him a lie and swear I was telling the truth about my sexual escapades.

Once, Robert Jr. dated a red-headed nurse. This woman had one gorgeous body and a pair of super fine legs. One night, the redhead's boyfriend was looking for Robert Jr. It just so happened that Robert Jr. was off that night.

We always walked home together, going down the parking lot, crossing Biltmore Avenue, and going down Choctaw Street. When crossing McDowell, I noticed that the redhead's boyfriend's car was behind me. He had two other guys in the car with him. The one in the front passenger seat had a face full of hair that was pleading for a shave. He threw a beer can out

41

the window and was swearing. Although I did not understand every word he was yelling, I completely understood Jethro's tone of voice.

It was time to play hide-and-go-seek. I ran between McMorris Service Station and a warehouse.

This was my neighborhood; there was no way these white boys could catch me, I thought.

There was one superhero I had something in common with: the Flash. I was probably the fastest dude on Southside, with the exception of Allen Pinkston, a distant cousin. He had beaten me in a fifty-yard race a couple of years ago.

Once I got my bearings, I could see the Paul Cox store. I came out of hiding thinking I was clear.

Wrong again.

They began flashing their headlights and blowing the car horn. The dude in the right back seat had half his body hanging out of the right rear window, with no shirt on, telling me to stop—they only wanted to talk.

I could see the newspapers printing: "Colored Teenager Beaten to Death; Authorities Rule Suicide."

There was no way I was going to stop.

Change of plans: I couldn't take them to Southside because they could catch up. So, I decided to take them to the water. The Choctaw Bridge was directly in front of Paul Cox's store.

I instantly became the Flash. They were about twenty yards away when I got to the bridge. I held up my middle finger at eye level, giving them a smile, and then turned toward the bridge and up and over into the Nasty Branch, praying not to land on something sharp like a board with a rusted nail or a broken piece of glass.

I lucked out, and I lost them.

Now it was time to find my cousin.

Robert Jr. was at the pool room, and when I told him what happened, he just laughed about it. He rewarded my heroics with pickled pig's feet and a Coke.

I enjoyed hanging with family and I also enjoyed hanging with my boys.

Saturday morning at the Y.M.C.A., we played basketball. If you loved the game, you were there. This was where the Stephens-Lee High School star athletes hung out. My game was somewhat marginal. The stars of the court were Henry Logan, who had the sweetest jumper and was an overall basketball scholar who went on to play for the ABA; Thomas "Hump" Hymes and Slab were the pros when it came to handling the basketball—they were quick and fast. They had no problems taking you to the hoop.

Hump, Henry, and Slab were the ones no one wanted to check because they would make a clown out of you. I remember Hump put a move on me one time; I thought I broke both of my ankles. I became the clown of the day. Slab and Fred Nesbitt teased me for about a week. Then there were Benny Lake, Willie Maples, and Lewis Bell, who were the 1962 4A Stephens-Lee High School State Champions.

Boyce "Beaver" Norris introduced me to pocket billiards and ping-pong. Massey helped my card games. The Dawkins brothers, Eddie "Moose" Johnson, and many others were the stars on Saturday. I wish you could have seen us—better than any NBA game you've ever seen. What made it so great was that it was all free.

Out of all the guys, Slab was my best friend and running partner. He lived in the Hillcrest Apartments. Nannie loved him and thought he was well mannered and a gentleman. That's probably why Slab was my first and only sleepover buddy. He just had a special charm about him. I guess that is also what made him a true ladies' man and a father before he was seventeen years old.

Ms. Eunice, Slab's mother, reminded me of an Egyptian queen, like Cleopatra, because of the way she wore her hair. She was definitely a beautiful woman. When I'd sleep over at Slab's house, she always cooked us breakfast. She made me feel so special. Slab's sister, Patricia, who was a spitting image of her mother and also my classmate, treated me like family.

Just thinking about it, there were so many strong Black women like Ms. Eunice and Ms. Ethel who were all single mothers who helped raise me.

I especially remember how Ms. Ethel looked after me one summer.

Nannie sent me to summer camp every year until the summer of 1958. When I was ten going on eleven, Nannie asked Ms. Ethel to keep an eye on me during my new summer camp—the bean field.

Ms. Ethel had six daughters who could sing, especially Willie Mae. Sometimes, we would sing leaving the bean field, and at times, I took the lead. We had the whole bus rocking.

The bean field bus arrived at the corner of Southside and Congress Street around six in the morning. Only tool required was a foot tub. Nannie expected the foot tub to be filled with beans upon my return.

The bus ride to the bean field took about twenty to thirty minutes. When we arrived, each of us claimed a row of beans that could run the length of a couple of football fields. We then had to pick up a wooden basket called a hamper. When fully packed, one hamper equaled a bushel. Each hamper of beans was worth a ticket, which was worth fifty cents. At the end of the day, we cashed our tickets in for money.

It seemed like everyone on the bus had two- to three-gallon buckets, and only a few of us had foot tubs, including Ms. Ethel.

Picking beans requires technique, patience, and consistency. It took me over an hour to fill up my foot tub and maybe four or five to fill up a hamper. It was hot—about eighty degrees.

There was a six-year-old girl, babysitting her three-month-old baby brother. She had a box of Nilla Wafers and they were sitting under a big oak tree, right next to a fifty-gallon tank of cold drinking water.

Ms. Ethel told me that if I wanted some real food, I should leave that child and her cookies alone. I think I must have eaten half the box.

The fried chicken from the food bus was smelling good, but I needed at least two tickets for the barnyard pimp. At the rate I was picking, I'd be going home hungry.

I started to take shortcuts. I started mixing beans, bean plants, and anything else I could find to help me fill up my hamper with a foot tub of beans on the top.

By one o'clock, I had two hampers of beans ready for pickup. When the bean truck arrived, three big, massive Black men were loading the truck with the beans and paying people with tickets. When they got to my hampers, they just smiled and dumped my beans on the ground. They picked up the bean plants, giving me a nasty, evil look while shaking their heads.

I was looking at three superheroes. They could have easily been Iron Man, Thor, and the Incredible Hulk, or all three in one. I got the message loud and clear.

Ms. Ethel came to my rescue.

"Okay, young man, dry up those tears. Collect your beans and put them in one hamper. Only beans," she commanded.

"You need about two foot tubs of beans to top it off. Once that's done, I'll give you three tickets. Go and eat, and at the end of the day, I want one ticket and three tickets tomorrow. Is that understood?"

"Yes, ma'am, Ms. Ethel."

At the end of the day, I had about two-thirds of a hamper of beans, minus Nannie's beans. I tried to sell Ms. Ethel the leftovers. She said those beans were payment for rescuing me.

After thinking about it, I agreed.

Lesson learned.

CHAPTER 7

SHEBA

One night, Slab and I were coming from a party in the East End. Walking down Patton Avenue, we separated at Cox Avenue, the halfway point between his house and mine.

I was hungry because all they had to serve at the party were chips and Kool-Aid. The bus station was on my route, and with good luck, I could get there before the snack bar closed.

A Black woman was asking the waitress at the snack bar for change for a five-dollar bill. The waitress was an older white woman with a mole on her nose that reminded me of a giant booger.

"Listen here, girl. Didn't I tell you I have no change to give you?"

The waitress had one hand on her hip and the other pointing a finger at the Black woman.

The Black woman was well-dressed, about five foot five, and kind of cute. The gap in her teeth was a subtle imperfection that made her even more attractive.

"Madam, I don't want you to give me anything. I just need some change to get some cigarettes out of the cigarette machine."

The waitress, getting annoyed, said in a loud voice, almost sinister in its delivery, "Girl, if you don't get out of here, I'll call the police."

The Black woman stepped back and was about to leave when I lightly cupped her elbow with my hand.

"I have change, Miss."

"Oh good."

She tried to hand me the five-dollar bill.

I shook my head and didn't take the money.

"Miss, I got enough to get you a pack of cigarettes."

The Black woman smiled for the first time and said, "That's sweet of you. I don't forget a favor, and I won't forget you."

"It's okay. The waitress is mean to everyone around closing time."

I had about seventy-five cents to my name, and cigarettes were thirty-five cents a pack. I could kiss the hamburger goodbye tonight; I thought as I was walking over to the cigarette machine.

"What's your pleasure?" I asked as I dropped the last coin in the machine.

"Oh, and a gentleman, too."

The woman smiled in appreciation, showing dimples that weren't there the first time she smiled.

"I'll have a pack of Salems," she said, displaying even white teeth.

I had done my good deed for the day. Nannie and Daddy would be proud of me tonight.

I was still hungry, and the smell of the food from the snack bar was driving my taste buds crazy. Well, easy come and easy go, I thought as I handed her the cigarettes.

"I owe you one. My name is Sheba Miller," she said, holding out her hand.

"My name is Tierron Madden, but my friends call me Tee."

Sheba's eyes widened with inconspicuous recognition.

"Well, Mr. Ti-err-on Mad-den," she replied, pronouncing each syllable correctly, "I'm glad to meet you. You really saved my life tonight. I was dying for a cigarette. I thank you again."

"No problem," I said with a little bit more bass in my voice this time.

Sheba smiled and waved goodbye, then walked out the door. I walked over to the snack bar to get something to munch on. The waitress was closing the snack bar but had not cleared the cash register.

"Yes, ma'am, I'll have a Milky Way," I said.

"I'm closed. If you had tended to your own business, you would be eating a chocolate candy bar as we speak," the waitress said, opening the cash register.

There were still ten minutes to closing, and this time, the woman was true to character. That was one mean old lady, I thought as I exited the building. I hope the Good Lord has provided some fried chicken and a piece of potato pie at 10 Congress Street tonight. I do hope you are listening, my

Father, I prayed as I crossed Ashland Avenue, heading for Southside.

Then I heard a car horn. When I turned around, it was Miss Sheba in a new white SS Impala with white bucket seats. She told me to get in so that she could take me home. I jumped in, and she floored it. The Impala took off like a rocket. I was grinning from ear to ear.

"This is a nice car. Is it yours?"

I ran my hands over the pure white leather and inhaled its new fragrance.

"Yes, Mr. Tee Madden, this automobile is mine. Bought and paid for. Would you like to see the title?"

"No, I believe you. I just want to lay back and take it all in."

As I relaxed, Miss Sheba put in an eight-track. Jackie Wilson's smooth voice rang out.

We sang in unison and did sound good.

"We need to get a contract. We'll call our duet Tee and Miss Sheba," I said after we sang the song's last verse.

"First, you can drop the Miss, and second, we'll call ourselves Sheba and Tee, like Peaches and Herb. Women are always first."

"Well, if I drove in something like this, I could settle for Miss…I mean Sheba and Tee," I joked, moving my head up and down and feeling the dashboard.

Sheba made a right on Southside and pulled over to the curb.

"I'm tired of driving. Would you do me the honor?"

I was in the driver's seat so fast that I began pushing her over to the passenger side.

"Are you hungry?" she questioned.

"I could eat a horse with saddle, but my funds are few."

"Didn't I tell you I never forget a favor? Now it's payback time. How about some pork chops and eggs?"

Sheba touched my right arm, and my stomach growled in agreement.

"Just point, Kemosabe, and I'll do the rest."

After adjusting the seat and the rearview mirror, I took a left on Choctaw and a right on McDowell.

"I'm going to treat you to a home-cooked meal, Tonto," she bellowed while patting my gear-shifting hand.

If my friends could see me now, I thought as I rested my arm on the center console.

Sheba told me she lived in Biltmore as we passed Lee Edward High School, an all-white high school that looked like a college campus. We always wanted to play against Lee Edward in football, basketball, or track.

Not a chance now with integration, I thought.

As we took a left off the Biltmore Bridge, the entrance to the Vanderbilt Estate was on my immediate right.

"Are you sure your last name isn't Vanderbilt, or are you just one of their cooks?" I joked, leaning as far back as I could.

"I assure you my name ain't Vanderbilt, and this colored girl doesn't cook for no white folks."

"I didn't mean any harm. It was just a joke. Any lady dressed like you are and driving an automobile like this couldn't be a house cook."

51

"My mother supported me and my brothers cooking and cleaning for white folks. That's not for me because I got plans, and they don't include housekeeping or cooking for a living."

"So, what are you telling me—that you can't cook? Am I your guinea pig tonight?"

We both laughed.

"Listen, my young friend, if there is one thing in this world I can do, I can cook. Just you wait till you sink your beautiful white teeth into my delicious golden-brown fried pork chops with my special seasoning. You might think of me as a goddess. I do believe that is one step up from the Vanderbilts."

"Whatever you say, Venus," I said, rubbing my stomach.

We had driven out of the business district and onto the Sweeten Creek Highway for about six miles, then made a left onto a dirt road, followed by a couple more rights and lefts.

"Are you sure we won't run into hostile Indians or maybe discover Atlantis?" I said, half-jokingly.

"We're almost there," Sheba said, patting my stomach.

Why would anyone live so far out in the middle of nowhere? No streetlights, just pitch black. Maybe this was not a good idea, coming out here with someone I didn't know. Nannie had always told me to beware of strangers bearing gifts.

We passed over some railroad tracks. About a hundred yards to the left stood a well-lit white house. As I turned into the driveway, the house was still a good fifty yards away, bordered on both sides by a white picket fence. As we drove into a double-paved driveway, I could hear a dog barking.

"Home sweet home," Sheba said as she exited the car.

When she unlocked the door, a little black French poodle jumped into her arms.

"Tee, I want you to meet my baby, Africa."

The poodle stopped barking as I rubbed her head.

"Nice to meet you, Africa," I said as I took the dog from Sheba.

"I hope you are not in a big hurry to eat. The chops are frozen."

Sheba took off her coat and reached for mine.

I could eat them frozen, hungry as I am, I thought.

"No problem," I said.

"Make yourself at home."

Sheba hung our coats on a wooden coat and hat rack. She then walked into the kitchen.

"It won't take long once this hot water attacks them," Sheba said jokingly.

"No problem."

I looked around and gave the house a thorough inspection.

The house was small and well-kept. The walls and floor were stained pine wood. The floor shined like glass. There was a long mahogany stereo console that ran almost the length of the large picture window, which was draped with floor-length white curtains. A black bearskin, complete with head and legs, faced a seemingly oversized fireplace. Right above the mantelpiece was a large picture of Jesus Christ, and under the picture of Jesus was this poem framed and written in bold red letters: "O Lord, help me to understand that you ain't going to let nothing come my way that you and I together can't handle."

That would be a nice present for Nannie and Daddy. I must remember this poem. I could freehand it in red ink and frame it in an 8x10, I thought as I read it aloud several more times until I had memorized it.

I was still entertaining Africa when Sheba came out of the hallway, wearing a housecoat, slippers, and jeans. She grabbed a small log from a brass log basket and added it to a log that had almost accomplished its mission.

"Take off your shoes and make yourself at home," she said as she entered the dining room.

"Mr. Tee, would you care for a little wine or apple brandy?" she asked after taking two round glasses from a mother-of-pearl china cabinet.

Nannie would kill me if she smelled alcohol on my breath, but I was a senior in high school and would be a man in less than four years. I can handle brandy anyway—that's a kid's drink. I'll just brush my teeth when I get home. Nannie will be asleep, I prayed, crossing my fingers.

"Why not? I'll take a shot."

I removed my shoes and felt the warmth of the floor. She walked in and handed me a half-filled glass of brandy.

"Now, drink it slow. Here's to pork chops and eggs."

After we clinked our glasses together, I hesitantly brought the glass to my lips and took a sip. I could feel the warmth of the liquid flowing down my throat. It was smooth and deliciously sweet. I could become a connoisseur of this wonderful brew in no time, I thought.

"I could really dig this stuff," I said out loud while holding up the glass she brought.

"I'm so glad you like it, Mr. Tee."

I smiled, feeling really good.

"The first time you called me Mister was all right, because I didn't know you, or you me. Now that you're fixing the pork chops and eggs, you got to be my friend because I'm your friend. Anytime you want a friend, just call Tee when pork chops are on the menu, and I'll be your friend. Can you dig it, Sheba?"

Sheba started laughing and could not stop; she was laughing so hard that she began to cough uncontrollably. I followed her into the kitchen, and she had fallen to her knees, she was laughing so hard.

"Tee, I am fine," she said, still laughing. "But it was just the way you said it. I'm not laughing at you; I'm laughing with you. I've never known anyone express their love for pork chops and eggs the way you do. I am definitely your friend. Now get out of here while I get the food ready."

"I'll take one more shot of brandy and I'll get out of the chef's way," I said with a little drag in my voice.

Sheba topped off my glass with more brandy.

"All right, just one more small one, that's it! Coca-Cola for you, Mister—I mean, Mr. Tee. No, I really mean Tee…I'll get it right after a while."

"Well, Sheba, you can call me anything except late for pork chops and eggs." I said humorously, noticing for the first time that she was nude from the waist up under the robe.

"Now get out of my kitchen if you still want to eat."

I quickly hopped out of the kitchen to the dining room, heading for the living room.

"Sheba, do you want to hear some music?"

"Yes, put on something with a fast beat. We need to liven up this party. The records are on the right side of the console."

She started snapping her fingers to an imaginary beat. I put on a couple of LPs with James Brown and the Fabulous Flames leading off. The first song was "Night Train."

At first, I was dancing with Africa; then it got good to me, so I put Africa on the couch. This seemed to piss her off because she began barking and running back and forth on the couch.

"Sorry, Africa, but I need to do my thing."

Sheba was singing to the music, and I could tell she had some gospel in her. I started to ask her to join me on the floor, but then thought she was too old to know the moves I knew. I didn't want to embarrass her.

If I didn't know any better, I'd think that I was a little tipsy. Nope, not the kid. I just had two glasses of this sissy drink. No real man can get drunk off brandy.

The music was sounding better than ever. I was doing the James Brown, with both thumbs inside my jacked-up pants. I was sliding across the glossy floor with ease. In fact, I was better than the man himself. It got so good to me that I played it again. Then "Green Onions" by Booker T. and the MG's. The song put me in the jungles of Africa. I could smell the chops, and I wanted to celebrate.

The warmth of the fire from the new log had erased any tension I might have had when I first entered Sheba's home. I still could not understand why she stayed out here all alone. Oh well, to each his own.

I am the chief warrior of the Mandingo tribe, celebrating a big kill of swine, I thought, as I was moving to the beat of the music.

"Pork chops, pork chops, they are on the way, pork chops, pork chops, they are on the way," I sang, as the smell of the pork chops got more intoxicating.

Or was it the brandy?

I think both.

My hips started moving in a slow circular motion, then faster and faster until my body began to rain perspiration.

"You need some help?"

Before I knew it, Sheba had wrapped herself around me from the rear. As our movement became more synchronized and our bodies became one, I could feel every inch of her. Talking about going to the mountaintop—I was almost there. I could feel the warmth of her body and smell her womanly fragrance. Then I felt her sliding and coiling around my leg like a python. I opened my eyes for the first time, and the first thing I noticed was that the overhead lights were off and the only light in the room was coming from the fireplace.

Her bathrobe and jeans were lying on the floor. Sheba was completely nude. She definitely didn't look like this with clothes on, I thought.

She was a work of art.

Sheba began to undo my pants. When I finally stepped out of them, she started kissing areas that had never been kissed before.

As she pulled me down to her, her head nestled on the bear's head. The fire that was consuming the log was an icicle compared to the burning desire that was growing inside me. So, this is the difference between a woman and a girl, I thought as our lips met.

Africa jumped on my back, hysterically barking like a mad dog. She started running up and down the length of my body.

"Not now, dog, go away," I demanded harshly, trying to wave her off with one hand while Sheba tightened her grip.

"Let her bark, Tee," Sheba whispered as her legs and feet intertwined with mine, reinforcing her grip.

Africa did not let up, and her little paws started feeling like razor blades as she struggled to stay balanced on my slippery back.

I was trying to pry myself away from Sheba because I was starting to feel the pain and discomfort of Africa's paws. Then Africa stopped barking and clawing my back. The next thing I felt was something warm running off my back.

"She pissed on me!"

"What?"

"She pissed on me. Africa pissed on me."

"Damn you, you little bitch!" Sheba screamed as I rolled over.

"I don't believe she pissed on me."

"Tee, don't you move a muscle. I'll be right back."

Sheba was breathing heavily and licking her lips.

She grabbed Africa with one smooth swoop and disappeared through the hallway. Wonder Woman had nothing on this African queen, I thought, as I tried to dry my back with Sheba's bathrobe, feeling a little pain as the robe irritated my scratched-up back.

"Thank you, my Heavenly Father, for what I am about to receive," I prayed under my breath with my palms touching and looking up with a grin.

"Thank you, thank you, thank you. I do owe you one."

I heard a door shut and Sheba's feet racing back to the living room. I could still hear Africa barking and clawing at the door like a wild dog.

Don't worry about your momma, Africa. I am going to take good care of her, I thought, as I finally started to relax.

"Oh my God! I don't believe this is happening," Sheba screamed, her eyes widening incredulously.

She ran past me toward the large picture window.

"No, no, please, Lord, tell me this is a dream."

Sheba was muttering incoherently as she peeped through the curtains.

"This has got to be a dream."

The sound that came from her was a cry of terror. Shock theater couldn't have duplicated it any better. This was definitely not the lady I met at the bus station and definitely not the sex goddess I was about to meet. She was scared, which frightened me.

"Put on your clothes!" she screamed as she grabbed her jeans. "You got to get out of here, Tee."

"What's going on?"

"Hurry, Tee!"

I pulled up my pants while Sheba picked up the rest of my clothes. I was zipping my pants up when Sheba grabbed my arm, pulling me toward the hallway.

"Ouch!"

"What's wrong?" she cried as she was pulling me through the hallway.

"I'm caught in my zipper!"

She opened a bedroom door and pushed me in, pointing to a window. "Tee, go through the window! He'll kill us both if he finds you here," she cried out in a voice raw with terror.

As she shoved me, my clothes, shoes, and then disappeared down the hallway, it dawned on me what Sheba had said: He'll kill us both. It took me no time to put on the rest of my clothes and penny loafers. Then I realized that the window was too small to get through. Now I was really scared.

But scared of who? I thought.

By this time, Sheba was back in the room with my coat and tears in her eyes. "Tee, take your coat. Now get out of here."

"I can't get through that window; it's too small, and who are you running from?" I demanded.

Sheba realized that I was right. "Tee, it's my man, and if he finds you here, we're dead."

Oh God! If you get me out of this, I'll go to church every day and twice on Sunday.

I prayed as I tucked my coat under my arms and raced out of the bedroom.

"Where are you going?" Sheba screamed. "You can hide in here till he goes to sleep."

"I got to get out of here!"

I was frantic. If I could just catch him off guard, I could run right past him, or if he was in my way, I could bump him to the side. I hope he isn't carrying a gun, I thought, as I passed the room that Africa was still raising hell in.

I was about to enter the living room when this giant in black-and-white pinstripe bib overalls, about six foot four or taller and about three hundred-plus pounds, was locking the door. I stopped dead in my tracks, but my heart must've run into him because I felt no heartbeat. He was big, black, and wide. Big Daddy Liston who played for the Baltimore Colts had nothing on this man.

I was looking at death as sure as there was a God in heaven. In fact, I would probably be seeing him real soon. There's no way I could have moved this man. I couldn't even see the door for his massive body.

Now I know what David felt like when he first saw Goliath. Yeah, but David did have a couple of rocks. I don't think a gun, let alone a rock, could stop this man. I know he had to bend down just to clear the door frame. I was in big trouble, and I never knew what the word really meant until now. He was the epitome of the Jolly Green Giant, a replica of John Henry. I was doomed. I didn't have to worry about graduation. This man was going to take it all away, I thought.

When he finally turned around to pick up his suitcase, our eyes met, and there was the coldest set of eyes I had ever seen. I just hope this is going to be quick, I thought, as John Henry straightened up, leaving the suitcase on the floor. Now he even seemed larger than he was before. I hoped he wasn't growing on me right in front of my eyes.

"Hi, baby! What are you doing home so early?"

Sheba's voice was chipper as she entered the living room fully dressed. This was definitely not the woman I had just left. Her whole attitude had changed.

"Who is this little nigga?" John Henry yelled.

"Don't you dare raise your voice at me, Sam."

"I said, who is this little nigga?"

"Sam, have you been drinking again?"

"I've had a few, but I ain't drunk, and I still want to know who this little piss ant is!"

"Sir, my name is Tierron LaVon Madden. My father is the Reverend A.R. Madden Sr.," I interrupted, hoping that he still wanted to talk.

"I know Reverend and Mrs. Madden. We used to call Reverend Madden Lil Daddy, and I also know their son, June Madden. In fact, little nigga, we grew up together. I don't recall him having a brother."

"Mr. Sam," I said, looking at Sheba for confirmation and getting the green light from her, "my mother is Delores, and I was adopted by my grandparents."

I could feel my heart double its normal beat.

"Well, I'll be damned. Of course, I know your momma," Sam said, smiling for the first time in recognition.

"Sam, we were about to eat. Are you hungry?"

Sheba walked toward the kitchen, not waiting for an answer.

"Tee, would you help Mr. Sam with his luggage? Just take it in the bedroom and put it on the bed," she calmly continued.

"Miss Sheba, I better be getting home. I don't want Lil Daddy to worry," I answered, hoping Sheba would catch the hint.

"Just do as I say," Sheba replied, pushing me toward the suitcase.

"I don't need any help."

Sam grabbed the suitcase and disappeared down the hallway.

The pork chops and eggs were not as good as I thought they would be. I just wanted to leave. Although nothing happened between Sheba and me, I still felt guilty. Sam was a gentle giant, but the stare I got from him when he saw me for the first time indicated to me that Sam could have run through me like water. Sheba told Sam what a good Samaritan I was, while Sam washed his food down with scotch and water.

After we ate, I grabbed my coat and hinted that it was time to go. I thanked Sam for his hospitality. Sheba and I walked out the door. As I was about to get in the car, Sam called me back into the house.

"Listen, Tee, or whatever they call you," Sam said. "This is my house, that's my car, and that's my woman. If I ever catch you out here again, Reverend Madden will have only one son. Now, what part didn't you understand?"

He was looking me in the eye as he stared me down.

"I understand, sir," I responded as I gulped apologetically

As I turned to exit, Mr. Sam chimed in again, "Tee, I believe you forgot something."

Then, he threw me my underpants.

I jumped in the back seat of the car, shocked by what had just transpired. The only thing that came to mind was what Daddy used to say to Uncle Young, Daddy's older brother, when he showed up with alcohol on his breath—"God takes care of fools and babies," and Uncle Young was no baby.

Uncle Young

I had to wonder which one I was at that moment.

We rode in silence until we hit a paved road.

"Are you all right?" Sheba asked.

"When I get home, I'll be fine," I replied.

"Listen, Tee, you were a perfect gentleman. You have nothing to be ashamed of. If anything, I was wrong in leading you on. My intentions were honorable; it just got out of hand. You must believe that. Sam works for the railroad as an engineer, and most of the time he is gone four to five days a week, sometimes more. He was due home tomorrow evening. I'm sorry that I put you through this. Sam's a good man. I love him dearly, and God knows I'm telling the truth. This is the first time that anything like this has ever happened."

She turned to look deep in my eyes, almost pleading for understanding.

"No problem," I lied.

Just get me home, I thought.

"Tee, I must confess that when you introduced yourself, I knew who you were. Your mother used to do my hair, and I know your father. You are the spitting image of Clarence with his fine self. I remember when you were born. Do you still stay on Congress Street?"

"Yes, but why didn't you tell me this from the beginning?"

"Oh, I don't know. I guess that I was so amazed at how much you had grown and what a gentleman you had become. I guess I was playing a game with you until I saw you on the floor dancing."

Sheba shook her head as if she was trying to clear her head.

"You looked just like your father."

I felt ten feet tall and even bigger than Big Sam as Sheba's words vibrated through my ears.

"How well do you know my father?" I asked, trying to get a better look at her face.

"No, there was nothing between us. Your father is older than Sam, and Sam is almost seven years older than me. Jesus, Tee, do I look that old? I'm just twenty-five."

"No, you look great," I said, thinking back to when she was lying on the bearskin. She was fantastic.

"Here we are, lover," Sheba said as she stopped in front of my house.

"Tee, I had a good time tonight, and I am glad Sam showed up before we got involved. Now I can go home and make love to him and not feel guilty."

Sheba reached for my hand and I gave it to her.

"Sheba, when Big Sam called me back into the house, he threw me my underwear."

I tried to search her eyes for fear, still holding her hand. I saw no fear, and for the first time, I saw the face of a remarkably beautiful lady.

"Listen, Tee, Sam loves me, and I know how far to go with him. Like I said before, this was the first time anything like this has ever happened. I know I panicked when I saw him driving down the driveway. I am deeply sorry that I put you through that. If Sam was really mad, you and I would be dead."

"Good night, Sheba," I said, squeezing and releasing her hand.

"No, this is goodbye, lover."

She grabbed my face with both hands and gently bit down on my top lip.

"You owe me that for those delicious pork chops I prepared for you. Goodbye, Mister Tee."

Sheba smiled as she gently pushed me away. And that was the last time I saw Sheba and Big Sam, but I knew I would never, ever forget them.

CHAPTER 8

DECISION TIME

Robert Jr. asked me about going to Washington, D.C. in the fall with him. He told me that the job market there was better than in any other place in the South. I told him that I would sleep on it and get back to him later. It seemed as if I was the last one of my classmates to make a decision. Everyone was leaving by September; they were either going to college, tech school, or somewhere else. I knew that I had to go somewhere, but Washington, D.C. would be my last choice. The city did not appeal to me, plus I didn't know anyone there.

It was Saturday night, and there was everywhere to go, but the rain was coming down like there was no tomorrow. I had promised Daddy that I would go to church with him and Nannie this Sunday, so I decided to lay low and spend some time at home with the folks.

Nannie was extremely happy because I hadn't been to church in a while, especially since my working hours changed after graduation. Money was always a problem around 10 Congress Street, so work was necessary to keep the money coming. I would give Nannie a third of my check and sometimes more if she needed it. Since "Uncky," my great uncle, died a couple of years ago, money had been tight. Uncky's army pension had been about a third of the household's income.

Daddy had three churches, and none were within the city limits. Saint John Baptist Church was in Fletcher, North Carolina. I became a member of Saint John when I was eight years old. I was the president of the Junior Choir.

I was really looking forward to going to church again to see my old friends and members. Just to see Daddy perform was like seeing James Brown live at the city auditorium. Daddy would scream, shout, yell, jump, dance, and do whatever else it took to get his message across. Nannie was his backup, his cheering squad. They were a team and a sight to behold.

The rain had passed. Daddy and I were watching a movie about World War II and the bombing of Pearl Harbor.

"I'll never forget that day, Black Sunday, the seventh of December 1941," Daddy said, not looking up from the television.

"How many Japanese did you kill, Daddy?"

"I didn't kill. I saved lives. I was a medic dragging the wounded to safety and tending to their wounds the best I could. I remember one time I dragged this wounded soldier to safety, and it had to be a hundred yards. I saw so much blood; the inhumanity of it all. Everybody called me Rev because I carried and quoted my Bible all the time. Each time I picked up a wounded soldier, I always quoted scripture while carrying the wounded back to safety."

I loved listening to Daddy talk about his time as a soldier. He had all of my attention as he continued to reminisce.

"But have you ever heard of Doris Miller? We used to call him Dorie Miller. He was a cook on the USS West Virginia on December 7, 1941. Dorie manned a .50-caliber gun with no training and shot down two Japanese fighter planes while his ship was sinking. He was one of the last to abandon the ship and had to swim close to three hundred yards to safety. They awarded him the Navy Cross. He was killed in action later, on another ship."

Daddy emphasized, "It's a shame they didn't give him his due. He deserved the Medal of Honor. The only people having a harder time than the Blacks during this period were the American Japanese. Everything was taken from them, and they were placed in holding camps."

Daddy enlisted in the U. S. Army in October of 1943. He was awarded the Asiatic-Pacific Campaign Medal and the World War II Victory Medal. He received an honorable discharge from the Army in 1945.

Pvt. Arthur Robert Madden "Daddy

"How about the women?" I questioned, knowing that this was an area he would avoid talking about.

"What about the women?" he repeated, looking up from the TV and searching for Nannie.

I had to put my hands over my mouth to keep from laughing.

"Daddy, are the Filipino women as beautiful as most men say they are?" I finally asked, almost laughing in front of him.

After making sure that Nannie was not around and not within hearing distance, Daddy smiled. Then, looking me in the eye, he said, "Yes."

This made me think back to the day I had my first sexual experience. I was twelve years old. The encounter cost me fifteen cents, a Nehi grape soda, and a five-cent bag of two-for-a-penny ginger snap cookies.

Angel lived in the Southside Apartments. She was fourteen, and I was very nervous. My orgasm felt so good, and then I felt drained of energy. It scared me so much that I ran home and into my room. Nannie knew something was wrong, so she sent Daddy up to investigate. I didn't know how to tell Daddy, but I knew that God didn't like what I had just done. I thought maybe He had punished me for the act I had just committed. The act hadn't taken that long, but the stimulation from the act had exploded in unfurling waves of pleasure. I had never felt so good in my life. I felt so good that I screamed at the top of my lungs—so loud that Angel had to put her hands over my mouth. Then, after the pleasure, I felt drained and weak. My body started shivering, and I broke out in a cold sweat, which scared the living daylights out of me.

At first, I thought I had the clap; then I thought maybe I got her pregnant; finally, I thought I was dying. Whatever had just happened, I was out of there. I jumped up so fast it startled Angel, and she knocked over the half-drunk Nehi grape soda. I pulled my pants up and ran out the door. Angel was calling me names that Daniel Webster couldn't define. The only thing I knew was that something that felt so good couldn't be right.

"Tierron, what happened? What's wrong?" Daddy asked, trying to pull the bed coverings off me.

I was in the fetal position and holding on tight to my bed coverings.

"Daddy, I'm dying," I whispered.

"What?"

With one jerk, I was on top of the covers, still in the fetal position.

"Daddy, I've been bad, and God is punishing me!" I screamed, shaking like a limb on a tree.

"What's wrong with my baby?" Nannie said, rushing up the stairs.

"Daddy, no!"

I moaned, looking him in the eye and shaking my head, begging him to stop Nannie before she came into the room.

"Liler, this is men talk," Daddy said as he caught her before she reached the top step.

"Everything is fine, Honey. Just give us a little more time."

"What's wrong, Rev?" she repeated.

"Men talk. We'll talk later."

Daddy gently placed both hands on her shoulders and turned her around.

When she had gotten to the bottom of the stairs, Daddy returned to my bed. I was seated in an Indian position.

"Now tell me, what happened?" Daddy asked, as he sat down on the bed.

I didn't know where to start and tried to read Daddy's eyes for reassurance.

"Daddy, I did a bad thing, and God is mad at me for doing it."

"Son, just come out with it. Say what's on your mind."

"Well, Daddy, ay... ay... ay... I..., I…"

"Come on, you can say it," Daddy pressed on, moving his head up and down.

"I've, I've been fucking!"

I cried out as the tears started to flow.

Daddy's bottom lip almost dropped to his belly button.

"What did you say, young man?" Daddy asked, his eyes almost popping out of his head.

"Daddy, I said, I've been fu—"

Daddy grabbed me with one hand and placed the other firmly over my mouth.

I started crying and gave him the whole story, not leaving out anything. As I started describing Angel's body, I became excited again. I knew then that I was going to bust hell wide open.

How could I possibly be sorry if I'm ready to do it again?

I tried to search Daddy's eyes for understanding, but now he was avoiding my gaze.

Why was he embarrassed?

Daddy let me finish my story, but I left my new excitement out. I didn't want to complicate matters worse than they were.

Daddy talked for about two hours about the do's and don'ts of life. He told me that I was going through puberty and that I had ejaculated, and the fluid that came out of my penis was baby-making stuff.

"Son, you are becoming a man."

"But Daddy, I'm twelve years old, and I won't be twenty-one for..."—counting on my fingers and looking up—"nine years."

What I learned was that you can only have sex when you are married, and if you have sex before you are married then you are fornicating. If you are married and have sex with someone other than your wife, you have committed adultery. I could tell this was going to be a big problem. I mean, thou shall not steal, thou shall not kill—no problem—but thou shall not fornicate is going to be a problem.

This ejaculation thing...I didn't tell Daddy that it felt so good. Better than Nannie's banana pudding or anything else that I experienced.

Daddy was finishing his sermon, and I could tell that he wasn't mad at me. In fact, I detected a little pride in his voice as he was preaching to me.

I just couldn't get over my new experience. Angel had busted my bubble, and I liked it. This little adventure cost me fifteen cents. That wasn't a problem; I always had lunch money.

Daddy promised that he would not tell Nanny about our conversation. I know he didn't tell Nannie the truth because the next day she made me a chocolate cake. I didn't ask the good Reverend any questions. I was just thankful that he belonged to me.

When I came out of my memory-induced trance, I realized Daddy was telling me how God had brought him through the war and safely back home to the family. I couldn't get my mind off the Filipino women—their long black hair and their high-hip grass skirts waving from side to side.

"That's it," I said. "I'm going to join the Navy and see the world."

I could see the approval in Daddy's eyes. Nannie, on the other hand, didn't think that was a good idea. Well, Daddy convinced her that it was in my best interest.

That's my old man, I thought.

Monday morning, bright and early, I was in the Navy recruiting office on Patton Avenue. We went through all the paperwork, and in a couple of days, everything was set. I was to report to Charleston Naval Reception Station in about two weeks. That would be a couple of weeks before everyone was off to college. My timing was right. I called my girl Sarah and told her the news. She was excited for me and couldn't wait for me to get off the phone so she could spread the gossip.

Then I called my main man Slab and told him the news. He started calling me a hero, and I started believing that I could be one. Vietnam was war, and my chances of becoming a hero in the Navy were slim to none. But we did have a war hero from these parts. Sergeant Alvin York, United States Army, was born in Pall Mall, Tennessee, the next state over. In World War I,

Sergeant York single-handedly crushed a German machine gun battalion, killing at least twenty-five and capturing one hundred and thirty-two soldiers. He was also a conscientious objector.

Was my man dealing with the situation or not?

Since we breathed the same air, maybe we had the same blood. I could see myself, riding down Patton Avenue, to a hero's welcome in a brand-new Cadillac convertible, my family and friends cheering me on. I liked the sound of it.

"I am going to Vietnam," I said to myself.

CHAPTER 9

GAMBLING WITH
MY FUTURE

My friends planned a surprise going-away party for Slab and me. Fred, our partner, couldn't keep a secret. He spoiled our surprise, though we played it up like we were surprised.

Daddy let me use his car, a 1956 Chevy Impala. The party was one of the last parties we had before the college season began, so everyone who was someone was there.

The Temptations kicked off the party with "My Girl," followed by "I Know (You Don't Want Me No More)" by Barbara George. Then my song to dance with Sarah was "The Entertainer" by Tony Clark. Now if you want to see the Black Fred Astaire and Black Ginger Rogers do the swing, Sarah and I had the patent on it. She had a small frame but was so well put together.

Everyone had high expectations of themselves. We talked about growing up in Asheville and how we were going to change the world. I was going to stamp out Communism all by myself. Slab was going to the NBA to break the all-time scoring record. Sarah was going to be a teacher and rid the world of illiteracy.

Two cakes were brought out: one had U.S. flags and my name on it, and the other had miniature basketballs with Slab's name on it.

"Don't Make Me Over" by Dionne Warwick, "The Tracks of My Tears" by Smokey Robinson, and "Will You Love Me Tomorrow" by the Shirelles, along with other slow songs, were all playing. Each time these songs came on, I was forbidden to slow dance with the many girls I had crushes on. I could only fast dance with them. What a waste.

I knew that next year at this time we would all be in different worlds.

The last songs were "Rainbow 65" by Gene Chandler and "You're Losing a Good Thing" by Barbara Lynn. The lights went out and the grinding began. Sarah and I were never intimate, and now I was wishing that we had gotten to know each other better. We sang our school's alma mater, and tears started flying.

Oh Stephens-Lee, Dear Stephens-Lee,
Our hearts are filled with love for thee;
A champion Brave, thy youth to save,
Thy children honor thee.
Home of truth, we do believe,
Noble Deeds thou wilt achieve;
In song or rain we shall remain
Faithful thee, dear Stephens-Lee

Oh Stephens-Lee, Dear Stephens-Lee
Our hearts are filled with Pride in thee,

A Warrior Bold- the right of uphold-
Alma Mater, Dear
When upon life's rugged sea
Oft our thoughts will turn to thee;
From day to day, Crimson and gray
Praise we Stephens-Lee

I kissed Sarah and told her I would write to her.

After leaving the party, Slab, Fred, and I just rode around for about an hour talking about old times. After I dropped them off by their homes, I went home and sat in the car for a while. I was going to miss my friends, and I was going to miss my family.

The next morning, Nannie fixed me one of my favorite meals: country ham, red-eye gravy, grits with three eggs sunny side up, homemade buttermilk biscuits with her apple grape jelly, and a big mug of coffee. We sat at the dining room table. Nannie placed her favorite tablecloth, chinaware, and sterling silverware as if it were our Thanksgiving dinner. Daddy prayed one of his mile-long prayers, asking God to protect me while I traveled through this perilous journey. We ate in silence.

Normally, Connie would have something smart to say, but she was quiet. I told Cookie that I was going to bring her something back if she continued to get straight A's in school. She couldn't hold back the tears, and of course, the family followed suit, including Connie.

After breakfast, I hugged and kissed everyone. Momma seemed especially happy, saying how proud she was of me.

Nannie continued to cry, hugging me very tight. Daddy told her that she was not losing a son but gaining a hero. I concurred with my old man. There is nothing good about goodbyes.

Daddy drove me to the bus station. He and I hugged for about two minutes. He slipped me three five-dollar bills and told me I could pay it back with my first naval check.

When I arrived at the reception station, I quickly made acquaintances with other Navy newbies. We filled out a lot of paperwork. Then we were told to get plenty of rest because the next day we had to take a series of tests, including a physical examination. After checking into our rooms and dropping off our personal baggage, a group of us checked out a movie. We watched *The Great Race*, starring Tony Curtis, Natalie Wood, and Jack Lemmon, which helped break the ice between us. The movie had us rolling in our seats. Jack Lemmon was extremely funny. Plus, I had always had a crush on Natalie Wood ever since I saw her in *West Side Story*. I need not elaborate on my man Tony Curtis because he was one of the coolest men in Hollywood. After the movie, we picked up some hamburgers, fries, and shakes and started playing poker.

The lights were out at ten, but we continued to play under the blanket with a lamp. We played nickel, dime, and quarter poker with three bump limits. I learned how to play High Chicago, which is high spade in the hole takes half the pot. High-low split: the high hand gets half the pot, and the lowest hand gets the other half. I was ahead by about twenty dollars before we realized that it was wake-up time. We showered and shaved, then we ate breakfast. We were then herded into a large room filled with seated testing cubicles. This tall sailor, who should have been playing in the NBA, explained the testing procedures.

The sailor said, "Begin."

The next time I heard his voice was, "Five minutes to go."

I fell asleep after the seventh question. I panicked, my heart beating so fast I felt dizzy.

Tee, get it together.

"God, I could really use you now. I'll stop gambling. I'll give the money back. Please, God, I'll never look at another card again," I prayed.

So, I began marking the answer sheet without looking at the questions. When in doubt, choose C, I thought. Then the sailor said to put our pencils down. As I looked at my answer sheet, some answers were marked twice. Most questions weren't answered at all. When I turned my test in, I knew I'd messed up. Then I started praying again.

"Oh God, you saved Moses from Pharaoh by splitting the Red Sea. Jesus raised the dead and turned water into wine. Just give me a passing grade, and I'll never play cards again."

I continued to pray, my eyes watering.

After the test, my name and the name of a fellow card player were called out to report to room 14. Once there, we were told that our test scores were not adequate to enter the United States Navy. In other words, I was too dumb to enter the Navy. I was flabbergasted beyond belief. I begged the officer in charge to retest me, insisting that there was a big mistake. He assured me that nothing was amiss, that their findings were correct and without error.

I was told I was leaving at 1400 hours for Asheville, NC. That's two o'clock civilian time. I couldn't hold back the tears. How was I going to face Nannie and Daddy and the rest of the family? How was I going to face my friends?

Everything was running together in my head. I couldn't concentrate. What was I going to do? I could kill myself and make it look like an accident. No, I can't do that. God doesn't forgive suicide.

"Heavenly Father, help me," I prayed.

No... no... no... no... this is not happening to me!

I yelled as the tears continued to flow.

Someone was shaking me, then I felt a sharp pain in the left side of my face. Someone had hit me. There was a crowd around me.

"Calm down," the officer in charge said, patting me on the back.

"Someone, get him some water."

It seemed like everyone was touching me. Some were so close I could smell the garlic and onions on their breath, which was turning my stomach. I was so hot that I couldn't breathe, and my shirt was soaked with perspiration. I began to hyperventilate. Then, all of a sudden, breakfast—and probably the hamburgers, fries, and shakes that I had yesterday—were gushing out of my mouth like a fire hose.

I caught the officer in charge square in the face, turning his all-whites into a peak of floral arrangements of digested and undigested food. He must have jumped back ten feet, cursing me out every foot of the way.

"Son, everything is going to be all right. I am Chaplain Harrison. What seems to be the problem?"

As the Chaplain spoke, he pulled me away from the mess I had just created.

Someone handed me a cup of water and some towels. Chaplain Harrison coached me into drinking all the water.

"I can't go back home because my mother's critically ill. That's why I joined the Navy—to help support her," I lied. I then told him about my test results.

"Son, you failed Navy requirements. Maybe in a year or so, you can try again, or even better, why don't you try the Army? They're looking for fine young men like yourself," he said politely.

By this time, I had regained my composure, and I was trying to think of what my next move was. I glanced up at the officer-in-charge; he was still wiping himself off and rolling his eyes at me. If looks could kill, I would be buried by now.

Think with what little brain you do have, I thought.

Then I thought of Sheba and Big Sam, the poem under the picture of Jesus Christ: "Oh Lord, help me to understand that you ain't going to let nothing come my way that you and I together can't handle."

"Chaplain, would you pray for me?" I asked in my most solemn voice.

"But of course, let us bow our heads," he replied as he grabbed both my hands.

The prayer was nothing like Daddy's and a whole lot shorter, to say the least. I thought about going to Pittsburgh to live with my father. Then I thought, he didn't want me then and he doesn't want me now. Then I remembered what Nannie had told me to do when things seemed to get out of hand.

"Relax, let go, and let God. Relax, let go, and let God."

I repeated Nannie's admonition as the chaplain was finishing his prayer.

"Thank you, sir, for being so kind and understanding."

"Are you going to be alright, young man?"

"Yes, sir," I lied. "I guess God is not ready for me to leave home."

Trying to create a smile, I called home, and Momma answered the phone.

"Momma!" I cried out.

"Man Boy, is that you? What's wrong?"

"Momma, I have some bad news. They found something wrong with my heart. They said that my heart skips a beat or something."

I was fighting back the tears, and Momma began to cry.

"Man Boy, everything is going to be alright. Bad hearts seem to run in the family. Just trust in the Lord, and he'll carry you through,"

"Yes, ma'am. Tell Daddy I'll be home about 9:30 tonight," I said as I hung up the phone.

I am sorry I told this lie, but this was one lie that I was going to stick with, come hell or high water.

Nannie and Daddy were waiting at the bus station for me. If I could have found a hole, I would have crawled in it and died. I had to lie to back up a lie. Then Nannie would ask me specific questions pertaining to my heart. I was lost and did not know how to answer her. She finally told me it was the will of God. I could tell she was not disappointed.

Daddy gave me a slice of sweet potato pie and a big glass of milk.

I finally made it back home. Yes, home sweet home.

CHAPTER 10

RECOVERY

I could not meet any of my friends for about a week or two. I knew I would die with this lie, even if I had to go to hell with it.

Recovery was slow and mentally painful. Knowing that I was too ignorant for the United States Navy was heartbreaking enough. I knew some guys in the Navy who were missing a few screws, who couldn't pour water out of a boot with directions on the heel. Yes, this was a major setback. I needed to get out of this place.

Where do I start? I need to get my old job back; that is a start, I thought. I have to stay focused. I have to be positive.

Now I saw what education was all about. I was an average student up until my sophomore year in high school. I even came close to making the honor roll a couple of times. Then the girls and wanting to belong started. I traded my education for popularity. I could have had both. What a fool I was.

I called Sister Mary Jane Francis, my old boss. I told her the same lie that I told family and friends about why the Navy turned me down. The good sister was a sight to behold, even in her nun's uniform. She personified beauty. Then again, I had never seen her without her white uniform, except a couple of times when she wore black and white. When she walked down the hospital hallway, my mouth dropped to the floor as I stared at her. I know on numerous occasions some of the nurses were pushing my chin up and laughing, saying, "It isn't nice to stare."

Sister Mary Jane Francis was about five foot nine or five foot ten. She wore no makeup, so what you saw was what you got. Her personality was one of her best qualities. When she spoke to me for whatever reason, she put me in a trance. Most of the time she had to repeat herself, which seemed to amuse her. I think she and most of the nurses knew how I idolized her. I remember when I first saw a couple of strands of her brown hair, I got excited and felt ashamed of my reaction. So, I prayed to the good Lord to forgive me for about a week.

I had never seen a Black nun before, but I was sure that there must be one because Blacks had been copying Whites as long as there had been a USA. I probably could not take it if I saw a Black Sister Mary Jane Francis.

I believe that women were made for men and men for women. God made man and woman to be fruitful and multiply.

I could never understand in a million years why the good sister was a nun.

That was beyond me.

The good sister was always in my dreams. I dreamed that we were married, and when we were just about to kiss, I would wake up in a cold sweat.

I remember Nannie discovering the results of my dreams from my stained sheets. I overheard Nannie discussing it with Daddy.

"Rev, you need to talk to Tierron. I know he's becoming a man and all, but what he is doing in his bed is immoral and sinful."

"Well, honey, he'll grow out of it," Daddy said, with a little humor in his voice.

"There is nothing funny about it, Rev. He's got two sisters, and it doesn't look right him carrying on that way. Hope you are not encouraging such behavior."

"Of course not, Liler, but he is growing up and there are things God put in him and young men his age that only time can heal."

"Rev, are you telling me God is putting him up to it?"

"No, Liler. I mean all boys his age are probably going through it. Arthur Junior went through it and even I went through it until you came along," Daddy joked.

I could hear some rustling and giggling going on. Daddy must be putting on the old charm, I thought.

"Rev, stop it! And keep your hands to yourself," Nannie said with a giggle. "I'm serious," she said in a softer voice.

"He'll be fine, sweetie."

"Rev, you know I've heard that it causes blindness."

There was a long silence, then a little giggling as Daddy tried to disguise his amusement by clearing his throat. Nannie exploded like a stick of dynamite.

"I'm serious, Rev, and you are laughing at me."

"No, sweetie, I'm not laughing at you. Your son is normal, he is going through something that boys his age go through. But I'll talk to him if it'll make you happy."

"Now that's more like it. What are you going to tell him?"

"To be more discreet."

"Rev!" Nannie yelled in a shocked voice.

Well, Daddy didn't approach me with it, and to save face, I started using a sock. No more evidence.

After all, this wasn't something that just started.

I remember Angel's sister Carla, who is a couple of years older than Angel. Now, Carla didn't go for the soda and cookie deal. She wanted—and got—two days of lunch money, which was fifty cents. A few times, I got it on credit, and when I did, she had no problem getting paid. Carla told all my friends how small I was. I was thirteen, and all my friends started teasing me by holding up their thumb and index finger.

Ronnie, a couple of years my senior, told me, "Now we know what the T stands for—it stands for tiny."

The word on the street was if you wanted to grow, you had to exercise yourself. That's how I started and have been at it ever since. I hear some women say size doesn't count, but size is everything to men.

I mean, in the gym showers, the older guys with the big penises held their heads high like they owned Sears & Roebuck, with their chests out and fists clinging to their hips, showing everything. Then there were boys like me who held our towels like a fig leaf and sometimes carried them into the showers with us.

I remember how big Grandpa was when I first noticed him. It was about the same time Carla made me aware of my humanity. Grandpa was drying off after taking a bath when I walked in to use the bathroom. I was staggered by the size and length of his penis. Daddy was big, but Grandpa was humongous in comparison. We are talking eight inches long and about two inches in diameter. The first thing I thought was, "What does he feed it? It looked so alive."

I'm thinking about the African black mamba—big, black, and deadly.

"Grandpa, why are you so big and I'm so small? I hope it runs in the family," I said in astonishment, still looking at the snake of death.

"Tierron, you would look ridiculous with my piece, and I would definitely look deformed with yours," he said with amusement. "Don't rush it, and get out of here."

"Yes, sir."

As I was about to close the door behind me, Grandpa yelled, "Tierron, it does run in the family."

I smiled as the door shut.

***

I got my job back.

The good Sister was just as stunning as ever in her angelic white habit. I guess being an orderly was not the worst thing you could do, especially when considering the alternative of not having a job. Plus, there is a little nobility in being a male nurse attendant. You are helping your fellow man get better. The pay is lousy, but every little bit helps.

Chapter II

Growing Pains

Everybody was off to college. All my friends were gone. I had become a little distanced from them because of the Charleston tragedy. I felt so ashamed because I represented my class when I took the battery test, and I failed them. This was something I would take to my grave; no one must know, including my family.

I talked to Sarah a couple of times on the phone. She told me she was having a good time and had met new friends and all. As the months rolled by, our relationship as girlfriend and boyfriend dwindled. The "I love you" and the "I miss you" were steadily disappearing from our conversations. The letters used to be two to three pages long, but now there were none. The last time we talked, she told me she was seeing someone else. I was not mad because I was also dating. I guess the saying is true: "Out of sight, out of mind."

I started dating a girl named Leslie. She was tall and slim with amazingly beautiful eyes. They were big and brown with long lashes that encircled her eyelids. When they moved, they seemed to be in slow motion and in perfect harmony with each other. Leslie and I would go out from time to time, but our relationship never sizzled. I think it was because Leslie and Connie were good friends.

Now, Connie had some nice running partners. One was Nicole, and she had to be the most beautiful woman on the planet. Some girls are attractive and become less attractive, and some are less attractive and become more attractive, like the ugly duckling syndrome. Nicole was different—she got prettier each time I looked at her. I remember when she was living in Lee Walker Heights, the projects. Momma and Uncle June lived there also, so it gave me an excuse for Nannie to let me go. I had bought Nicole some chocolate kisses and had Nannie gift wrap them in aluminum foil. When I got in sight of Nicole, she was wearing a light blue dress trimmed in white lace and a plethora of shoulder-length braids with matching light blue ribbons on each braid. She was more beautiful than ever. I had practiced over and over what I was going to say to her. I got within thirty yards of her when all hell broke loose.

Nicole's brothers saw me and turned their mean-ass black-and-white cocker spaniel on me. I turned to run and tripped over something. I fell, tearing my Sunday pants and dropping the chocolate kisses. I could hear the kids laughing at me. Instead of running to Momma's or Uncle June's apartment, I just ran home. I was so humiliated I never tried to approach Nicole again.

Then there was Jackie, and this was one fine, bow-legged creature. I do believe it was a lust thing. Jackie, as a kid, was a tomboy and could beat your butt if you weren't careful. I had always thought she had the prospect of becoming a fine young lady. I had no idea she would turn out to be so fine. I started dating her, although she had a child with one of my classmates and ex-friend, Frank Towers.

What seemed to bother me about dating Jackie was having to deal with the knowledge that she was Frank's ex. I had always been attracted to his previous girlfriends. I had dated two of Frank's girls, and they had dropped me to go back to him. I guess the reason Jackie hadn't dropped me was because I had learned from the first two. Or was it because Frank had joined the United States Air Force? I knew that he would always be in her life because of the baby.

Frank and I had fallen out a while ago.

I remember it was a Saturday morning, right after Valentine's Day. It had snowed about three to four inches. Frank lived about five or six houses up from me. He had gotten in a car accident and didn't have a driver's permit. He came over to the house with one of our friends, Samuel Stone, to borrow my permit. Well, I didn't see any harm in giving him my license. We were friends, and I had always had a little crush on his sister, Barbara. I had taken her to the junior and senior prom as a junior. It was a night to remember, although nothing happened. Just being with her busted my bubble.

Frank had dated Connie for about six months, so he was something like family. Frank and Barbara were two of the most popular students in our class. I really thought he was my friend because I thought we were close. Well, anyway, Frank returned my license the same day, and all was forgotten until the Department of Motor Vehicles in Raleigh, North Carolina, wanted six hundred and fifty dollars or my license.

Frank entered the Air Force soon after graduation. I tried to contact him with no luck. I told his family about my dilemma, and I am sure they informed him. Still, Frank made no effort to contact me. Of course, I should have told Nannie and Daddy about it, and maybe I could be driving legally today, but this was a decision I made on my own. Daddy had always told me to accept my responsibilities and deal with them, so I sent my license in by mail because six hundred fifty dollars was like a million dollars to me.

Wow!

Do good guys always finish last?

It just doesn't seem right that some people seem to have all the luck, and then there are people like me.

I had really prepared myself for the driver's examination on my sixteenth birthday. The patrolman told Daddy that I was the first one in about two weeks to make a perfect score. Daddy was so proud of me, and when he told Nannie, she just beamed with joy.

There was this poem hanging up in the living room that Nannie loved to recite: "God grant me the serenity to accept the things I cannot change; the courage to change the things I can; and the wisdom to know the difference."

I didn't have the wisdom to know the difference, but I was learning.

I could never tell Nannie or Daddy how I had lost my license, although I still drove the car from time to time.

CHAPTER 12

211B

Now here I was, a certified male nurse attendant. I had two weeks of training at Memorial Mission Hospital. That's the hospital across the street from Saint Joseph's, where the Blacks go to recover from their illnesses. I had never seen a Black patient at Saint Joseph's. I was told that Blacks could not afford the cost because it was a private hospital.

Anyway, how proud I was when I received my training certificate. Nannie hung it on the wall. I had been an orderly for about two years. Before then, I worked in the dietary department cleaning pots and pans and doing any other work that had to be done, including delivering food and retrieving the empty plates. It was a promotion.

Russell, another orderly that I worked with, was putting two kids through college. I graduated with his daughter, Starlett. Now she was going places. She received an academic scholarship to Spelman College in Atlanta. The girl was smart, a real bookworm, and Russell made sure we all knew it. Russell had an older son who was playing college football. So, I guess being an orderly wasn't too bad.

Working from three to eleven is the worst shift when you like to party. I also like to sleep, and Nannie let me sleep late, so I chose sleep over partying. I guess my party life was over. At eighteen years old, my life as a high roller was done. That's got to be a record.

I really missed the Castle on the Hill. That was the local name of Stephens-Lee High School because it was set on top of a hill, looking over the city of Asheville. My class was the last to graduate from her walls.

I let the fond memories of my time at Stephens-Lee roll through my mind as I approached the nurse's station.

Miss Porter was sitting at the desk, watching the clock but pretending to go over the work charts with Mrs. Carson, the seven-to-three head nurse. Miss Porter was the head nurse of Second North on the three-to-eleven shift. The woman should have been a doctor or nurse practitioner. She knew her job, mine, and everyone else's associated with the hospital, and she knew them well.

"Good afternoon, Miss Porter and Mrs. Carson," I said, picking up my worksheet without looking up.

"Well, good afternoon to you, young man. You are three minutes early," Miss Porter said, peering through her half-moon glasses that were balanced on the tip of her long, pointed nose, and looking at the wall clock. "This is a record; just keep up the good work."

"Yes, ma'am, anything to put a smile on your face."

"Tee, how's your heart? I hope you are getting enough exercise. It'll help to strengthen your heart," Mrs. Carson said as she bit down on her lower lip to reset her upper dentures.

"Yes, ma'am, my heart is fine. I do get a good workout when Miss Porter is in charge," I answered, staring at Miss Porter.

Both women looked up at me with amusement.

"That was very good, but we need a rectal temp in room 211B," Miss Porter said, still with a little humor in her voice.

"Yes, ma'am, but it is not on my worksheet," I responded, going over the sheet again.

"Yes, I know. The patient's doctor just called it in. Go ahead and complete your task, and I'll enter it on the log."

Miss Porter gave the order as she and Mrs. Carson walked toward the medicine room.

"No problem," I said.

Got to keep those drugs accounted for, I thought, as Mrs. Carson unlocked the medicine room door.

I was about to go to the utility room to pick up what I needed for the rectal temp when I heard laughter coming from the hospital cafeteria. The main cafeteria entrance and exit were directly in front of the Second North nurses' station. Three young women were coming toward me: two white girls and one highly light-skinned Black girl. She was a yellow bone— that's what we call a light-skinned sister. The Black girl stood out because of her height and attire. She stood at least a head taller than her friends and was dressed like a model. I could have sworn that I saw her in a JCPenney catalog. She was not from here, that's for sure.

Yeah, she must be a college student.

When they got closer, she looked up, exposing a face that I knew I was going to know better. I checked her out from head to toe and could not find a flaw anywhere. So, this is why the Almighty kept me here.

She was wearing a solid white blouse with a V-neck and Southern-laced sleeves that covered her long, slender arms. She wore a tan skirt, about an inch above her knees, that revealed perfectly shaped legs covered with white tights. Her shoes were tan, strapped at the heels with an open toe. Her hair was as black as a cypress swamp and shoulder-length, which reminded me of Liz Taylor in Cleopatra. Her skin was the color of cream with a touch of bronze. Her eyes were perfectly centered and draped with long lashes. Her gumdrop nose could have only been made for her oval face, and her smile seemed to light up the dimly lit corridor, exposing flawless ivory. A stone replica of Lena Horne.

When our eyes met, there was a tingling sensation that started in my groin and ended at the top of my head and the bottom of my feet simultaneously.

"Hello," she said with a smile.

I could only nod my head because my mouth was as dry as the Sahara Desert after being open so long. You could have flown a jumbo jet in and out of my mouth without touching the sides. When they were some distance past me, I was trying to check out her rear, which is a true indicator of a real sister, but my queen had moved in front of her friends. I must get a clear shot of her buns, I thought, as I was walking toward the departing three. Then I heard this familiar, irritating voice.

"Young man, young man, leave those young ladies alone and get to work," Miss Porter said.

"Yes, ma'am, but I need to get a thermometer out of the utility room," I said, not looking at her but still trying to zoom in on my queen's behind.

Yes, she was a sister, I thought, after getting a glimpse of a perfectly round butt.

The utility room was located on Second South. With a little bop in my stride, I walked in. Russell was washing his hands with his orderly cap molded in the shape of a Navy cap.

"What's happening, Youngblood?" he asked.

"Man, I am in love," I said, staring out into space.

"Let me tell you something, young Don Juan," he said as he dried his hands with a paper towel. "If you don't leave that married woman alone, you are going to have some big trouble."

Russell was almost whispering as he gave me his warning.

"What are you talking about?"

"You know what I am talking about. I heard about you and Nurse Maya. I wasn't born yesterday, Youngblood."

"Russell, we broke up weeks ago."

I started that lie with Robert Jr., and he must've told Russell. Now it had blown out of proportion. I just hope Maya didn't get wind of it. When you lie, you must continue the lie with another lie, I thought.

"Well, I hope so," he said.

I put my hand over my heart and said, "Russell, I just saw the woman of my dreams."

"I hope you are not talking about one of those white girls that just walked past here. Boy, don't you know that is D-E-A-T-H and not L-O-V-E."

"Russell, one of them was Black."

"Youngblood, listen to me. There is no future with a white woman. Society has already made your move for you. You can't take her out to dinner or dancing because you are always defending yourself. There is a white man who will take your life in a heartbeat to protect what he thinks is his, and the law protects him. I have lost a couple of friends thinking that times have changed, and they ended up disappearing from the face of the Earth."

"How many times do I have to tell you, one of them was Black!"

"As flat as their asses were. Boy, as soon as you get paid, I want you to invest in a pair of glasses. There wasn't one colored gal in the bunch. Why don't you get a young colored gal and stick with her?"

"I would, but she's in college and when she comes home, she stays with you," I fired back with a smile.

"Now you are talking, Youngblood. But you need more than this job is paying to support my baby."

"When me and Starlett get married, I'm going to quit my job, then both of us can stay with you, Daddy."

"Well, I know they taught you better than that at Stephens-Lee," he said, flipping his cap over his forehead and walking out the door grinning.

When I reached 211B, the patient was a burn victim, which meant he was highly sedated. He must have weighed at least

260 pounds and was about five foot six. The room was saturated with the smell of burnt flesh. Seventy percent of his body was burned, and half of his right ear was missing.

It took me about ten minutes to get him positioned. Then I put on my gloves, lubricated the thermometer with KY Jelly, and inserted it.

I just couldn't get that lovely creature I had just seen out of my mind. Russell was crazy. She was Black! Her ass was round as a basketball, not flat like a pancake. I told myself I would see her again and she would know me. I just knew Nannie would like her.

Yes, this is love and lust, I can live with both.

The patient moved a little, bringing me back to reality. When I went to remove the thermometer, it was gone.

"Shit! Where's the thermometer?" I shouted.

I felt around but couldn't locate it anywhere. It was inside of him. He had rolls of fat and the hairiest ass and crack I had ever seen.

Jesus!

How many times had Miss Porter told me to keep my hands on the thermometer when administering a rectal temp to a patient?

She is going to have my ass this time!

I rolled him over to one side, resting him on the side rail. I could go to jail if he dies. Oh God! I've done it again. I just knew they hadn't fed him in a while, and maybe his body thought the thermometer was food. If the thermometer breaks, the mercury could kill him.

I had just graduated from high school and was on my way to reform school.

Oh shit!

Where's that damn thermometer?

By now, I was hysterical and talking out loud. I was in the bed and on my knees, pushing layers of fat away with one hand and searching with the other. I couldn't find it anywhere! I was going to jail, and my life hadn't even started yet.

Maybe I can see it, I thought, with my face less than an inch away from his rectum. The patient let me have it. He sprayed me, and I felt the mist, like a skunk defending itself. The smell was unbearable, and I knew that smell didn't come from an empty stomach. When I jerked back, he rolled over and I was under him. I began to struggle for my life because I couldn't breathe. I tried the nurse's button, but it was out of reach. As I struggled to get out, I heard the door open.

"What are you doing, young man?" Miss Porter asked, with laughter in her voice.

After she got me out of my predicament, I told her what had happened. Well, it took two nurses and two orderlies to get one thermometer out of one big ass hole.

That was a crazy lesson learned!

CHAPTER 13

ROMEO AND GLENNA?

Glenna Aravia Thompson "Glen"

It was payday, and Nannie fixed my favorite dish: fried chicken, collard greens, rice and gravy, deviled eggs, and banana pudding for dessert. Daddy made his famous grape Kool-Aid with freshly squeezed lemons.

The family was seated at the dinner table. Anthony, Uncle June's oldest son, had joined us. Anthony rode his bike down on the weekends. We had all grown up together, and I considered him my little brother. He was five years my junior. He and Cookie were the same age. We called Anthony "Chicken Smeller" because he could smell chicken in the middle of nowhere. I do believe he smelled Nannie's chicken that day.

Daddy asked me to lead us in prayer. It was short and to the point.

Daddy always got the first piece of chicken, and then the grabbing began. I didn't have to worry about my piece getting grabbed; the chicken back was mine, and that was the law—Nannie's law! I wanted to request a change in the chicken parts because the main reason I chose the back several years ago was that it looked bigger than the rest of the pieces. Well, it was the biggest piece but the smallest in meat portion. I guess I had been lame in the brain for a long time now.

I had already given Nannie a third of my check and Momma a ten spot.

"Nannie, could I keep my check next payday?" I asked. "I need to get my sports coat out of layaway at JCPenney. I got it on sale. It's really nice."

"I'll pray over it, but money is very scarce around here. Things haven't been the same since Uncky and Grandpa left us. There are bills to be paid. You know we have Feast in the Wilderness in two weeks," she said.

Feast in the Wilderness was given to Nannie by God. She said one night God came to her in a vision and instructed her on an all-day service. In other words, we would eat, worship, eat, worship, eat, and worship.

"The junior choir is singing, and we are to dress in black and white. What color is your coat?" Nannie asked, passing the cornbread to Cookie.

"It's green pinstriped."

I was proud of my fashion choice, although I had nothing remotely close to wear with it. It just looked good.

"Well, you need a black coat for church. The one you got is getting too small, plus it is tearing at the seams."

"Yes, ma'am, but I just met this girl, and she is so together. I just know when you meet her you all will love her too."

I was hoping for some understanding from the boss lady.

"Tee, I know you are not talking about Jackie Mason, are you?" Connie asked sarcastically, speaking with a full mouth of food.

"No, I am not talking about Jackie."

"Can't you like her in a black coat?" Nannie said with jest.

"Now, Liler, he's old enough to know what he wants," Daddy said, looking in the air. "Son, I got a black vest that's way too small for me. With a little doctoring up, it'll go fine with your white shirt and black tie."

"Man Boy, what's her name?" Momma asked enthusiastically.

"Well... I... ay... ay don't exactly know... ay her name, Momma. We haven't... ay... met yet," I stuttered, not looking up from my plate.

"You don't even know her name," Connie said with a sly grin, looking at Nannie.

"That's right, but I will know her, and she is going to be my girl," I promised.

I didn't know where that came from, but I knew it to be the truth. It felt like my heart was beating a thousand beats per minute. I could feel the adrenaline as I spoke of her. This has to be love because no one has ever made me feel the way she has.

Everyone's mouth dropped and all eyes were on me.

"I do believe my son is in love," Momma said, beaming with joy.

"Suppose she is one of them Jehovah's Witnesses, or even worse, one of them Black Muslims? Now, Tierron, you know what the Good Book says: 'Thou shalt have no other gods before me,'" Nannie quoted.

"Mama, can't you see that our little boy has grown up? I do believe he is in love," Momma said.

"Praise the Lord," Nannie said.

"Nannie, she is not a Jehovah's Witness or a Black Muslim," I said, with my fingers crossed under the table.

"Tee, don't forget you promised to take me to the carnival," Cookie said, changing the subject.

"I want to go, too," Anthony added.

"I promise," I said, looking at them both.

"Well, if she is a model, I believe God wants you to have that coat," Nannie said with a smile.

I jumped up and kissed Nannie and Momma before Nannie could change her mind.

"I just know you all will love her," I said, returning to my seat.

Daddy gave me a wink, which confirmed his approval.

"What makes you think that she wants you? Plus, she probably doesn't know you exist," Connie said.

"She will be my girl, and you can take that to the bank," I said rolling my eyes at her.

Connie stuck her tongue out at me, and Daddy commanded us to behave ourselves.

Earlier that day, Nannie had been staring at my collection of twelve 5 x 7s of my classmates' graduation pictures, and of course, they were all female. There were a couple of photos of me and my date to the junior and senior proms. They were distributed all around the living and dining rooms. Most of the pictures were located on top of the piano and on the mantel over the fireplace. They were just friends, although I had an intimate imaginary relationship with them all. I knew what she must have been thinking.

"Nannie, they are just my friends, but you will meet my future bride," I said as she shifted her attention to me.

"Well, son, when are we going to meet my future daughter-in-law?" Daddy asked after clearing his throat and looking at Nannie.

"Soon, Daddy," I replied when I noticed tears rolling down Nannie's cheeks.

"What's wrong, Nannie?" I asked, and all eyes went to her.

"Oh, Tierron, you've grown so fast, and you are the spitting image of C. Ray. I love you so much, and I just want you to do what is right," she cried. "You are not forced to marry her, are you?" she asked, looking me in the eye.

"Mama, he said they were never formally introduced," Momma said, passing her a napkin.

"Nannie, Momma is right, but I will bring her here to meet you."

I put more bass in my voice and patted her hand.

This was one introduction I had to make, I thought as I watched Nannie dry her eyes.

After dinner, Connie and Cookie began clearing off the table. I whispered in Anthony's ear that I needed his bike to go over to Jackie's house. It was going to be a great day. I just knew it was. In fact, I couldn't remember the last time I was so excited, although it had been a week since I had seen that lovely creature.

As I grew to appreciate the fairer sex, I was constantly in front of the mirror, trying to perfect perfection—and that's an impossibility. But the comb was my mortal enemy. Just getting it through my head was an act of God.

My father had thick curly hair, and so did his brother, Uncle Jesse. His hair was a lot straighter than C. Ray's hair. I know they didn't get up in the morning cursing their hair out for it to act right. My father and his older brother had what most Black people call good hair. Momma said there was no such a thing as good hair or bad hair. Hair is hair, she would say.

Butch was the spitting image of his father from head to toe. I, in turn, got C. Ray's big nose. He's got a big mustache to camouflage the enormity of his nose, and I have peach fuzz, which doesn't hide my big nose.

Now, don't get me wrong. I am not complaining about my physical appearance, because my old man is one handsome dude. I pray to the Almighty every day to be just like him in body and soul, except in the parental department because I will take care of my own.

I guess I have always been in competition with Butch, although he probably hasn't given me a second thought. The reality of it all is that I've always envied him for having a caring and tangible father. As far back as I can remember, Butch was always the prince, and I the pauper.

I am now fighting over time spent in the bathroom with Connie. I even started taking regular baths instead of once a week, which Nannie would have to make me take. I had always been a strong believer in the stand-up wash at the bathroom sink. Connie was always telling me I stunk, and I was constantly telling her that I smelled like her breath. I guess you would call our bickering sibling rivalry. Cookie, on the other hand, was my baby sister and the apple of my eye. Most of the time, whatever I had, if Cookie wanted it, it was hers.

It was time to make a truce with Connie because I wanted to know all I could about what makes girls happy. I could not get my queen out of my mind. I had told God and my family that this girl was right for me, and she was going to be my wife. Although I still didn't know her name, I knew she would be mine one day.

"Connie, I got a proposition. If you help me out, I'll take you and Cookie to the YWCA dance this Friday."

Connie and Cookie were not allowed to go without a male chaperone—or should I say, me.

"Who do I have to kill for this?" Connie calmly asked.

"I just need some information about what girls like in boys. I mean, I know you and Nicole talk to each other about what you like and don't like about boys. I need all I can get to catch this trophy."

"First thing, I don't believe you will take me and Cookie to the dance because you are working. Why don't you just march yourself into the kitchen and tell Nannie that you are taking us on Friday night to the dance, and you are paying our way in? Plus, five dollars now, cash in hand, and when you return, I'll tell you something that Nicole said about you"

Connie laid out her demands as she parted her long hair in small patches to grease her scalp.

"Jesus, girl, this better be good," I moaned, reaching for my wallet and knowing I would give anything to know what Nicole said about me. "I'll give you three and not a penny more."

Connie took the money, and I walked into the kitchen where Momma was doing Nannie's hair.

"Nannie, will it be all right for me to take Connie and Cookie to the dance at the Y on Friday night? I'll start working from seven to three Thursday morning. I am switching with one of the orderlies for about a week."

Knowing I didn't say anything about paying their way in, I still might just get what I wanted for only three dollars and a trip to the dance, which I was going to anyway.

"Well, it's about time you took an interest in your sisters, and God's got great things in store for you for being so considerate. Just don't keep them out too long. Now come over here and give your Nannie some sugar."

I marched over like a toy soldier to receive my rewards, then did an about-face and marched back to the bathroom where Connie was finishing up her hair.

"Now, tell me everything Nicole said about me, and don't leave a thing out," I thundered.

I didn't want to seem too anxious, but I was displaying that I was.

"Wait a minute."

After putting the last touches on her hair, Connie grabbed my hand and led me into the kitchen. Her hair was long, thick, and jet-black. Connie was becoming a young lady, I thought, as she pulled me into the kitchen.

"Nannie, did Tee tell you that he was paying our way into the dance Friday night?" Connie asked, turning my hand loose.

"Now Tierron, you know I don't have any money to give these girls for the dance," Nannie said, leaning to the side while Momma was straightening her hair.

I looked at Connie, and she smiled back.

"Yes ma'am, I was going to pay their way in," I groaned, not trying to show my frustration with being outsmarted by my younger sister.

"But Nannie, we are going to need some money for hot dogs and Cokes," Connie said in her best Shirley Temple impression.

I must admit I would have given her an Oscar for that performance.

"Okay, I'll give them five dollars apiece," I finally surrendered.

"No, Man Boy, five dollars together should be enough if you are going to pay their way in," Momma said, not missing a stroke with the hot straightening comb.

"But Momma!" Connie protested.

"Connie, you heard what your mother said. Five dollars is plenty," Nannie finalized.

"Yes, ma'am," Connie said, as I followed her out of the house to the porch.

"Alright, you little gold digger, let me have all of it," I said, knowing I had just been conned.

"Well, don't get mad when I tell you this, and I hope you can accept constructive criticism."

"Yeah, yeah, come on. Tell me what she said."

"Let's go down and sit on the driveway wall."

Connie led the way, and I followed close behind.

Oh! This must be good, I thought.

Connie sat on the wall and motioned for me to do the same.

"Right now, if you had a choice of being with Nicole or your new friend, who would you choose?" she asked.

I had always had a big crush on Nicole for as long as I could remember, but no one had made me feel the way this queen had made me feel.

"That's easy, my new friend," I proudly said, as my feet dangled off the brick wall.

"Well, if that's the case, forget about Nicole."

How could I forget one of the most beautiful girls in the city, if not the world?

"Girl, I just paid you, so tell me what she said," I angrily demanded, while waving my fist.

Connie knew that she had my dander up and she was ready to push the right buttons.

"Tee, Nicole said..."

Connie was now almost bursting with laughter and holding her air-filled jaws with both hands. She was laughing so hard, air was occasionally escaping through her fingers.

"Sh-sh-she said, you are cute, but if you cut off your head you would look a hundred percent better."

Connie's jaws exploded with mocking laughter.

The next thing I knew, Connie was racing through the gate and locking it behind her. I was madder than Samson was when he found out about his new haircut. I cleared the gate with one bounce and caught her before she got to the top of the stairs.

"Girl, you're going to feel some pain!" I shouted.

"Momma... Momma!"

Connie screamed, scratching and clawing with her long-manicured nails.

"Ouch!"

I felt pain in my side.

Momma had a chunk of my side, squeezing and twisting.

"Tierron, leave your sister alone. Don't you dare hit her. You don't ever, ever, hit a girl regardless. Do I make myself clear?"

Momma shouted at me, with nostrils flaring and tightening down on her death grip.

"Momma, shiiit!" I cried as the pain intensified, with both my hands in the air and fingers fully extended and separated.

"Tierron, watch your mouth!" Nannie yelled.

"Momma, I swear, I didn't do anything to him!" Connie cried with tears running down her face.

"Connie, stop swearing!" Nannie shouted.

"Momma, please turn me loose, you're hurting me!" I pleaded.

Momma finally removed her clamps from my side.

"Delores, I just know she started it," Nannie said, staring at Connie.

"I don't care who started it. You two kiss and make up," Momma said as she gently pushed me toward Connie.

"Momma, I ain't kissing her."

I stuck out my bottom lip and began wiping away the tears with my upper arms.

What I wanted to do was put my foot up her ass, I thought, as Momma pulled Connie toward me.

"Now do your Momma proud, Connie, and kiss your big brother."

"Momma, I don't—"

Momma cut Connie short by placing her index finger over her lips.

Connie leaned over and pecked my jaw. I could have thrown up right in her face and not spared a drop anywhere else. Momma gave me a notch, so I figured when Momma made a request—which she seldom did—take heed or feel pain. Momma had a patent on pinching. So, I pulled back my lips and touched her jaw with my face because I'd be damned if I was going to put my lips on her.

"Now that's more like it," Nannie said as she walked back in the house.

"You two should always love each other, and you are not setting a good example for Cookie. Now don't you feel a lot better?" Momma asked.

Before we could answer, she kissed both of us on the forehead and grabbed Connie by the arm, leading her into the house.

Connie turned around and gave me a victory grin, as Momma's words "Now don't you feel a lot better" sank in.

I surveyed my present condition. My side still hurt, my shirt was torn, and my chest looked like a herd of alley cats had danced the twist and shout to the beat of the Isley Brothers. I just knew it was time to leave Asheville.

Feel better, my ass, I thought, as I began nursing my wounds.

***

I started going to work on time, sometimes arriving ten minutes early. Miss Porter began treating me with more respect—I could hear it in her voice. She used to issue orders like an army drill sergeant; now, they seemed more like requests. Russell even mentioned how much he welcomed the change. I attributed it all to a woman I had never met and whose name I didn't even know.

Thursday morning, I walked to work with Robert Jr. Since the incident with the redhead, he had switched shifts. I told him about the fox that had changed my life, and as it turned out, he knew her. He had dated her cousin, Coleen. The queen's name was Glenna Thompson, and she and Coleen were student nurses. They were from Canton, North Carolina, which was about twenty-three miles from Asheville. Glenna was assigned to Saint Joseph Hospital, while Coleen was assigned to Memorial Mission Hospital.

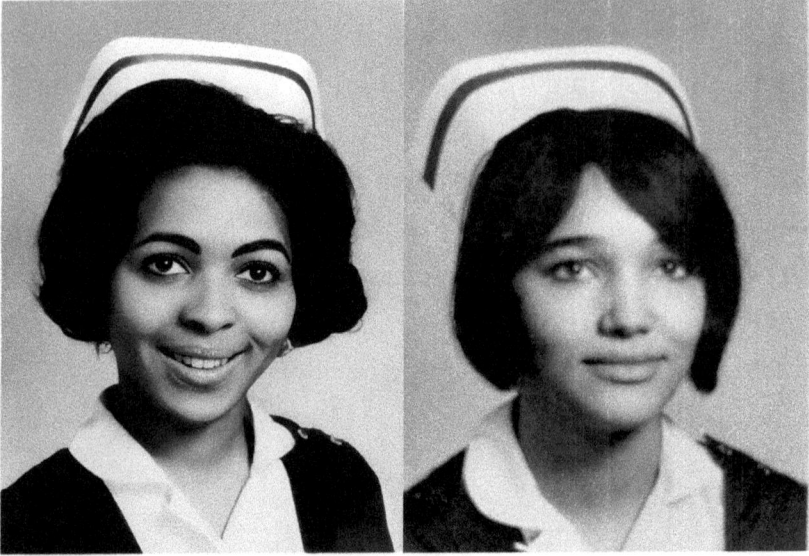

Glen   Coleen

The morning shift was a lot livelier than the evening shift. I guess because that's when the hospital was in full swing. Word was already out about the new foxes. At lunchtime, all the eligible bachelors would fight over the best seats in the employees' dining room, which was adjacent to the main cafeteria. When you paid for your food, the entrance to the employee dining room was about five paces to your front. The doctors and nurses ate in the main cafeteria. The orderlies, dietary staff, and housekeeping department, who were all Black, ate in the employees' dining room.

When Glenna walked into the cafeteria, you would've thought that Diana Ross had just entered. The low whistles and catcalls brought unwanted attention to Glenna and her class. I would only marvel at her style and grace.

Bae Bae worked in the housekeeping department and was much older than me. Our families had known each other for many years, and he thought Glenna and I would make an ideal couple. Mary Rose, a Black LPN who worked in the emergency room, also believed we were the perfect Romeo and Juliet. She warned me that Roy, a fellow orderly and eligible bachelor with a new car, was making his interest known and that if I wanted Glenna, I had better act quickly.

One day, while taking a patient back from an x-ray in the elevator, Glenna joined us. My heart felt like it was about to leap out of my chest. She was even more beautiful than the first time I saw her, dressed in her student uniform, looking like a model.

"Hello, Tee. How are you today?" she asked, turning to press her desired floor.

I stumbled through a response as my patient started coughing uncontrollably. When I looked up, she was gone. I cursed myself for not responding promptly, like a man should have.

I talked to Bae Bae, and we decided to have a party at his house. It was Wednesday, with payday a couple of days away.

Now it was time to put the icing on the cake. I finally located Glenna in the gift shop, having a Coke with her classmates. I walked up to their table, cleared my throat, and said, "Excuse me, ladies."

"Yes, may we help you?" Glenna asked, with all eyes on me.

In my most masculine voice, and looking into her large brown eyes, I said, "Glenna, my friends and I are throwing a party on Saturday night. Would you like to go with me?"

"Oh! You do know my name," she said sarcastically.

"Yes, I've known your name since the first time I laid eyes on you," I lied.

"Is that so? Have a seat and let's talk about my invitation," she said, pointing to the empty chair at the table.

"Thanks, but no thanks, I'm still working," I said.

"Glen, maybe we would like to go to the party, too," the redhead said, giving her a wink and a smile.

Wow! This white girl knows me too. They must have been talking about me. This is good, I thought.

"Excuse me, but I seem to be at a disadvantage," I responded, looking into a full face of freckles.

"I'm sorry. Tee, this is Brittany—Britt for short," Glenna said as the redhead nodded in recognition.

"And this is Valarie, who we call Val."

The brunette extended her hand.

"And my name is Glen," she said, moistening her sensuous lips with her slow-moving tongue.

"Of course, any friend of Glen's is a friend of mine. So, you ladies are cordially invited to the party of the year, hosted by yours truly."

"I like him, Glen!" Val said while looking at me.

"Well, if I go with you, do you promise to treat me like the queen of the party?" Glenna asked.

I grabbed the vacant seat and sat down, pulling the chair closer to her and looking into those big dreamy brown eyes. With my right hand cupping her left upper arm and my left hand holding hers, I said, "Pretty lady, I'll treat you better than any man has ever treated you, and you can put your daddy at the top of the list."

I didn't bat an eye.

I was surprised at how naturally the words came from my heart and out of my mouth. It must have been the truth.

Glen smiled and squeezed my hand. Britt and Val raised their Cokes in approval.

"Yes, we accept your invitation," Glen said, looking at her friends and then back at me.

"Good, because I guarantee you all a good time."

I got up from the chair and, while still holding her hand, kissed it lightly.

"Tee, wait a minute," she said, releasing my hand.

She grabbed a napkin, wrote on it, folded it, pressed her painted lips on it, and handed it to me.

"Anytime, Tee," she continued, giving me a smile that could have melted the sun.

"I must be getting back to work, ladies. It's been a pleasure," I said, looking at Britt and Val.

I waved the note high, giving a bigger smile.

Glen whispered, "Call me," but no sound came out. I turned and walked out of the gift shop.

When I got to the elevator, I quickly unfolded the napkin. It had her name, number, and the word "KISSES."

I neatly folded it and smelled her freshly pressed lips. When I stepped off the elevator, you couldn't hit me in the ass with a red apple. I had a smile Muhammad Ali couldn't knock off, and Wilt "The Stilt" Chamberlain was a midget to me.

I started stepping high and slow, with one hand in my pocket holding tight to the note. I should frame it for our grandkids, I thought, as I strode toward the nurse's station.

I called Glen that night, and we talked for over two hours. We were both born in 1947. She was a Cancer, and I was a Leo, born a month apart. We are perfect for each other, I thought, as I thanked my heavenly Father for another blessing.

CHAPTER 14

BELLE OF
THE BALL

O n the day of the party, I began by picking up snacks. Charlie's Market had the best cold cuts, and Paul Cox offered the widest variety of cheese. Ms. Nora had the cheapest corn whiskey. I had already scored two bottles of Wild Irish Rose, or "Little Men" as we called it, from Mr. Snag, the neighborhood wino who fancied himself a "Connoisseur of the Grape." I had hidden the bottles under my mattress.

I'm going to win Glen's heart tonight, I thought.

As I started polishing my church shoes, Connie walked in.

"What's happening, big brother?" she asked, grabbing the bottle of aftershave on the nightstand and sitting beside me on the bed. "Is this a brand-new bottle of Old Spice?"

"Yes, nothing is too good for my baby."

"So, you're serious about this girl?"

"Yes, she's got good possibilities."

"What kind of possibilities?"

"She has a great possibility of becoming my wife," I replied, grinning.

"I can tell you're nervous."

Connie covered her mouth to stifle a laugh.

"You don't know what you're talking about. I'm cool as a cucumber on the Alaskan front," I stated arrogantly.

"Well, Mr. Cucumber, why are you polishing the sole of your shoe?"

"Shit!" I whispered, and we both laughed.

"Listen, Tee, I know you're going to be the best dancer and the best-looking boy there. Just don't get carried away like when you and Slab get together and act a fool. When I saw that bottle of Old Spice aftershave, I knew she was someone special. So, brush your teeth and wash your rusty butt. After the SOAP and WATER comes the Right Guard and aftershave, because I've already checked you out when you mix the funk with the Right Guard," she said, folding her top lip under her nostrils.

"Plus, you don't want to put too much aftershave on; you might just rub off what little peach fuzz you do have," she said jokingly, letting out a giggle.

"Thank you for that lecture on personal hygiene, Miss Clean. Now get out of here so I can get ready."

My frown turned into a slight grin as I ushered her out of my room.

I made a final inventory of my clothes. My new green pinstripe sports coat fit me like it was tailor-made. Cookie did a good job of starching and pressing my black shirt and pants. My black socks had lost their elasticity, so by the end of the night they would be down past my ankles. Well, no one would be able to tell if I didn't sit down, plus the lights would be low.

Now, my Fruit of the Looms had more holes in them than a fisherman's net, and these were my best ones. Nannie always said, "Make sure your drawers are clean, in case you must go to the hospital." Well, I hope I don't break a leg tonight.

After taking a long and deserving bath, I touched up my nails with a little clear polish. Momma always said my fingers looked better than any professional model she had ever seen. I kept my fingers manicured and my nails a quarter inch, with my pinkie fingers about half an inch. Then I'd use Momma's eyelash brush to highlight my eyes because most of the girls I knew always told me how beautiful my eyes were. After that, I darkened up my mustache and sideburns because it made me look older and always got me into the Gay 90s Night Club on Biltmore Avenue.

One thing about me is that if a woman gave me a compliment, you could bet your last money I tried to improve it.

Glen and her cousin Coleen were rooming with Miss Young, an English teacher. She lived on Victoria Boulevard, which was within walking distance of both hospitals. You could ride a bike from her house to mine without pedaling, but you needed good brakes.

I arrived at Miss Young's house at about a quarter to eight. It was a red-brick two-story house with black shutters on each window. It looked more like a red box with the top flaps raised diagonally to each other. The house was surrounded by a four-foot chain-link fence. I could tell that the grass was freshly cut and well maintained. I rang the doorbell, and moments later, Glen opened the draped multi-window door.

She was breathtakingly beautiful. She wore a red silk wrap-around mini dress that revealed long, well-shaped stockinged legs, based with black patent leather strapped medium heels. The gold crucifix she wore around her long slender neck seemed to be the dividing point for her voluptuous breasts, which rose and fell with each breath. Her cleavage seemed so deep that I just wanted to jump in headfirst and get lost in the abyss. Her face showed no hint of makeup except for the cherry-red lipstick—the same lipstick she had earlier displayed to me when she pressed her lips on the note she passed to me in the hospital gift shop. I knew before the night was over, I would be that note.

She wore large hoop gold earrings that sparkled against her face. Her hair was a mass of curls, not a strand out of place. That was going to change, because my hands had already decided they were going to explore her, starting at the top. I knew by the end of tonight, Glen was going to change my God-given name to Hans. That tingling sensation that started in my groin when I first laid eyes on her had returned. Yes, this is what the old people call love, and I liked it. I was totally lost in oblivion, and as I began to come back to reality, I felt shaken.

"Tee…Tee, are you all right?" Glen asked, half smiling, with both hands on my upper arms.

"Yes… ah, Glen, I'm fine," I stammered, still captivated by her presence.

"You look marvelous."

"Why, thank you, Mr. Madden, and you are just as handsome as ever," she replied while grabbing her black leather jacket.

"Thank you, Miss Thompson. Let me carry that for you."

I took her jacket as she closed the door.

"It's a beautiful night."

We both looked up. There wasn't a cloud in the sky.

"Yeah, it is, but it ain't got nothing on you, sweetheart," I assured her, moving my head from side to side and admiring perfection.

"That's sweet; thank you again. Are you ready?" she asked, almost halfway down the cement walkway while I was still stationed in front of the door.

"Listen, just turn around and walk to the gate. I want to get a good look at all of you."

I stood perfectly still with my arms folded and my right hand cupping my chin, still captivated by her.

She hesitated for a moment. "Whatever you want," she giggled as she spun around like a professional model, strutted her stuff, then spun around again laughing.

The bright light over the door, aided by the streetlights, illuminated her as if she were performing at the Apollo Theater. I could only applaud her, but I think I was congratulating myself on my big catch.

"Yeah, you passed my inspection, pretty lady," I said, walking toward her, totally satisfied with my findings.

"You look fantastic in that coat. I've never seen one like it before. Did you get it here?" she asked, feeling the material.

"Oh! This old thing?" I retorted, opening the car door.

We got to the party and the hounds were out. Glen was the belle of the ball. The women were jealous, and the men were envious. She stood out because she was much taller than most of the women. She spoke the English language with the ease of an English professor, showing no hint of her southern heritage. She was very articulate in her pronunciation, which impressed everyone.

I became self-conscious about my street slang. I hated English all through high school and always got the minimum grade. Now it seemed I was ashamed to speak in front of her. Well, this was one big flaw I had to live with because I'd be damned if I was going to drop out of her class.

Britt and Val showed up about fifteen minutes after we did, with two of their classmates. Becky, a tall, slim brunette who wore braces, seemed nervous and out of her element. I think this was the first time in her life that she was playing the role of a minority. Amy, a petite little blonde, could have passed for twelve, but Glen said she was one of the oldest ones in her class. She was twenty-four years old.

I could tell Glen was more relaxed because her classmates were there. I felt more relaxed because there seemed to be enough women to go around. Plus, Black dudes seemed to go wild when white girls were around. I guess it's because they are the forbidden fruit. The old saying is that there are only two free people in the United States: a white man and a Black woman. Black men have always resented this. I don't think that Black men have a special craving for white women. I think that, just like the forbidden fruit in the Garden of Eden, the more you say they can't have it, the more they want it.

Well, there were enough women there to keep my competitors occupied, but every time I tried to sneak out with Glen for a little playtime, someone would ask her to dance. She would smile at me and squeeze my hand.

"I'll be right back; don't go anywhere," she'd say.

The party was in full swing. Robert Jr. was with a woman in her thirties named Allison. She worked at Memorial Mission as a nurse. She was a blonde and kind of cute, but she wasn't someone I'd write home to Momma about. Robert Jr. let it be known that she wasn't a bottle blonde. She seemed to fit right in at the party, plus she had style and rhythm. I must call a spade a spade: Robert Jr. was resourceful.

Allison was having a ball. She seemed to know the lyrics to all the songs and had a voice to boot. Bae Bae was spinning the 45s and laughing and talking stuff.

Glen and I danced back-to-back to the beat of "Do You Love Me" by the Contours and "Stubborn Kind of Fellow" by Marvin Gaye. After Marvin finished his tune, I decided to go upstairs to one of the bedrooms that Bae Bae said was our love nest, so Glen and I could be alone. I was leading her to the stairs when Roy accosted us.

Roy and I were about the same age, but he was about two inches taller and weighed about twenty pounds more. A lot of people thought we were related, which pissed me off. Jimmy Stewart's slow jam "I Do Love You" was playing and the lights were turned down.

"Hi, man! You gon' hog the lady all night?" Roy asked in his heavy bass voice.

"Roy, I give you more credit than others. You figured that out all by your damn self. I'm really impressed. Hoggin' my lady is a twenty-four-hour job."

"Well… ay ay… Why don't we…ay… ask Glenna?" he stammered, reaching for her arm.

I just hope she follows my cue, I thought.

I pulled her toward me and tried to stick my entire tongue down her throat. She met my eagerness with equal desire. I had always worried about my kisses because up until now, it all seemed like such a big hassle. I could never get my mouth right. Either my mouth was open too wide or not enough. Now I seem to have mastered it.

My hands did what they said they were going to do—explore. They were in her hair, down her neck, all over her back, and finally massaging her NBA trophy. My hands were second-rate compared to hers because her hands were all over me, and I could feel myself about to explode.

Shit!

I forgot I wasn't wearing any underwear. What seemed to be a simple gesture of who was in control ended up being who wasn't in control. I prayed that Roy was getting a front-row view of love in action.

I quickly but gently pushed myself away before I messed up my freshly pressed slacks. A couple of months ago, in the same situation, I would have had some wet pants. I guess this is what you call maturity.

Joe Tex was singing "Hold What You've Got," and we embraced again.

As the song was winding down and our kisses became more civilized, I knew she was the one. Out of all the disappointments in my life, I knew in my heart that I couldn't afford to lose her.

Glen was something special and needed special attention, I thought, as our lips disengaged and I held her face close to mine.

As I examined her eyes, they told me all I needed to know. They told me that we were falling in love.

Glen led me back to the middle of the floor after Bae Bae had dedicated a song to us. "My Girl" by the Temptations came on. Roy and Val were in a corner chair kissing all over each other. He found a toy to play with.

Good! Now he can leave my lady alone, I thought as the record ended.

"Hi! Glen, give Tee a break—you've got a lifetime to be with him," Britt said, losing her footing.

I grabbed her.

"OOPS!" Britt laughed.

"Britt, what are you drinking?" Glenna asked, turning up her nose.

"White lightning… and I could use a cigarette about now," she said, searching through her purse.

I reached into my inside coat pocket and flipped out my pack of cigarettes. I lit one and passed it to her.

"Here you are, Britt," I said.

"Thanks, Tee."

She took a long drag and slowly released the smoke from the corner of her mouth. She finished the contents of her drink in one gulp, showing off a sizable rock on her finger.

"Is that real?" I whispered to Glen, not taking my eye off the ring.

"Yes, it is. Her family is rich. I think they're in the tobacco business. Are you sure that's the only thing you're looking at?" Glen asked, glancing at a pair of forties that could have belonged to Jayne Mansfield.

"Well, my sweet, I'll take the ring, and you can have the baby feeders," I said, squeezing her jokingly.

"Can anyone join in this powwow?" Val shouted as she and Amy approached us arm in arm.

"Hi Val, where's Becky?" I asked.

"She's outside getting some air, and maybe something else," Val joked, then she and Amy burst out laughing.

"Tee, what's in that damn punch? Becky's had about two cups, and she's laughing and talking to everyone," Amy chuckled.

"Oh, just some of my special brew," I bragged.

"Well, I like it," Amy said.

"So, Valarie, you finally came up for air," Britt said sarcastically, looking at Roy who was now talking to Bae Bae.

"Brittany, Brittany… Brittany, do I detect a hint of jealousy?" Val bellowed, and everyone laughed.

"No, I'm surely not. I just think you should act more dignified in the company of strangers," Britt retorted in her most southern dialect.

"Brittany, you are jealous. I never would've believed it—you really are jealous!" Val yelled.

Everyone laughed again.

"Valarie Hoffman, if I want a man, any man in here, and especially Lurch over there, no problem," Britt shouted, fluffing her fiery red hair back.

"Any man?" Glen joked, squeezing my arm.

"I said any man, Glen. I wasn't talking about Tee," Britt said.

"So, you're saying my man is not a man?" Glen chuckled.

"Oh, Glen! You know what I mean," Britt replied.

This was my cue—I could see that everyone was having a good time, especially my lady and her friends. I needed to check on the rest of the party.

I squeezed Glen's hand as I walked off to the beat of "Beat You to the Punch" by Mary Wells.

"Don't go too far," Glen whispered.

I threw her a kiss. I walked into the kitchen and poured myself some punch with a little splash of Wild Irish Rose. We had two five-gallon containers of punch—one was straight, and one was labeled "Good Stuff," which had over a quart of corn whiskey with a little gin chaser. I had to leave the "Good Stuff" alone or suffer the wrath of Nannie, Momma, or both. You didn't want both on your tail. I would rather go through hell with gasoline drawers on than have the "Dynamic Duo" rain pain on their beloved son.

I had bought three small bottles of Little Man for sippers like me. I grabbed a couple of chicken salad sandwich quarters and washed them down with my mix. After straightening up and making an inventory of the remaining refreshments, I was satisfied.

Robert Jr., Bae Bae, Roy, and Joe, another one of Saint Joseph's finest, were in deep conversation. When I strode up to them, I had a cup in hand and was in time with the music.

"Listen, man, Asheville's got nothing else to offer me. I'll be out of here in a couple of months, right, Cuz?" Robert Jr. said, slapping my hand.

"Nigga, you're still working for the man, even if you had to go to the moon," Joe said, taking a sip of straight moonshine.

"Listen, man, have you noticed there are no Black patients at Saint Jose's? You know why? Because it's about money. We don't have the economics, and until we do, Blacks and whites will always be segregated. Now, in D.C., Blacks run everything—not like this one-horse town. Ya hear me?" Robert Jr. said.

"Not if Rev. King has anything to do with it. The man is moving, and the world is changing for the better," Bae Bae retorted, taking a long drag of his cigarette.

"Man, don't you know, if they think Martin Luther King is moving too fast, they'll kill him. They'll probably get a Black man to do it," Robert Jr. said, looking at me for approval.

"You know, if something mysteriously happens to Rev. King, the colored folks and some of the good white folks wouldn't stand for it," Roy countered.

"They shot the President of the United States, a white man, in broad daylight. You know what they'll do to a Black man," Robert Jr. said, opening a pack of cigarettes and offering me one.

I grabbed one, and he lit both of us up.

"Robert Jr., tell it like it is," I said sarcastically.

I just couldn't keep my mind off Glen. Damn, she looks good.

"Listen, my brothers, the world is changing. Sidney Poitier just won an Oscar. President Johnson just signed the Civil Rights Act of 1964 and Voting Rights Act of 1965," I said.

"No more Stephen Lee. Man, I pray we don't lose our souls," Joe drunkenly whispered.

"Man, I just wanted to play Lee Edward in some football and kick some ass," Roy said.

"Shit, fuck football, how about the girls?" Joe laughed.

"Yeah! Happily ever my ass. Then how are we going to deal with the Black women? Just look! They're ready to start some shit right now," I joked back, pointing to a group of Black women standing next to Glen and her friends.

We all laughed.

"Wait a minute, Tee, now I occasionally mix it up because variety is the spice of life. I love all women, but it seems the white women got the positive cash. You know that ready flow of funds that gives them the power of independence. Independence creates individual thinkers, and intelligence is born. We all know intelligence equals domination over one's destiny. Black women have been denied independence. Don't you see, my brothers, that's why I want a woman to stimulate my loins as well as my pockets. Now there is always an exception to the norm. Now Glen's got potential; that's why I—"

"Don't even try it," I interrupted Roy before he could finish his thought.

"Tell him, Tee," Bae Bae said.

"Man, you are just as lame as the rest of us. You are so into the white woman thing that you are missing the point. You can't take your white woman to a white establishment, and if you take her to a colored one, the colored women will hate you, and the colored men can't wait to find a weakness in your game so they can replace you. If you get stopped by the police, regardless of whether you are right or wrong, your Black ass is grass and you will get a citation, and if you are stopped by the wrong cop, your ass will be fertilizer for that grass. So, nigga spare us the bullshit, and give your brother some respect," Joe said, giving everyone the low-five.

"No more politics for me, my brothers," I said as I parted between Robert Jr. and Roy like an NFL running back.

I moved into the back end of my woman. My arms slid in between her arms and body, with my hands caressing and exploring the rest of her firm and narrow waist, as our bodies synchronized with "A Lover's Concerto" by The Toys.

I wrapped my arms around her and kissed her with the passion of a long-lost but recently found love, and she responded to my call. I was in heaven as we harmonized with The Toys. The party was going strong, and everyone was laughing and dancing, but my mind was on one thing. Well… two things. One was in my arms and the other was what I was going to do with the rest of my life.

I felt a tap on my shoulder. "Hey Cuz, let's get some air. It's family time," Robert Jr. said.

"I'll be right back, Glen," I whispered with a light kiss.

We walked outside, and the cool mountain breeze was almost sobering. When we got to Robert's car, we sat on the hood.

I lit two cigarettes and handed Robert Jr. one.

"I love you, man. I'm going to miss you," I said, blowing a perfect ring of smoke out of my mouth.

"I love you too, Cuz," he said, blowing an equally sized smoke ring.

"I'm falling in love, and I know how many times we said love is for losers. Well, I'm no loser, and if I'm a fool, then let me find out the hard way. I can't learn it from you; I must live it," I said, blowing out a larger smoke ring.

"You sure it ain't lust? We are too young to be committed to any woman."

"Man, when I am with her, the world doesn't exist. It's like we are alone on a tropical island. With every word that comes out of her mouth, I beg for more. Each time I bat my eyes, she seems to get prettier and more intriguing than ever."

"Cuz, I think you should leave that woman alone before she has you barking at the moon on a cloudy night."

We both laughed out loud.

"Hey, Robert, is that you?" came a voice from one fine sister.

"Yeah, this is me and who… Coleen, is that you? Yeah, it is… girl, you are still fine," Robert Jr. said, breaking our bond.

"Why, thank you, and is my cousin in there?" she asked as she and Robert Jr. hugged.

"So, Coleen, I finally get to meet you. I'm Tee."

"Well, Tee, it's about time we met. Glen talks about you all the time."

"Well, I hope some of it was good."

"It was all good."

"You know, you got here just when the party is really getting started."

"Oh, Tee, this is not a social call. Glen's grandfather has taken ill and is asking for her. We tried calling but no answer."

"I hope it's nothing serious."

ᅟ

"We don't know," she replied as I opened the door to the house.

"Well, how about a cold cup of punch before you go?" I offered.

After I poured three cups of punch and distributed them, I told Bae Bae to play "I'm So Proud" by The Impressions. As I walked across the floor toward Glen, the clock on the wall said it was ten to twelve. Glen must have anticipated my next move because she passed her leather jacket to Coleen and met me halfway.

"May I have this last dance, my princess?"

"Yes, you may, my prince."

Glen fell into my arms, and we held each other like it was our last dance on God's green earth. At that moment, I knew that she was my Cinderella, and I was her Prince Charming. And when the clock struck twelve, her glass slipper would be embedded in my heart forever.

As the song was ending, I knew our relationship would get better.

Chapter 15

Back to
Business

I was back on the evening shift, regretting it even more. I hadn't seen or talked to Glen since the party. She had told me her hours were from nine to four, Monday through Friday, and she did volunteer work on Saturday for extra credits. Each time I called Miss Young, the phone would ring and ring. I wanted to call her home in Canton, but Nannie had prohibited us from making long-distance calls after Connie had made a call to Savannah, Georgia, to a departed classmate and had talked for hours.

Glen had my mind, and that was something Robert Jr. and I said we would not let happen.

I just could not get my mind together at work. Miss Porter was constantly on my case for daydreaming. I just couldn't seem to get it right. A patient had defecated in bed, and I changed the linen, but I forgot to remove the old ones. Of course, Russell told everyone that the love bug had taken a double chunk out of my tail.

Then the next day, I had to prep a patient for hernia surgery, and I got my rooms crossed. Mr. Brayshaw was in room 304 and Ms. Bradshaw was in room 314. I knocked and entered room 314, not looking up. I pulled the covering down from the bed before I realized Mr. Brayshaw was missing something.

Ms. Bradshaw screamed, "What do you think you are doing, orderly?" while pulling up her bed covering.

I accidentally dropped my prep kit, rubber gloves, and tray on the floor from the shock of exposing a bottle blonde with varicose veins the size of milkshake straws and the ugliest feet I had ever seen.

"Mr.… Ms., I am so sorry. I made a mistake," I said. "I thought I was in Mr. Bradshaw's room and—"

"Do I look like a Mr. Brayshaw?" she interrupted. "Are you calling me a man, orderly? When you exposed me, did you see a man or a woman?"

The anger was in her eyes but not in her voice. I was in trouble, because men shave men and women shave women. I could see my walking papers as Miss Porter entered the room.

"Orderly, what is the problem, and why are you in Ms. Bradshaw's room? Mr. Brayshaw's room is 304," she screamed.

"I got my rooms mixed up," I said as I was retrieving the prep kit, rubber gloves, and tray from the floor and looking at Ms. Bradshaw to see if she was still pissed off at me for our encounter.

I saw no anger. Thank you, Jesus, I thought as I passed Miss Porter on my way to room 304.

The next day, I kept thinking of Glen and the song "You've Really Got a Hold on Me" by the Miracles. Yes, Glen had a hold on me, I thought, as I slowly walked toward room 314. I tried to remember what Ms. Bradshaw looked like. I only knew she was not a real blonde. I had practiced my apologies for what I was going to say to her. I knocked lightly and pushed the door open. It was a private room filled with flowers, get-well cards, and two large baskets of fruit. Ms. Bradshaw was a middle-aged white woman with high cheekbones. Her platinum blonde hair reminded me of Jean Harlow, yet she could have been Susan Hayward's twin sister. She was reading a book with round, frameless glasses parked on the tip of her nose, sitting in an overstuffed recliner.

"Good evening, Ms. Bradshaw."

"And good evening to you, orderly," she smiled.

"Ms. Bradshaw, I am really sorry."

"Listen, young man, no more apologies," she said. "I had some fun yesterday."

"Yes ma'am," I said, reading her eyes and returning her smile. "I just came by to check on you."

"I am fine, but I need my feet and ankles rubbed. Can you help me out?"

"Yes ma'am, I will tell Miss Porter—"

"No," she interrupted. "I want you to massage my feet. I've already cleared it with Nurse Porter."

Ms. Bradshaw pointed at a bottle of ointment and a box of disposable gloves between a bouquet of assorted colors of carnations.

"I love flowers, especially carnations," I said while inhaling the sweet fragrance of the flowers.

Ms. Bradshaw fully extended the recliner after removing her bedroom slippers and adjusting her housecoat, exposing those feet from hell.

"Ms. Bradshaw," I said, looking down and pouring a little ointment on her feet, "I'm going to pray for these two; they need Jesus."

Ms. Bradshaw screamed with laughter, and her book went flying into the air and landed on the floor. The title read *The Origin of Species*.

"Do you think that your prayers can help my feet?" she asked, drying the tears of laughter from her reddened eyes with her pink floral housecoat sleeve and still trying to hold back her laughter.

"Orderly, what is your name?" she asked, pulling some Kleenex from the table.

"Tierron LaVon Madden. But Tee for short."

"Tierron LaVon Madden is beautiful. What does it mean?"

"I think it means bastard," I said, looking down.

"Why do you say that?" she inquired, with no more laughter in her voice.

"My momma and my biological father weren't married. So instead of calling me a bastard, I'm called an illegit. Listen, I am cool with it. One day I will be legit!" I said with confidence.

"Well, if this is true, then Jesus was conceived out of wedlock, so Jesus is a bastard too," Ms. Bradshaw said, reaching for her book.

Oh my God!

Did this woman call your Son a bastard?

Please God, if anyone needs forgiveness, Ms. Bradshaw does.

"No ma'am," I said, with my heart feeling like it was about to jump out of my chest.

I was still waiting for God to send a bolt of lightning to light up this room.

"No ma'am," I continued, then looked down at my hands realizing I wore no gloves, and my hands were wrapped around Ms. Bradshaw's claws.

Oh my God, please don't turn my hands like Ms. Bradshaw's feet, I prayed, and I could feel the sweat running down my face.

"Tee... Tee, I did not mean you any harm. I just meant that you and Jesus were conceived out of wedlock. Are you alright?" she asked.

"Yes, ma'am," I said, cleaning up and placing her slippers back on.

"Tee, your hands are gentle and firm. My feet feel like cotton. You are a good masseur. Thank you."

As I rushed out of her room, still thinking about her calling Jesus, the Son of God, a bastard, I thought, I'm going to pray for Ms. Bradshaw as I continued my rounds.

Around eight o'clock, Miss Porter said Ms. Bradshaw needed my assistance getting into bed. I asked Miss Porter about Ms. Bradshaw's feet, and she said that as a child, Ms. Bradshaw had developed foot fungus, which is why her feet were in such bad shape.

I knocked, got an okay, and entered. Ms. Bradshaw was still seated in the recliner next to her walker.

"Hey Tee, I'm ready for bed," she said as she placed a bookmark in the book and handed it to me.

I grabbed the book with one hand and helped Ms. Bradshaw to her feet with the other. After tucking her in, Ms. Bradshaw said, "Do you think your God can heal my feet?"

"Yes, ma'am, I know he can… I mean, my family and I watch Oral Roberts almost every Sunday. It's amazing how God heals the sick and the lame on television. Just believe while he prays for everyone who touches the screen. I've seen him perform miracles through God," I said reassuringly.

"Well, young man, if that's the case, then we don't need hospitals, and with no hospitals, you've got no job."

Ms. Bradshaw looked at me, grinning from ear to ear.

Now this poor woman is going straight to hell, I thought, trying not to lose my cool.

"May I ask you a question?"

"Of course, you may ask me anything."

"Do you believe in the power of God?"

Without hesitation, she answered, "No, I am an agnostic."

"You don't believe the Bible, God's word?"

"The word 'Bible' is a Greek word that simply means 'book.' The Bible is a good book, but it is not the only book in the library. You need to read more books because books will take you on a world tour of knowledge," she preached.

I started to give her an amen, but then I realized that this woman was going to hell, and if I gave her an amen, I might accompany her.

"Ms. Bradshaw, I will pray for you."

"Tee, have you heard of Charles Darwin?"

"Yes, he was Black, and he died in a car crash here in North Carolina," I said with a reassuring smile.

She returned that reassuring smile with a shake of her head.

"No, young man, I think you are talking about Charles Drew, and yes, he was in an auto accident, and he bled to death because the hospital refused to treat him. I'm talking about Charles Darwin. He supports the theory of evolution."

"So, you think we come from apes?" I humorously replied, which almost turned into laughter.

"You should read his works. You might think differently."

"Good night, Ms. Bradshaw, and I will still pray for you," I said with a smile.

"I'm counting on it. Good night!"

I turned off the lights and quietly shut the door.

***

It was Friday night, and the carnival was in town. For three nights and two days, Blacks would be spending their hard-earned money. The only event that was larger than the carnival was Stephens-Lee High School's homecoming. Now that homecoming was gone, the carnival was number one.

It was held at Walton Street City Park. It had the only swimming pool for Blacks in the city. Daddy Bill was a swimming instructor and lifeguard at the pool. I remember when Daddy Bill threw me in nine feet of water, trying to teach me how to swim.

"This is for your own good. You'll either sink or swim," he said.

Well, he got that right. I sank and damn near drowned. He had to come to get me. I could have sworn that he was trying to kill me. I didn't speak to him for about a week after that. I told Nannie, and she confronted Daddy Bill. He was trying to explain his intentions, but Nannie wouldn't let him get a word in. So consequently, I didn't learn how to swim.

There were so many foxes that lived en route to the pool, like Ketery, Marlene, the Baird sisters, Lolitta, Wanda, just to name a few. Catching a glimpse of one of those foxes was my mission in going to and from the park. I've heard various reasons why so many Blacks couldn't swim—some say it's because we have no buoyancy or too much muscle mass. I knew a couple of heavyset Blacks who couldn't swim a lick or float. There are major studies from renowned universities and colleges supporting those theories. We just needed access to water, and the rest would fall in place according to Daddy Bill.

Cookie was so excited and filled with the joy and cheer of a thirteen-year-old. Her excitement spread through the household like gospel music on Sunday morning. I used to feel the same way when I was her age. That's when I was spending someone else's money. Now I was spending my own, and it wasn't as much fun, if you can dig where I am coming from.

Most of the time, Daddy Bill would support the cause, plus I could always borrow a five spot from him. Connie and Cookie would con Momma out of some money. So, most of the time, we had enough money to support our fun.

The first night of the carnival was always the best time to go because everybody would be there.

The aroma of fresh roasted peanuts and popcorn mixed with the smell of hamburgers and hot dogs stimulated our taste buds. For dessert, cotton candy and candy apples were a must. The most popular attraction at the carnival was the Swing, always located on top of a hill overlooking the forest. As you swung around over the trees, you could see the mighty French Broad River in the distance. The Swing had more than twenty-five seats and could rotate, reaching speeds of more than thirty miles per hour. We would hold each other like a train with our feet in the forward swing seat. As we picked up speed, our feet would act as rocket launchers, now achieving speeds over fifty miles per hour. This ride alone consumed a third of our money.

There were other rides, such as the Bullet, that were a little shaky, but of course, I could not show fear because I was the big brother. If you had any loose change or valuables in your pocket, most of the time the Bullet would claim them. So, you really had to watch yourself after the washing machine-type ride the Bullet produced. I was always the first to go on the so-called scary rides, especially when there was a pretty girl around.

Now the carousel, what we called the merry-go-round, was for profiling. If there was a girl you wanted to be seen with but knew she wouldn't give you the time of day, or if she was new, like from another town, this was your card to the players' club. Here's how it worked: You were with your boys, scoping out this fox. You told your boys to wait while you took care of a little business. You approached the fox and said something funny like, "Do you mind going on this ride with me 'cause Momma said I couldn't go alone?"

That line always got a laugh.

Now, if she was already waiting in line, this was much better because you wouldn't have to pay her way on.

Once you are on the carousel, you keep her laughing while maintaining your pose. Your boys are checking you out, thinking the two of you are having so much fun. They will be asking you questions about her all night and tomorrow, too. Last year, I met this pretty girl named Helen from Hickory, North Carolina. I ended up paying her and three of her cousins' way in. You do what you can to keep up the image.

Well, we had been on the Swing and Bullet a couple of times when Cookie pulled me toward the Ferris wheel. Although I had never been on it before, I always thought it was a sissy ride. I asked Connie to go with Cookie, but she insisted that I accompany her.

"Okay, but after this let's get some hot dogs; I'm starving," I said.

"Me too," Connie said.

Cookie and I got on and made two complete 360-degree rotations. On the third rotation, we stopped at the twelve o'clock position. You could see all of West Asheville from there. I felt so relaxed with the mountain breeze hitting my face and oh, how peaceful and calm everything was up here. I closed my eyes and thought about Glen. Oh, how I wished she were here with me. I would wrap my arms around her like a giant octopus and never let go.

Then suddenly, the wind picked up, rocking the cart. Cookie thought this was fun, so she began rocking with it. There were signs all over the place that said, "DO NOT ROCK."

"Cookie, stop rocking!" I yelled.

"Why?" she asked, laughing, rocking, and scaring the shit out of me.

"Girl, can't you read? Now stop!"

I realized that the cart wasn't designed to make a 360-degree loop. If we flipped upside down, we would surely fall to our deaths. I was almost in tears, and Cookie knew it. My demands changed to a plea. She still refused to stop. Big brother started praying to the Almighty.

Lord, if you get me on solid ground, I'm going to wring her neck, I prayed.

Finally, the Ferris wheel began to move. I was going to tell the operator to stop the wheel as soon as we got to the six o'clock position.

As we were getting closer to the drop zone, I could see Connie and Nicole and a couple more of her fine friends, talking and looking up at us. I straightened up, wiping my tears, because I couldn't show any fear. I tried to look cool. I sat back with my arm resting over Cookie's shoulder. What I really wanted to do was put my hands around her neck and squeeze. I waved at Nicole, who, showing that beautiful smile, waved back. I forced a smile but felt like taking a dump, and before I knew it, we were on the way back up. Cookie didn't lighten up a bit. When we got to the nine o'clock position, the wheel stopped. Now we were directly over Connie and Nicole's heads. Cookie continued to rock, and if I said anything, they would hear me. I reached into my pocket and fumbled with my wad. I unfolded it and pulled out a five-dollar bill.

"Cookie, this is yours if you stop the bullshit!" I whispered, shaking like a leaf on a tree.

"I'm going to tell Nannie you said a bad word," she said, reaching for the money.

"Listen, baby sister! I better not hear about anything that happens up here, because if I do, I'll never take you anyplace again. Now, do we have a deal?" I whispered, holding her upper arm and squeezing.

"Tee, you're hurting my arm," she screamed.

"Girl, you better be glad it isn't around your neck. Do we have a deal or what?" I bullied, squeezing just a little tighter.

"Okay, okay, it's a deal."

"Not a word," I said, releasing her arm and the five-dollar bill simultaneously.

The wheel began to rotate the final 270 degrees. Cookie sat like an angel, and for a moment, I could have sworn that I saw a halo hovering over her head. I've got to get off this thing before I lose my mind, I thought, as the operator unfastened the safety bar.

"Hey Nicole, with your fine self," I said, smiling and hoping to mask my most recent encounter.

"Hi handsome, it's my turn," Nicole chuckled, looking at the Ferris wheel.

"How about some hot dogs? My treat, I'm starving."

I didn't care if the good Lord himself asked me—I was not getting back on the wheel of death for anyone.

"Okay, I'll take a Coke instead of a hot dog. Gotta watch my weight," Nicole joked.

After looking at her from head to toe, I still could not find a flaw anywhere. I gave her my best smile and, while staring into those big brown eyes, said, "Girl, you could gain one hundred pounds and still look good to me."

"Girl, you know he's lying," Connie said. "Gain a few pounds and see if he's still talking the same stuff."

Connie grabbed Nicole's arm, spun her around, and headed toward the hot dog stand, with their entourage in hot pursuit.

"Don't worry about them, big brother. I still love you," Cookie chuckled, grabbing my hand and pulling me toward the departing females.

"So, you think I'm going to buy you something to eat after the way you acted?"

"Tee, I'm just following big brother's advice: taking care of number one. Plus, you must admit, I earned this," she said, smiling and holding up the five dollars.

"Cookie, what you did was dangerous back there," I said, trying to sound serious.

"Maybe. But you can't live forever."

"Yeah, but I'd still like to see nineteen if you don't mind," I said, now getting a whiff of those good-smelling hot dogs.

Everyone got a hot dog with all the fixings and a Coke. I guess Nicole decided not to watch her weight, and neither did the rest. I figure that's a small price to pay when you've carried a torch for someone for as long as I have. When I looked at Nicole laughing, talking, and having fun, I figured the best thing we could ever have been is what we have now.

Out of my eighteen years on God's green earth, no one had ever made me feel the way Glen had, I thought as I put the last piece of chili dog in my mouth.

CHAPTER 16

CONVERSATIONS

It was Saturday morning, and the country ham Nannie was cooking was like an alarm clock, ringing in my nose. I had promised her that I would help her in the yard pulling weeds and planting flowers. So, I dragged myself out of bed, washed up, and stumbled into the kitchen.

Daddy was reading the newspaper while Nannie was skillfully dealing with the pots and pans. The rest of the household was fast asleep. Nannie let the girls sleep late because after breakfast, they had four loads of clothes to iron. Nothing was excluded: towels, sheets, face cloths, I mean nothing.

"Good morning, everyone."

I stumbled into the kitchen, still half sleepy, pulling the chair from under the table.

"Morning," Nannie and Daddy said in unison.

Nannie placed a large cup and saucer in front of me, then gave me a kiss on the forehead.

"Your cousin Lonnie called last night. It seemed important. He wants you to call him before twelve today," Nannie said.

"Yes, ma'am, after breakfast."

I poured myself a cup of coffee out of the electric percolator I had given them last year on their wedding anniversary. Nannie always kept it shining like new.

"Drink your coffee, Rev, before it gets cold," Nannie ordered.

Daddy took a sip of coffee and placed the cup back on the saucer.

"You know, Liler, I've always agreed with Rev. Martin Luther King's philosophy on nonviolence, but now he is protesting against our boys in Vietnam, and this Cassius Clay is right along with him."

"Well, I think he's stirring up a lot of trouble for us colored folks."

"Muhammad Ali, Daddy," I interrupted.

"What?" Daddy asked, looking up from his paper.

"Cassius Clay changed his name to Muhammad Ali."

"Well, whatever he calls himself," Daddy said. "I think all the colored men should go and fight for their country. Not only to show the white people that this is our country, too, but because every man has a personal obligation to serve his country, especially in crises like these. A man who doesn't believe in his country doesn't believe in himself. Uncky served in the Army during World War I and I served in World War II. I believe your father also served. We came back better men."

"Rev, the Bible tells us, 'He that lives by the sword shall perish by the sword,'" Nannie quoted.

"Yes, Liler, I am aware of that verse, but it also says in the third chapter of Ecclesiastes, first verse, 'To everything there is a season, and a time to every purpose under the heaven.' And he further breaks it down, I believe in verse... ay... eight," Daddy said, tilting his head back and closing his eyes.

Then he opened them and lowered his head, piercing over his glasses which seemed to balance on the tip of his big nose. He turned his head toward me and looked up.

"Yes, verse eight, 'A time to love, and a time to hate; a time of war, and a time of peace,'" Daddy continued, satisfied with his memory.

Then he went back to reading his newspaper.

"Daddy, Muhammad Ali believes in himself more than anyone I know, and his religion prohibits him from going to war," I said.

"This Muhammad fellow, wasn't he a Christian before turning to an idol god?" Daddy asked, looking up from the paper.

"Yes, sir, Muhammad Ali was a Christian and now he's a Black Muslim."

"Jesus, Lord help him, 'cause he knows not what he is doing," Nannie shouted.

"Well, son, he doesn't have to worry about going to that war over there or going to jail over here, because when you turn your back on God, you forfeit His love and mercy. He thinks he's got problems now, wait until he faces the Almighty!"

Daddy slammed his fist on the table, causing the coffee cups and saucers to rattle.

I jumped back, waking up from my half-sleep.

"I truly feel sorry for this young man because he has no idea what is in store for him," Daddy continued, after regaining his composure.

Daddy folded the newspaper and placed it on the table. He grabbed a napkin, blew his nose, wiped the tears from his eyes, and got an amen from Nannie. Daddy reached out and grabbed my hand.

"Son, Nannie had a vision about you last night, that you will be leaving us soon and you'll become a traveler. That you will see things and do things that most men dream about. You gotta promise me that you will keep the faith and always believe in God because He's real! Real as you and me sitting here," Daddy said, as he gently squeezed my hands.

As I studied his eyes, for the first time, I saw eyes of joy, wisdom, compassion, love, and understanding. I knew Nannie had always had "The Gift" to foresee the future. She had made a believer out of me numerous times.

I remember Cousin Robert giving Robert Jr. a car on his sixteenth birthday. It was a brown and tan two-door sedan, Star Chief, 1956 Pontiac. It had whitewall tires, fender skirts, and not a scratch anywhere. It was as clean as the Asheville City Board of Health although it was several years old. Robert Jr., Roach, and I had made plans to go to Shelby, North Carolina, to see some girls we met last Fourth of July at our church picnic.

I asked Nannie if I could go a week before the trip, and she said she would pray over it. Well, as the departure day drew near, Nannie kept saying that the Lord hadn't directed her yet. Then Friday, the day before the trip, Nannie said she saw danger and that I couldn't go. She told Cousin Robert and Mrs. Roachen what the Lord had revealed to her. Well, they thanked Nannie for her concern, but the trip was still a go. I begged and pleaded, and with a little help from Momma and Daddy, she finally surrendered. She said as soon as I got there to call her.

We were all excited. We dressed alike, looking like the Three Musketeers. We wore blue and gray beanie caps, blue and white checkered short-sleeve shirts, blue jeans, and brown penny loafers with a brand-new penny for good luck. You couldn't hit us in the ass with a red apple. We knew we were clean.

Shelby was about eighty miles from Asheville. We sang, joked, and laughed to celebrate our newfound independence. We exited off Interstate 40 onto the ramp when we lost engine power. The car was equipped with power steering and power brakes. We were entering a secondary highway with no brakes or steering. There was a '57 light blue Chevrolet that didn't see us until it was too late. It plowed into the left door, hurling Robert Jr. into Roach. I was in the back seat watching everything. I was thrown to the floor. I just knew Robert Jr. and Roach had bought the farm.

As it turned out, none of us were seriously hurt. Robert Jr.'s left arm was bruised, and Roach's right arm was banged up, but otherwise, they were okay. I had not a scratch on me.

When I called Nannie, the first thing out of her mouth was, "Is anyone hurt?"

She said she felt a sharp pain in her right arm about the same time the car crashed into us. After that, she made a believer out of all five of us.

Traveler of many lands... What does that mean?

I would never forsake my Heavenly Father like Muhammad Ali, I thought.

I felt Nannie grab both our hands. When I looked up at her, tears were rolling down her face like Niagara Falls. I knew she knew something, but I was too afraid to ask.

"Rev, let's pray for Mr. Ali because it's never too late," Nannie said, bowing her head and closing her eyes as she squeezed my hand.

Daddy began to pray with the power and conviction of a man on death row. What was even more moving was that I was praying right along with Daddy because I truly believed in Ali. He was my hero. I believed in him the first time I saw him on television, down at Robert Jr.'s house, when he said he was going to knock out Sonny Liston. And my admiration for him hadn't changed after the second fight with Liston when he turned his back on Christianity. I didn't agree with his religious philosophy, but I loved the man the same.

That was when I started calling myself Black instead of colored or Negro. I think what amazed me about Ali was how he stood up for what he believed in—a Black gladiator against the pride of hungry lions. I didn't expect Nannie or Daddy to understand what I was feeling because I didn't quite understand it myself. The only thing I knew was that I loved this man and I saw him as my big brother. No man had ever made me so proud of being Black.

When Daddy finished his prayer, his eyes were swollen with moisture and as red as a cherry. Daddy held my hand long after Nannie had released mine.

"Son, you will have trials and tribulations, and there are going to be times when you think that God ain't around, or He's not listening, but you got to keep the faith and believe, because He may not come when you want Him but He's ALWAYS!... ALWAYS ON TIME! God takes care of fools and babies... always be... the BABY," Daddy said, clamping down on my hands as I flinched with pain.

"Yes, Daddy," I moaned.

When he finally released my hand, I could still feel it throbbing.

"Now, how about some breakfast before you two start on the yard," Nannie said, wiping her eyes and smiling.

I called Cousin Lonnie, and he told me there was a job opening at the Grover Arcade Federal Building starting in a couple of weeks. The pay was a little better, and the hours were from seven to three. No experience necessary, and on-the-job training. If I wanted the job, I had to be ready for an interview at ten o'clock sharp on Monday morning. I said yes, even before he stopped talking. I couldn't wait to tell Nannie and Daddy the good news, although the job wasn't mine yet. I could tell in his voice that the interview was just a formality.

Monday morning, I got up early and put a pot of coffee on. Daddy was already up working in the basement.

"Morning, Daddy."

I walked down the back steps while he was pulling boxes out of the basement.

"Morning, son. You want me to drive you into town? I have somewhere else to go this morning."

"Well, Daddy, if you're busy, I can also take the city bus, which will take me to Pack Square. It's about a block or so from the federal building."

"Well, son, it seems like you know what you're doing."

"How about some coffee, and I can toast up some of Nannie's biscuits."

"Seems like you have got a plan. Let me finish here; give me about fifteen minutes or so."

"Daddy, can I help you?"

"No, I got this. You know how I like my biscuits. I'll take two."

The coffee was made, and Daddy liked his coffee black. I looked in the bread box, got three biscuits out, and split them in half. Then I got out Nannie's grape jelly and apple butter and toasted them in the broiler, 'cause that's how Daddy liked his biscuits. I served Daddy his biscuits and coffee once he sat down. Daddy said he remembered when the federal building was built.

"I worked there for a while. In fact, your Uncle Abe, Uncle Young, Uncle Prelow, and I helped clear the land that the building was built on. Your Uncle Prelow was one of the foremen who helped build the building. I remember it like it was yesterday. There were plenty of jobs at that time."

I arrived at the federal building at 9:40 a.m. with fifteen minutes to spare. Two white boys were waiting for the same interview. A tall, lanky redheaded kid with freckles named Jamie, and the second one was about my size with dark brown curly hair. His name was Bruce; he wore thick bifocals and talked with a lisp. We all hit it off well, talking about the Asheville Tourists, the city's baseball team. Jamie and Bruce's interviews lasted about five minutes apiece. My interview lasted about fifteen minutes. We were told we would be contacted in a couple of days with their decision.

When I got home, Momma told me Glen had called. She was staying in Canton until Wednesday and asked if I would please call her Wednesday evening at Miss Young's house.

Momma was impressed with Glen's conversation. She told me how mature she sounded over the phone. Nannie was eavesdropping, pretending to be snapping string beans in the kitchen.

What she really wanted to know was the outcome of the interview. After telling Momma that she would meet my mystery lady, I hastily walked into the kitchen and told Nannie what happened at the interview, from the moment I got off the bus on Pack Square till I walked out of the federal building. Nannie was overjoyed. She kissed me and said that the job was mine. Well, of course, I believed her because I felt the same way when I first walked out of the interviewing office.

"Nannie, I'll be making fifteen cents more an hour, and I'll be given the title of Assistant Archivist, keeping weather files."

"God is good!" Nannie shouted as she patted my arm.

"What's going on in here?" Daddy asked, opening the refrigerator and pulling out a pitcher of lemonade.

"Daddy, I think I got the job. Just keep your fingers crossed."

"Well, Tee, you forget who made those fingers. He's already told me the job was yours. Luck is for that Muhammad fellow. Praise the Lord," Nannie shouted, looking at Daddy for confirmation.

"Praise the Lord!" Daddy replied, raising his iced lemonade-filled one-quart mayonnaise jar.

"Well, I'm glad to receive some good news because we have our share of bad news," Daddy said.

"What's wrong, Rev?" Nannie asked, snapping her last bean and placing the bowl of beans on the table.

"Well, Liler, the car's water pump is out."

"I don't want to add to the problem, but the washing machine is going out, too. Mr. Welch said the motor is probably burned up and he could replace it for twenty-five dollars," Nannie said.

"'Twenty-five dollars! Liler, that washing machine is practically brand new. It couldn't be no more than three years old."

Daddy had finished his drink and was shaking the ice-filled jar.

"Rev, get a hold of yourself, and please stop rattling that jar of ice. You know it drives me crazy."

Daddy dumped the ice in the sink, then rinsed the jar with hot water and placed it on the drain board.

"Liler, don't worry about the washing machine. I'll fix it. That Mr. Welch is a Jew, and you know how they love money."

"Now, Rev, you remember when it was raining cats and dogs, and the porch light went out. You were soaking wet trying to fix that light fixture, and you blew yourself and every light in the house out. I thought I had lost you. You were out for almost ten minutes. Now Mr. Welch is a God-fearing man, and he's got six children and that lovely wife of his… bless her heart. She still brags about that apple pie she won a blue ribbon for at the county fair almost two years ago. Now you know her pie is nothing compared to my own. Anyway, Mrs. Welch always orders a German chocolate cake and a pound cake every year for Christmas from me. And I'm sure we won't have any more rat problems," she said, eyeballing me.

"Nannie, I don't think it's the motor," I said, feeling a little guilty for the rat problem. "Daddy just forgot to pop the circuit breaker before working on the porch light."

Daddy frowned and thought about it for a moment. "Well, Liler, I didn't mean to imply that he was dishonest. Like I said, me and your grandson will handle it," Daddy said, giving me a wink.

I have seen Nannie cry and beg for the house when an agent from Raleigh, North Carolina, came up to evict us, right after Uncky died. I remember when the agent left the house, he was weeping. Nannie had a way of making you feel guilty.

Yes, the Lord works in mysterious ways.

Now, Daddy had to get the car fixed because ministering was his income. Sometime in the middle of the night, Daddy would get up and travel miles to one of his church members who was grieving over a loved one or on request. Sometimes the offering was so small it just covered the gas it took to get there. There's no way I could have the patience to be a preacher.

One preacher in the family is enough, I thought.

"Daddy, I'll go to the junkyard, and I'm pretty sure I can find a water pump. Mr. McDaniel owes me a couple of favors," I said.

"What favors does he owe you, and who is Mr. McDaniel?"

"Daddy, he works at the junkyard, and I've helped him and Uncle Ben remove auto parts like tires, generators, mufflers, and engines. I also helped Mr. McDaniel remove a windshield. Uncle Ben said I am a natural with my hands. He said, 'With the right tool, you can build a new world.'"

Plus, I've picked up a couple of jars of moonshine for Mr. McDaniel, I thought, being careful not to mention my involvement in the whiskey business out loud. I knew where most of the liquor houses on Southside were.

"The yard can wait," I said, walking toward the washing machine and giving it a thorough inspection. "Nannie, I don't think it's the motor, and for half the price I can fix it," I said, giving Daddy a wink.

"Tierron, I know you didn't say what I thought you said."

"Nannie, I was just joking," I said, while giving her a big smile and a kiss on her jaw.

"Yes, the car is first," Daddy said, looking at Nannie.

"All right, the yard can wait, but after the car, the washing machine, because I got two more loads of clothes and hand washing is out of the question."

I called Mr. McDaniel, explained my situation, and asked how much he would charge me. He told me he had a water pump, but I had to remove it from a junker and could use his tools. He said he needed me to help him move some junk cars around the yard and help him drop an engine next week, and then we would call it even. It took me less than three hours, and I had Reverend Madden's 1956 Chevy Impala back on the road.

Now, the washing machine, like Daddy said, was less than three years old. When I checked the power plug, it had vibrated itself out of the socket, and I found a sock between the tub and the outer frame. Just killed two birds with one stone.

Feeling like a winner, I decided to play the numbers since my luck was running good. I went to the Southside Apartments to find my numbers man. I found Jake standing over a dice game, watching the local bums playing nickels and dimes. He was tall and slim with a beer gut and blacker than the ace of spades. He always wore a brown derby hat with a dirty white feather in it, on top of that dyed, fried process that looked like it took a recess. A half-chewed toothpick protruded out of the corner of his mouth, with lips so big and long that he could eat popcorn out of a Coca-Cola bottle. He had this one gold tooth in the middle of solid yellow teeth. If the gold didn't sparkle, you never would have suspected that he had a gold tooth. If you told him he wasn't sharp, you'd have a fight on your hands.

"Hi, Jake! I need some numbers, man," I said, giving him a quick handshake.

"Hi, little brother, haven't seen you lately. Since you scored on me in front of my lady."

"Man, it was just luck," I said in my most masculine voice.

Jake and I were in a poker game a couple of weeks ago. Sandy, his lady, had always had a crush on me, and Jake knew it. We were playing seven-card stud with a five-dollar limit. I had cashed my paycheck from the bank and went straight to the game. All my money, except Nannie's money, was in the pot. Jake had four red hearts, with four more showing across the board, including my hand. Jake was laughing and talking shit when everybody dropped out except me. I called him with a pair of nines. His mouth dropped to the floor, although his lips were halfway there with his mouth closed anyway. After scooping up the money, I told them I had to go to the bathroom. I slipped out of one of the backroom windows and was history.

I had to pay Sandy back for telling me Jake was bluffing, and she didn't want money.

Thirty-three was my lucky number. That was the age of Jesus Christ when he died on the cross. I just hoped I lived that long. Eighteen was Momma's lucky number because she said that was her age when I was born. I've hit it once, and Momma about three or four times. If Nannie caught these tickets on either one of us, Momma would get a tongue-lashing, and I an ass-lashing.

**

All day Wednesday, I couldn't get Glen out of my mind. I went uptown to The Block, which comprised Eagle Street and Market Street directly behind the police station. This was where the city's Black community congregated for a little chit-chat, a little fun, and where Black businesses were in full operation. Momma's shop, the Venus House of Beauty, was located on Market Street, about twenty yards from Eagle Street. We had two drug stores with malt shops, right across the street from each other. Steele Drug Store was located on the corner of Eagle and Market, three doors down from Momma's shop. The YMI drug store was located on the opposite corner of Eagle and Market. Both had large sectional windows on both streets with booths and tables and chairs, offering a front-row seat to the action on The Block.

When your parents took you to town for some shopping, your treat was to eat at one of the booths, sucking on an ice-cold malt or a thick, rich milkshake, and indulging in a delicious banana split or a creamy sundae.

Stephens-Lee was less than a half mile away. Every Christmas and high school homecoming, the Stephens-Lee marching band would strut our stuff down Market Street, make a left turn on Eagle, and head towards the Castle on the Hill. This is where I played my drums, and the band marched with more enthusiasm and pride than any other place we marched. It didn't matter if it rained or snowed—we were expected to give all we had when we marched on The Block.

You could share a Coke with your girl after school or just hang out with the guys. The YMCA had a full basketball court, and if you wanted to see some NBA talent, you just had to show up every Saturday morning. They had a ping-pong table and two pool tables. This is where I learned to play ping-pong and shoot pool—in other words, table tennis and pocket billiards.

We had an ABC store, a funeral parlor, scores of restaurants, cafés with dance floors, billiard rooms, and a record shop that had outside speakers. There were also lawyers' offices, a movie theater, barber shops, shoeshine parlors, beauty parlors, hotels, a bowling alley with ten lanes, and scores of other Black businesses.

Now, Martin Luther King was marching for integration and equal rights. Stephens-Lee had shut its doors for a new high school. Change was inevitable, and The Block had already taken on a ghost town appearance. This was not the town I once knew. It was changing, and not to my liking.

Since I had the day off work, and all my running buddies were off to college. I stopped by the pool room and got in a game of 5- and 9-ball with K.C. and Skip, two of the regulars.

I hadn't played them since I graduated, and I knew I was the boss, although their games had improved tremendously.

We were playing fifty cents on the five and one dollar on the nine. My game was marginal. I would lose one and then win two or three in a row.

I had a combination of the three-ball into the five-ball in the left corner pocket with the nine-ball about two inches in front of the right corner pocket. This was a wonderful opportunity to strut my stuff. In other words, it was time to talk trash. You see, talking shit deflates their ego and inflates yours.

I learned a long time ago that if you can't shoot a good game, talk one, and most of the time everything will fall into place.

"Gentlemen, back in 1926, three years before my momma was born, I made a similar combination in the corner pocket," I bragged, spinning my cue stick like a baton and reaching for the powder.

"Man, you gon' shoot or what?" Skip asked, chewing on his nails.

"In 1910, before I sank the Titanic, I made a combination shot with the three into the five-ball left corner pocket and the cue ball into the nine right corner pocket," I boasted, chalking my cue stick and taking my time.

K.C. and Skip seemed irritated. K.C. was gritting his teeth, and Skip seemed to be having lunch with his fingernails.

"Tee, I got ten dollars that says you can't make both," K.C. shouted, pulling out a small roll of bills, peeling off a ten, and slapping it down on the table.

"Yeah, man! Put your money where your mouth is."

Skip chuckled but didn't pull out any money.

"Listen, K.C., you know you can't afford to lose ten dollars. What you need to do is give that money to those illegits that you have acquired over the years," I joked.

Now all the eyes and ears in the parlor were keyed to our table. Small laughter echoed through the smoke-filled room.

"Shit! I don't know what you are talking about. I've already given your momma five dollars for your ugly ass!" K.C. shouted, and everybody busted out laughing.

"Nigga, give me a break," I said, raising my voice over the laughter. "If you could produce something like me, your dry ass would be in the White House!" I shouted back, which increased the intensity of the laughter.

When the laughter and idle chit-chat had stopped, all eyes and ears were on our table.

"Nigga, you gon' bet or what?" K.C. asked, his voice showing more contempt than before.

It was so quiet that the only noise you could hear was the outside sounds of a busy metropolis.

"Listen, K.C., I want everyone to know I tried to save you some money. You got a bet. Shoot stick," I commanded, letting the cue stick slide slowly back and forth through my powdered fingers until the cue tip mated with the cue ball.

I hit the three-ball into the five-ball, which fell into the left pocket. The cue ball bounced off the forward cushion, kissed the nine-ball, and bounced off the left cushion. The nine-ball rattled the sides of the right corner pocket and fell in. The crowd went wild with cheers and applause.

I looked at K.C., and he returned my look with a smile.

"Good shot, Tee," K.C. said, throwing a ten- and a five-dollar bill on the table.

Skip could only nod his head up and down, putting his lost wager beside the fifteen dollars. I put down two crisp one-dollar bills and lightly picked up the fifteen dollars.

I was about to break the rack when I heard a familiar voice.

"Still on the hustle, I see."

"Jimmy!" I yelled as we embraced each other.

Jimmy looked so handsome in his Army uniform.

"Man, let me look at you. Little Tee has grown up," Jimmy chuckled.

"Tee, you gon' break the balls?" Skip asked, tapping his cue stick on the floor.

"No, man, you break," I said, putting my stick back into the wall rack. "Skip, K.C., good game," I continued, pushing Jimmy toward the door.

"Man, I am hungry. Does the Blue Ribbon still sell those ten-cent hot dogs?"

"No, man, but you can get two for a quarter," I joked.

Jimmy had changed, and I must confess, for the better. I remembered a bashful, bucktoothed skinny kid who wore Clark Kent glasses, although he was a couple of years my senior. The uniform and about twenty pounds had turned him into Superman.

He joined the Army right after graduation. Jimmy Singleton had lived with his aunt on Blanton Street, a block away from me. His parents were killed in a car accident up north somewhere, I think.

Jimmy pulled the screen door open as we entered the Blue Ribbon Cafe. The place was filled with smoke and conversation. The counter and the twelve stools were occupied, and everyone was feasting on today's special: pig's feet, collard greens, rice, candied yams, and cornbread. A group of painters was getting up from a corner table, and we grabbed their seats. After the table was cleared and wiped off, we ordered.

"I'll have three slaw dogs, an order of French fries, and a Coke, please, ma'am," Jimmy said, straightening his tie.

"Sally, how are you today?" I asked, thumping a piece of cornbread on the floor.

"Hi, Tee! Long time no see. Where you been hidin'?" she asked, looking at Jimmy.

"Oh, I joined the Army," I joked, while Sally was still looking at Jimmy. He was blushing.

"Oh, that's good, now what... Oh, Tee!" Sally yelled, snapping her head away from Jimmy.

Jimmy and I burst out laughing.

"I know you. Where do I know you from?" Sally asked, looking at Jimmy's Army name tag.

Jimmy sat back in his chair, exposing his military medals and ribbons. "Sally, are you telling me you don't remember one of your best-paying customers?" Jimmy asked.

"Honey child, if you've been in here before, I would have remembered you," she said, pushing her lips out and narrowing her eyes at him.

"Sally, I used to come in here after school, order a slaw dog, and I always paid in pennies," he said, reaching into his inside coat pocket and bringing out a pair of glasses and putting them on.

Sally's eyes almost jumped out of her head. She dropped her order pad and stepped back.

"No, you are not Jesse James," she said, pointing her index finger and shaking her head from side to side in disbelief.

"That's me in the flesh."

Jimmy stretched his arms out in recognition.

"I don't know what the Army has done, but it worked. You look great. I know you're going to give me a hug."

"You better believe it," Jimmy said, almost leaping into the awaiting arms of Sally.

I cleared my throat.

"I'd like the special with extra pig's feet," I ordered, picking up the order pad off the floor.

After Sally and her pad had left, I looked at him. "Jesse James?" I asked.

"Yeah, Tee, that's me. Almost every day after school I would pay for a slaw dog in pennies. Auntie had this five-gallon glass piggy bank filled with pennies, so I would take two handfuls of pennies and put them in my pocket. Smiley, the cook, started calling me Jesse James, and the rest is history. The highlight of my day back then was chomping down on their slaw dogs," Jimmy chuckled.

"Well, Jesse James, I agree with Sally. You do look different. How long are you going to be here?"

"I leave tomorrow for Nam," he said.

"Man, you just got here."

"Tee, I've been in Newark, New Jersey, for a week visiting my mom's brother, Uncle Raymond. I had to come and see Auntie. You know she is getting old, and I was trying to convince her to move to Newark with Uncle Raymond. He's got plenty of room, but no, she'd rather be here with her three cats. Auntie told me how you come around and check on her, and you still only charge her a dollar to cut her grass."

"Listen, Jimmy! Miss Henrietta pulled me out from the Burning Bush."

That is what Jimmy used to call Nannie for reciting scripture to us about the do's and don'ts of life according to God.

"It was right after you went into the Army. I had gotten into a poker game and lost all of Nannie's money. It was twenty dollars that she had sent me to the store with. I borrowed the money from Miss Henrietta, and I worked it off after school and on Saturdays. She told me it didn't seem right for me to do all that work just to pay back a debt. So, every Saturday, for about three hours of work, she gave me a dollar. It took me a month to work it off. In that time, I learned every inch of her house."

"Man, she got money everywhere. Under her mattresses, under the floorboards, and in coffee cans. And I know she must have over three hundred dollars in her bra. I told her to put her money in the bank, but you know what she said—"

"'Got to be able to feel and touch my funds,'" Jimmy and I quoted, and we both laughed.

"Well, she must have listened to our advice because she opened up a savings account. She put me down as her beneficiary, and she does have a lot of money. But where I am going, you don't need money," Jimmy said, adjusting his military beret.

"Don't you have enough medals? But I guess you haven't heard, men are dying over there," I said, looking at his decorated chest.

"I'm in the 82nd Airborne Special Forces, and this is my second tour. I've been shot twice and still got some shrapnel in my leg. Man, I love it over there. I'm not afraid to die anyway. I'm just here on borrowed time. I should have left here with my mom and my dad," he said, taking out a handkerchief and blowing his nose.

"Jimmy, there is no such animal... borrowed time. When it's time for you to go, you are gone. Man, you can be in a burning house, and everybody burns up but you. In fact, you may come out without a scratch. You are not lucky because God doesn't deal in luck; that's for the unbelievers. You survived because He didn't call you. So, forget about borrowed time. God doesn't deal with time because man invented time. How can you borrow something that doesn't exist? God is real and everything belongs to Him. He doesn't need to lend something out when He can duplicate it in a wink of an eye. God is not in the lending, renting, leasing, or selling business. He's in the giving and taking business. So, if you believe you owe God something, then give Him your heart and soul, because He's got everything else," I preached.

"Boy, you sound like Rev. Madden. How is Little Daddy and the Burning Bush?"

"They're fine. What you need to do is stop by and say hello. Daddy will get a rise seeing you in that Army uniform."

"You know, when I first moved here, I was down in the dumps. I remember you were collecting for the March of Dimes. Auntie gave you a dollar, and you convinced me to help you out. We must have collected twenty dollars. You took the money and split it with me. Then you taught me how to play blackjack and you took it all back. Then you brought me over to meet your folks. I will never forget what the Burning Bush said: 'Now come over here and give your Nannie some sugar,'" Jimmy said, giving his best impression of Nannie, and we both laughed.

"Tee, you know, you ought to think about becoming a minister. You'd make a good one."

"Tee, becoming a preacher man? That young man has got too many oats to sow. He's too much like his daddy C. Ray," Sally interrupted, setting plates down in front of us.

"Sally, when I finish these pigs' feet, then I'm going to start sowing my oats on you," I joked.

"Child, you know this is too much for you to handle. So, you better call your daddy and your granddaddy too," she said, making an about-face and shaking her stuff in front of Jimmy.

We burst out laughing.

Jimmy ate four more slaw dogs, and I cleaned my plate. We got down on some blackberry cobbler. I told him about Glen and how I felt about her. He told me how blessed I was and how happy he was for me. He said he was still missing his parents, and when they died, so did he.

Jimmy blamed himself for their deaths. Jimmy said on that fateful day, he had complained to his parents about stomach pains on their way home from a picnic. His father said his stomach was also upset and that it must have been the potato salad. His mom never liked potato salad and her stomach was fine.

He was standing up in the back seat looking over his father's shoulder when he threw up. The distraction caused his father to veer into oncoming traffic and right into an eighteen-wheeler. His mother and father were killed instantly. Jimmy suffered a mild concussion and a few superficial wounds, but otherwise, he was fine. He said he talked to his parents every night, just before going to sleep. Although Jimmy's physical appearance had changed, he was still Jesse James.

I don't have The Gift like Nannie, but I knew in my heart that I wouldn't see him again, not in this life anyway.

CHAPTER 17

THE DATE

I called Glen and set up a date for eight o'clock. I needed a car, and everyone was busy. Daddy was at church, and Bae Bae was out of town. I was not going to walk.

I was ten minutes late and did not believe a bike could be so hard to pump going uphill. I had pushed it most of the way.

I must be getting out of shape, I thought, as I rested the bike against the chain-link fence.

I rang the doorbell, and moments later, Glen opened the door. She was more lavish than ever, and I couldn't help myself. I grabbed her and kissed her with the passion of a Christian crusader coming home to his woman.

"Wow! Did you miss me?" she asked.

"I've answered that. The question is, did you miss me?"

She held my face in her hands and absorbed my tongue in her mouth. She eagerly outlined my lips with her tongue, and then she gently bit down on my chin, which indicated to me I was missed.

"Didn't your momma tell you, you should never answer a question with a question?"

"Wow, you did miss me." I said, still holding her in my arms.

"Tee, where are we going tonight?" she asked, looking for a car and finding a Schwinn bicycle.

"Anywhere you want to go, my princess."

I was still lost in her arms and smelling her was driving me crazy.

"Yes, my prince, but don't you think we are just a little too old to be riding a bike together?" she asked in a low and girlish voice.

"What?!" I said, coming back to reality.

Shit! I had forgotten about that.

Think, Tee, and quick.

"Yeah ... ay., yeah, I thought that ...ay ...we could ay...yeah, could go for a walk. It's just a beautiful night, and the moon is full and not a cloud in the sky."

I hoped there would be a full moon tonight.

"A walk...tonight?" Glen asked with hesitation.

"Yeah," I answered, still holding her in my arms with my back to the door.

"That sounds like fun," she said with reluctance.

Whew, I breathed a sigh of relief.

"Come on in. I need to run upstairs and change my shoes."

She closed the door behind me. "Make yourself at home. I'll be back."

Well, I could tell no kids lived here. The house looked like a museum with a Persian rug centering a rectangular living room. The furniture was antique with plastic to protect it from the elements. A small low-hanging tear-drop chandelier pivoted the room. There was an old black-and-white picture of a Black man sitting and a Black woman standing. I could never understand why back then nobody smiled. I guess they didn't have too much to smile about. Maybe that's why Martin Luther King is giving white folks hell.

I refused to sit because I didn't want to mess up anything. Nothing was out of place. There were four large ashtrays, and they were spotless. I started to move them around to indicate that people lived here. I knew some kids that could really deal with this house, I thought when Glen returned.

"You ready?"

"Sure nuff," I said, wondering where we were going to walk to.

As we approached the fence, Glen pointed and asked, "This is your bike?"

"No, it's my cousin's bike. I use it for exercising," I lied.

"You know, this is a perfect night for a walk," Glen said, looking up at the starry sky.

"What did I tell you?" I affirmed, closing the gate after pulling the bike inside the yard.

I grabbed her hand and headed toward uncharted territories. I figured we'd walk and then come back and cool out at the museum.

"I had a great time at the party; how about you?" I asked.

"I had a ball, and you know I felt like Cinderella. Val is still talking about it. I think she and Roy got together. That's all she talks about: Roy this and Roy that."

"Good, then he can keep his paws and fangs off you," I said, giving her hand a gentle squeeze.

"Tee, the only person you have to worry about is Tee."

"You know, the first time you kissed me over at Bae Bae's house, you really rocked my world. Where did you learn to kiss like that?" she said, resting her head on my shoulder.

"I watch a lot of Rock Hudson and Elizabeth Taylor on television."

"Yeah, I bet."

The truth of the matter is that I considered myself a poor kisser until I kissed her, and it all seemed natural.

"Hey look! Did you see that?" I asked, looking and pointing to the sky.

"See what?"

"A shooting star."

"Did you make a wish?"

"Sure did, and it's already come true," I said, turning around to her, now holding her face in my hands and tasting her delicious lips.

If this isn't love, then I'm in big trouble, I thought when our lips unlocked.

"I didn't know there was a horse ranch over here," she said, pointing at a sign hanging on a long wooden fence that read Horse Ranch and underneath it: No Trespassing.

June Gibson
"Daddy June"

"My grandfather raises and sells horses. I've been riding since before I could talk. Let's see what kind of horses they've got," she said, pulling me across the street.

"What's the big thing about seeing a horse?"

I wasn't too sure about this venture. The No Trespassing sign meant do not enter. If you've seen one horse, you've seen them all. I wasn't worried about seeing a horse; I was worried about seeing the man with a double-barrel shotgun. I couldn't show my yellow streak, although it had run the length of my body.

"Oh Tee, a horse is the most beautiful of all God's creatures."

We went through an opening in the fence and down a graveled road. It seemed so peaceful. The moon was full, and it seemed to light up the night. We could hear water, and we followed the sound through the tall pine and oak trees until we came upon a brook. Glen wet her hands and soothed my face. She felt cool and soft. This was nice, and we were about to embrace when we heard something.

"Glen, I heard something," I said.

"I did too," she whispered.

"Listen, you get back to the dirt road, follow it back out to the street, and I'll catch up."

I pushed her toward the road.

"What are you doing?" she asked, coming toward me.

"I'm going to stand by this tree, and when he creeps by, I will deal with him. I'll be damned if I'm going to get shot in the back. Okay, baby, go!"

The sound was getting closer. She was about twenty feet away when she stopped. Now footsteps were on the other side of the tree, and I could swear that I was hearing more than one set of footsteps. Then I heard giggling.

It was Glen.

Shit!

This woman is crazy.

The footsteps were right beside the tree. It's now or never, I thought, with fists balled and my adrenaline flowing like the mighty Nile River.

I sprang with fists moving...

SHIT!

I saw this huge set of eyes with a white streak down the center, and it wasn't human.

The next thing I know, Glen was standing over me shouting, "Tee, Tee, wake up, baby!"

She slapped my face with water.

"What happened? What was it?" I cried.

My head felt like a ton of bricks lying on her lap. Everything was hazy and foggy. Then my eyes began to focus on something, and there it was again. I jumped back, screaming. I almost crushed Glen's soft body into the tree.

"Tee, it's just a horse!"

Glen tried to hold back the laughter while dousing my face with more water.

"A horse?"

My heart began to slow down, and my breathing became normal. I then realized that the alien from outer space was just a horse. The horse was no more than five feet away, with his head lowered, making eye-to-eye contact. I could have sworn that the horse was grinning at me.

"Yes, my prince, a horse. I believe the medical term for your infraction is called a blackout. In other words, you fainted," she chuckled, and then burst out in a scream of uncontrollable laughter, and the horse hee-hawed in confirmation.

I then realized if this got out, I, the fearless, would become I, the gutless.

I got to my feet and dusted myself off. She was still laughing. She walked over to this majestic animal and began rubbing his face.

"Come here," she said, waving her hand.

I kept my distance.

"That's a big horse."

"Tee, come over here," she said, kissing the horse above his nose.

"Now I know you don't expect me to kiss you after you put your mouth on that animal," I yelled, backing up a step.

Secretly, I hoped she would fall for my bluff and leave the horse alone because if she dipped her head in a bucket of shit, I'd still kiss her.

"Oh yeah?" she said, walking toward me, wrapping her long slender arms around me like a giant squid.

She began drinking my lips until I got thirsty.

"Hey, let's get out of here. I need something to drink," I said, returning her kisses.

"How about some hot chocolate with marshmallows, Roy Rogers?" she teased, grabbing my arm and leading me toward the graveled road.

I turned around and got a good look at the horse. With a white streak between those big eyes and those pointed ears, I could see someone mistaking this horse for a monster from outer space. This was an honest mistake.

"Hey, my princess, you're not going to tell anyone about this, are you?" I asked, lightly squeezing her arm.

"Of course not, my prince, of course not," she sheepishly chuckled without losing stride.

When we got to the house, Glen was still amused as we walked into the kitchen.

"Where is Miss Young?" I asked, watching Glen pour milk into a saucepan and place it on the stove.

"PTA meeting tonight. Why did you ask?" she said, opening a cabinet door over the refrigerator and pulling out a bag of mini marshmallows.

"This house just seems so empty. The night of the party was the same way."

"The house can get pretty crowded, with three females fighting for time in the bathroom," she chuckled.

"Why do women take so long in the bathroom? They have less to wash than men do," I joked.

"Well, I wouldn't know about that," she teased, looking down at her large breasts. "Have a seat," she said, motioning toward a three-chaired table.

"Wait a minute! I know you know these are real," she said, looking down and sticking her chest out.

"I don't know nothing. The only thing I see are protrusions. As far as I can see, those could be fake," I chuckled, slapping my knee.

"Tee, you know they are real. You couldn't keep your big, beautiful eyes off my breasts the night of the party. You weren't talking to me; you were talking to my breasts all night long. So, I know you know they are real," she retorted, reaching for my groin.

"Hey! What are you doing?"

"Well, since we are talking about protrusions, how about yours?"

"What about mine?"

"Well, maybe you are faking it. Maybe what I felt over at Bae Bae's house was a cucumber stuck down in your underwear," she said, laughing and still reaching.

"Girl, you crazy! Stop before you get bitten by a North Carolina black snake."

"Oh, it's a snake?"

"Yeah, a big black one at that," I said, with a serious grin on my face.

"You sure it's not a worm? Because worms don't bite," she teased.

"Worm!" I shouted, jumping up and grabbing my crotch. "This has plenty of bite!"

I wanted to take it out and slap her with it to let her know this was all real, I thought, as my manhood hardened along with my anger.

"Then let me see this big black North Carolina snake."

She had one hand over her mouth, trying not to laugh, while the other was reaching for my crotch.

"Stop! Believe me, you will be introduced, but now is not the time or place," I said, with both hands protecting my crotch.

"Listen, my prince, I am a nurse—or soon-to-be one. I have seen big ones, small ones, old ones, young ones, black ones, white ones, and I even saw red ones. So what makes yours so special?" she asked, backing me into the corner of the kitchen.

"Because I'm special, and everything on me is special. So back off before you start something you can't finish!"

I knew if she touched me, I would explode.

"Hello, you lovebirds," Coleen interrupted, walking in and carrying an open book in her arms.

"Tee, I had a wonderful time at the party, for what little time I spent there," she continued, putting the book down on the dinette table.

"You are welcome," I said, spinning Glen around and pushing her toward the table.

"Girl, your timing is bad," Glen teased, as she gently grabbed my crotch, and I flinched.

"Coleen, your timing was perfect, because she was about to discover powers she doesn't fully understand."

I patted Glen on the butt and gently pushed her away.

"I am sorry if I interrupted something," Coleen apologized.

"Well, you did," Glen chuckled while looking down at the book.

"I won't be long. I just need some help."

"Make it quick," Glen joked, elbowing Coleen in the side.

"Okay, I'm looking for information on uterine cancer, the most common form of gynecological cancer. I've looked all through this medical journal and can't seem to find it anywhere," Coleen said, turning a page.

"Let's see," Glen said, thinking for a moment. "I know it usually affects postmenopausal women ages fifty to sixty. Bleeding and uterine enlargement are typical symptoms. Treatment is often effective but includes a complete hysterectomy."

"Thanks, Glen, I just knew you'd know it. Now, I'll leave you two lovebirds alone. Tee, this girl has been talking about you nonstop since the party. I think Cupid has finally shot his arrow into her."

Clearing her throat, Glen said, "Didn't you say you had some studying to do?"

"Okay, okay," Coleen said, looking into the refrigerator and bringing out a Coke.

Glen handed her the medical journal after she had opened the Coke.

"Tee, I'll see you later," Coleen continued, rushing out of the kitchen.

"See ya!" I yelled, and before I knew it, Glen was in my arms.

"Now, after being rudely interrupted, let's start where we left off," she said, giving me a savage kiss.

Then we heard the front door open and close.

"That's Miss Young!" she whispered, and we quickly sat down and pretended to drink our cold chocolate.

"Good evening," Miss Young said, placing a dozen red long-stemmed roses in the sink.

"Good evening, Miss Young," Glen and I said in unison.

"Those are beautiful," Glen said, getting up, walking over to the sink, and smelling them.

"Yes, they are. This is my gift from the school for ten years of service. I would have enjoyed smelling a raise, though," she chuckled, then finally located a long glass vase.

"It's the thought that counts, Miss Young," Glen said, picking up a rose and bringing it to the table for me to smell.

"Well, honey, they could have thought up a raise."

"Tee, how's Delores? I know I haven't seen her in over three or four years."

"Momma's fine," I said.

"You tell the family I said hello, ya hear?"

Miss Young cut the last stem with a butcher knife and placed the flowers in the clear vase.

"Yes, ma'am, I will," I said, getting up and handing her the rose Glen had brought to the table.

"That's yours, my prince," Glen said, pushing my hand away from Miss Young.

"My prince—I like that, Glen," Miss Young said. "It is wonderful to be young and in love. So, young man, you better take good care of her. Now, it's getting late, and I know you and I have school in the morning, young lady."

"Okay, I can take a hint. Good night, Miss Young," I said, grabbing Glen's hand and leading her out of the kitchen to the front door.

"Listen, my prince, this weekend I am driving my grandmother to Knoxville, and I'll be back Sunday night. I'll call you at the hospital before you get off if I am back in time, OK?"

"Well, if all goes well, I'll be working at the federal building starting Monday morning at 9:00 a.m., if it's the Lord's will."

I pulled my bike out and straddled it.

"That's great! Now we can be together in the evening. I just know the job is yours," she said, grinning from ear to ear with her eyes sparkling like diamonds.

"Good night, my princess," I said, gently kissing her waiting lips.

When I pedaled away, I waved good night to Miss Young, who was peeping through the white curtains in an upstairs window.

CHAPTER 18

NEW BEGINNINGS

I got the job at the Grover Arcade Federal Building, which was built in 1929—the same year Momma was born. Its builder, E. W. Grove envisioned the first indoor mall. Although he passed a few years before its completion, the Arcade became the commercial hub of city life in Western North Carolina. During WWII, the Grover Arcade Building was closed by the federal government and used by the military for the duration of the war. Seventy-four shops and 127 offices were evicted with less than one month's notice. In 1951, the Grover Arcade Federal Building became home to the National Weather Records Center.

My job was moving boxes of files from one place to another in chronological order. Most of the files went back over a hundred years. These files were important to business investors, as well as city and state planners. If a city planner wanted to build an airport in a certain area, it would be critical to know the chronicles of adverse weather conditions for that area. My hours were from 9:00 a.m. to 5:00 p.m., and payday was every two weeks.

On my first day on the job, I had to report to Mr. Darren Johnson, my immediate supervisor. Mr. Johnson was a big man, about two hundred and seventy pounds, and about six foot four. He used to play for the North Carolina State Tar Heels and was an All-American offensive tackle for three straight years. Playing in the last regular season game, his knee was permanently damaged. Mr. Johnson walked with a cane as a result of the many knee operations he had undergone. I remember reading about him in the newspaper. He was the talk of the town and destined for the pros, no doubt about it.

Man, the world can throw you some lousy passes sometimes, I thought, as I sat down in front of his desk.

"Listen, Tierron, we can get along fine if you do two things," Mr. Johnson said, looking me in the eye. "Be on time for work and follow my instructions. Now, what did you not understand about my two commandments?"

When he was talking, I could see he was a decent man. He had a strong face, but his eyes were gentle and showed honesty. I knew we would get along fine.

Nannie would always tell me, "If you want to know a man's heart, look into his eyes, not his skin, and God will tell you all about him."

"Yes, sir, I understand your commandments," I said enthusiastically, looking Mr. Johnson in the eye.

"You come highly recommended. Do you know a Mr. Lonnie Burton?" he asked.

"Yes, sir. He was one of my high school teachers," I said, not telling him that he was also my cousin.

"Well, you should be very proud to be a member of the last graduating class from Stephens-Lee and to graduate with honors. You know, we're going to miss the Stephens-Lee Marching Band—the best damn band in the state, might be in the country."

"Yes, sir. I was a drummer in the band. We were the best in the country, if not the world."

People would come from miles away just to see us perform. The Stephens-Lee Marching Band was the talk of Western North Carolina. Yes, we were the best. I knew he had already checked my references and knew I was a good worker. So, nothing more needed to be said on my part, I thought.

"As you know, this job is only until the beginning of spring. It pays decently, and you never know what may come if you play your marbles right. The key to it all is hard work."

I was a little shocked when Mr. Johnson said I graduated with honors. But then I was brought back to reality when he said that the job was only temporary. I knew I could not go back to Saint Joseph Hospital. I left the hospital after giving them less than a week's notice. Sister Mary Jane Francis was more than a saint after I returned to the hospital from bombing out on the Navy the first time.

"Well, Tie...rron, I think you and I will make a good team. I want you to report to Mr. Mark Abrams three doors down to the left, and he'll show you around the shop. You can leave the tie and your Sunday best at home. We dress casually around here."

"Yes, sir, Mr. Johnson," I said, standing up and holding his hand firmly until he released mine.

When I walked into Mr. Abrams' office, there was this little man standing by a filing cabinet. He was about five feet tall, about Daddy's height, and weighed about one hundred pounds soaking wet. He was bald on the top, although he combed his hair from the side trying to cover up some of his baldness. His mustache was identical to Charlie Chaplin's, although I'm sure they had nothing in common. He wore black-framed glasses that were too big for his pug nose.

I could tell we were going to hit it off fine.

"Mr. Abrams?" I asked.

"Yes," he said, looking up.

"Mr. Johnson sent me over. I am the new hire. My name is Tierron LaVon Madden, but everyone calls me Tee."

"Yes, of course! Mark Abrams here," he said, closing the file cabinet drawer and gripping my hand. "Follow me."

I followed him to the basement, and he introduced me to people on our way to my work area. When we finally got there, there were bundles of dusty files everywhere. Mr. Abrams told me I had to arrange them in chronological order by state. As I surveyed my job, I removed my tie, rolled up my white sleeves, and went to work.

About twelve o'clock, Mr. Abrams walked in with a brown bag and two Cokes.

"Lunch time," he said.

"Great! I'm starving."

I dusted off my clothes and grabbed my brown bag, which Nannie had prepared for me: two sandwiches—bologna and cheese and peanut butter and jelly—wrapped in aluminum foil, cut diagonally, and an apple.

He had a pork chop sandwich and a bag of chips.

"You know this Martin Luther King?" he asked.

"No, I don't know him," I said, opening my Coke.

"You mean to tell me you never heard of Martin Luther King?"

"Yes, I've heard of him, but I don't know him," I calmly stated, taking a bite of my sandwich.

"You know what I mean. I know he's your leader, but I think he should slow down a bit because he's causing a lot of trouble between your people and mine."

"First of all, he's not–"

I stopped before I let my words get away from me.

Taking a deep breath I continued, "No, Dr. King is not my leader. President Johnson is my leader. My great uncle, who served in WWI, his leader was President Woodrow Wilson. My grandfather, father, uncles, and cousins who were in WWII, their leaders were Presidents Roosevelt and Truman."

"So, who is your leader?" I asked, with a smile on my face.

With a moment of silence, his whole facial expression changed. "Well, I... I... I... Well, I voted for Barry Goldwater. Though I wouldn't call him my leader."

"Well, who's your leader?" I repeated.

As he looked up, he said, "Well, I mean Martin Luther King isn't your leader, but how do you feel about him?"

"I'm still not understanding the question about what you mean by 'your people and my people.'"

He didn't have an answer.

"I am too young to vote, but if I could, I would've voted for President Johnson."

I could tell he was enjoying our conversation. He hadn't taken a bite out of his pork chop sandwich, and I found this intriguing. I had finished my sandwiches and was polishing my apple with my shirt.

"Why would you vote for Johnson?" he questioned, still not eating his sandwich.

"Because he approved the Civil Rights Act of 1964 and the Voting Rights Act of 1965 for all U.S. citizens."

"You had better eat your sandwich before the flies get to it," I laughed, looking at my watch and seeing that lunch was almost over.

"Oh, don't worry about the time. Mr. Johnson has a doctor's appointment, and he is gone for today."

"So, you are the boss," I said.

"Yes, I am," he said, biting into the pork chop sandwich and washing it down with a Coke.

"So is the President any relation to Mr. Johnson?"

He almost choked, holding the napkin that his pork chop sandwich was wrapped in. "Oh, no, no relation, I'm sure," he said.

"So why do you like King?" he continued.

"I like Dr. King because he was instrumental in getting the Civil Rights Act and the Voting Rights Act passed."

I didn't tell him that I didn't believe in his nonviolent resistance tactics, because I believe if you hit me, I hit you back.

"Why do you call him Doctor? He is a preacher, for Christ's sake," he thundered.

Wow, he doesn't know anything about Dr. King and it's going on one o'clock. Let me extend this conversation a little longer. I'm really enjoying this, I thought.

"Yes, sir, Dr. King is a very smart man. He graduated from high school when he was fifteen years old, from Morehouse College with a bachelor's degree at nineteen, and received his doctorate in systematic theology at twenty-six from Boston University."

"Well, I had no idea he is a doctor. I dropped out of college for medical reasons in my sophomore year," he said.

"I was told he shoots a mean game of pool, but I can take him," I said with a grin.

"I thought you didn't know him."

"I still don't know the man, but he was raised by a preacher man, and so was I. So, I know we are not all bad."

"Well, Tee Madden, that was a wonderful history lesson. I'll let you get back to work," he said, looking at his half-eaten sandwich.

Wrapping the remaining sandwich in a napkin and throwing it into the trash can, he added, "A bit dry."

I looked at my watch; it was a quarter to two. Yes, I like this job.

Daddy was waxing the car when I got home from work. When I walked into the house, Nannie was in the kitchen dealing with the pots and pans, and whatever she was cooking had my nostrils vibrating.

"Hey, Nannie!"

I placed a kiss on her jaw and got a drinking jar out of the cabinet.

"Hey, baby! How was your day?" she asked, looking up after pouring some milk into a bowl of cornmeal.

"Just fine."

"You got a call from Jackie. She said to call her before you go out."

Nannie relayed the message to me while cracking an egg into the batter.

"Yes, ma'am. Did anyone else call?" I asked, crossing my fingers.

"No. Were you expecting someone else?"

"Yes, ma'am, but it's not a problem," I said, walking into Nannie's room and dialing Glen's number.

There was no answer, so I hung up and dialed again, and the same thing happened.

She must have come in late last night, but she should be here by now, I thought, looking at the Big Ben alarm clock on the dresser.

It was a quarter till six.

I then called Jackie, and she said she needed to talk to me in person. I told her I would see her around seven. I went back into the kitchen, poured myself some Kool-Aid, and flopped down on a chair.

"Got female problems?" Nannie teased, pouring some hot bacon grease into the batter.

"No, ma'am," I said, still thinking about Glen.

"You know, Jackie is a pretty girl, and that baby of hers is so cute. You better watch it before some young man comes along and takes your prize."

"Nannie, I got someone else, and she is also beautiful with no kids and a promising future."

"So does she have a name?"

"Oh yes, ma'am. Her name is Glenna Aravia Thompson, and she is going to school to become a nurse."

"Well, we will have to meet this nurse."

I would definitely make sure that happened soon.

"What is that smelling so good?" I asked, getting up and investigating.

"Your Daddy's favorite: neck bones and oxtails, collard greens, rice, and cornbread," she said, slapping my hands.

"Nannie, just a sample, to make sure you haven't lost your touch," I teased, knowing she would let me sample the whole pot to prove she hasn't.

"Now just a little. Don't get more than that. That's it. Now, what do you think?" she asked, all up in my face.

"You forgot something," I said, after thoroughly sucking the neck bone clean.

"I forgot what?!"

"You forgot to put a plate of these down for me," I laughed.

"Gone away from here," she chuckled, pushing me away from the pot.

"Nannie, just one more," I begged.

"No, you don't want to spoil your appetite. Now go on and wash up for dinner. The cornbread will be ready in a minute, and tell your daddy dinner is ready," she said, pushing me out of the kitchen.

"Where's Momma and the girls?"

"They went to town to get Connie's dresses and shoes out of layaway. They should be back by six thirty. Connie is having choir practice over here tonight."

Daddy and I pigged out. Nannie kept telling us to save the girls something to eat. Knowing Connie and Cookie, they were probably feasting on hamburgers and french fries and washing it all down with a thick chocolate milkshake on The Block.

I washed up, changed clothes, and walked over to Jackie's house, which was all uphill. I was going to call it quits tonight.

I was going to tell her about Glen and that was it, I thought.

CHAPTER 19

PLAYING WITH FIRE

Jackie opened the door, looking fine as ever. Her golden-brown skin matched her gold hoop earrings. She wore my light blue long-sleeve shirt with the sleeves rolled halfway to her elbows. The collar was turned up, and the first three buttons were undone, revealing her maturing, firm breasts. The hem of the shirt was tied in a knot, exposing a flat stomach. She wore a blue miniskirt that enhanced her lotioned-down, big, bow-shaped legs.

It was hard to believe that she had a five-month-old baby, and I knew with that sexy smile on her face I was in trouble.

"Well, hello, stranger," she said, smiling and revealing even white teeth.

"What's up?" I asked, kissing her partially on the lips and walking into the house.

The house had a long hallway with three rooms on each side. Jackie lived there with her baby boy and her mother, Miss Willie Mae. Miss Willie Mae was quiet and always kept to herself. I guess we never said more than six words to each other since I'd known her.

"That is all I get?"

"I can hear your momma in the kitchen," I whispered, trying to skip the subject.

"That's never stopped you before."

Jackie hugged me around my waist from behind.

"Good evening, Miss Willie Mae," I yelled toward the kitchen, the third room on the right.

"Evening, Tee," she yelled back.

"You better be nice," I said, dragging Jackie into the living room, the first room on the left.

"Where have you been hiding? I know Miss Nannie gave you my messages."

As she spoke, Jackie pushed me onto the sofa and jumped into my lap.

"I've been busy. I started a new job today. Girl, you are looking at a government employee," I bragged, trying to push her off of me before I changed my mind and decided not to let her up.

"That's good. Now, we don't have to wait. Now we can get married sooner," she said, bouncing enthusiastically on my lap.

"Whoa!" I yelled, bouncing her off my lap and onto the sofa.

"What's wrong?"

"Marriage? Where did that come from?" I asked, not wanting to seem angry, but agitated nevertheless.

"Yes, I said marriage. That's what you said when we first started dating!"

There she was, spitting fire and brimstone. The madder she got, the sexier she became, and the more vulnerable I became.

Maybe I had used the term "marriage" in the act of passion to achieve the ultimate goal, but that was before Glen entered my life. Daddy had told me when you married into a ready-made family, you could never be the king of the castle, only the hired help.

Anyway, I came up here to tell her about Glen, and I figured now was a bad time.

"Listen, I just started working at my new job. I need to get a car and money in the bank before we even try to go that route," I lied, moving closer to her.

I quickly grabbed and twisted her onto her back. Looking down at her, I saw Dorothy Dandridge in *Carmen Jones*, and you know who Harry Belafonte was.

I tried to kiss her with the same passion as Harry did Dorothy, but when I closed my eyes, I saw Glen.

"Oh, Tee, do you still love me?" she moaned, receiving my kisses and returning them with equal passion.

"Oh yes, yes, my princess!" I whispered, trying to drink her mouth dry while thinking of Glen.

"Tee, I love you too, and I'll make you happy. Just give me a chance," she said, tonguing my ear and blowing her hot breath into it.

I moaned with delight. "Oh, Glen," I cried as my hand felt the seams of her cotton panties.

"What did you say?"

My mind snapped back to Jackie as she yelled, pushing me away from her.

"What? ... I said ... Jackie," I stuttered, trying not to look into her eyes.

"You called me Glen, didn't you? And who the hell is Glen?"

"Girl, you are crazy! You have been in this house too long. I think the outside air will do you some good."

"Jackie, is everything all right?" Miss Willie Mae asked, rushing into the living room.

"Everything's fine, Momma," Jackie said after we both sat up straight on the sofa.

"The baby's crying. I think he needs changing, and I already warmed his bottle," Miss Willie Mae said. Then she turned to me. "And how's your folks?"

"Yes, ma'am, they are fine," I said to a departing back, and she was gone.

"Tee, I'll be right back. Momma fixed some chocolate pudding. Do you want some?"

"Yeah, I'll take a little. Me and Daddy pigged out just before I came up here," I said, patting my stomach and forcing a fake smile.

She started toward the door and spun around with one graceful move. With one hand on her hip, she could have been Dorothy Dandridge's twin sister if she had one, I thought.

"You know you have some explaining to do," she said and disappeared into the hallway.

What I needed to do was get out of here, I thought as I fumbled with my wallet, searching for the napkin with Glen's number on it. I found it, memorized it, and pocketed it.

"Jackie! I need to call home," I yelled.

"Okay, you know where it's at," she yelled back.

I snatched the black receiver and dialed quickly from the phone on the end table.

The phone rang, and on the third ring, "Hello," Miss Young said.

"Hello, Miss Young, this is Tee. May I speak to Glen?" I whispered.

"Who?"

"This is Tee. May I speak to Glen, please?" I asked, elevating my voice a couple of notches.

"Oh, Tee! Yes, Glen and Coleen went out about an hour or so ago. I'll tell her you called."

"Thank you," I said and hung up.

"Is everything all right?" Jackie asked, walking in the door and handing me a cup of chocolate pudding.

"The line was busy," I said. "What is this stuff on top?" I asked, looking down at the pudding.

"Oh, that's crumbled-up Nilla wafers. Go ahead and try it," she said, looking at me suspiciously.

"Hey, this is good. Tell your momma it's delicious," I said after taking in a couple of spoonfuls.

"Okay, I'll be right back."

I spooned a couple more mouthfuls and quickly dialed home.

Daddy picked up the phone.

"Daddy," I said, hearing gospel music in the background. It sounded good, and I knew the house was rocking.

"Son, where you at? You got company, a Miss Thompson, and she is a ni—"

"Daddy, I'm on my way! Tell her not to leave," I interrupted and hung up the phone.

I downed the rest of the pudding and headed for the kitchen. I met Jackie in the hallway, carrying the baby with the bottle in his mouth.

"Listen, a friend of mine that I haven't seen in ages is in town and is looking for me," I said, rushing past her and putting the cup on the kitchen table.

"What friend?" she asked suspiciously.

"That's why marriage is going to be a big problem. You women always want to know everything," I replied while heading for the front door.

"Tee, wait a minute. Aren't you forgetting something?" she asked, grabbing my arm.

I turned around to kiss her, and she bit down lightly on my tongue. Then she held me in check until she clamped her arm around my neck. After, her tongue did the twist and shout in my mouth. I was struggling for air, and I knew the baby was, too, because the baby let out a cry, and that's when she released her grip.

"Jackie, I gotta go," I said, backing up toward the door.

"Tee, your kisses are getting better. Maybe this Glen's been giving you lessons."

She looked at me with distrust in her eyes while sticking the bottle back in the baby's mouth.

"Girl, you crazy," I said, closing the door behind me.

It took me about four or five steps to clear fifteen stairs from the porch to the sidewalk. I was on the move, heading for 10 Congress Street in a race with Jesse Owens.

I couldn't believe I didn't tell Jackie about Glen. I had planned out every word and how to break it to her gently. Then, when she opened the door looking so fine, I knew my plan had to wait.

I turned onto Congress Street and stopped on the bridge to catch my breath. When I got to the porch, the house was rocking with gospel music. Looking through the window, I could see all of Connie's partners were there, including Nicole. Glen was singing and clapping. I could tell she was enjoying herself.

After wiping the sweat from my face, I pushed the door open and joined in the singing.

Glen looked exquisitely beautiful, all dressed in yellow, and I was so proud to show off my woman. I could tell everyone had fallen in love with her, especially my family.

After the song, I politely walked up to Glen. "Hey, my princess," I said, looking into her eyes and laying a light kiss on her lips. I hoped that Nicole would get a little jealous.

"Hi, my prince," she said, returning my kiss.

Nannie started clearing her throat and gave me a "not in here" kind of look. I dropped my embrace but held Glen's hand. Then I reintroduced her to everyone, and she just fell right in. We sang one more song, and I had to drag Glen away from her newly acquired family.

"Oh, Tee, I just love your family," she said as I led her through the gate.

"Yes, and I know they love you too," I said.

"Are you hungry?" I asked, pulling her across the street to the café.

"Yes, I'm starving."

Nannie and Daddy used to run this café about six or seven years ago. Directly above the café, Nannie was co-owner of a beauty salon. Since she found the Lord, it was all about church now. Miss Dean and Miss Williams, who were sisters, were the current proprietors, and they were known for their fifteen-cent sweet potato pies.

"Good evening, Miss Dean and Miss Williams," I said, helping Glen onto the backless stool.

"Evening, Tee," they replied.

I introduced Glen, and they instantly fell in love with her. They asked me if there were any future plans, and I said it was on the drawing board. They really got a kick out of that. I ordered two hamburgers, Cokes, and pies to go because it was about closing time. I dropped a quarter into the jukebox, which got you three songs. I punched in "For Your Precious Love," then "He Will Break Your Heart" by Jerry Butler, and "My Girl" by the Temptations.

"May I have this dance, my princess?"

"I thought you would never ask," she said, spinning around and leaping off the stool.

I led her onto the dance floor, and while Jerry was beginning to sing "For Your Precious Love," we wrapped ourselves in each other's arms. I felt her soft velvet skin next to mine. I separated the perfume from her feminine fragrance and inhaled all that was not man-made.

As Jerry was ending his song, we spoke not a word because our bodies were in deep conversation. Although I said nothing to Jackie about Glen, I knew in my heart it was over between

Jackie and me. Glen kissed my Adam's apple and I knew there was no other woman for me.

We sang along with Jerry on the second song, and on the last, we swing danced. After we finished, we got cheers and applause from the proprietors and some of the departing customers. I paid for my order, and we were out of there.

The house was still rocking with gospel music when we started walking up Congress Street toward Victoria Drive.

"Tee, your family is so friendly. I must admit, coming down here, I was a little afraid," she said, sliding next to me.

"Coleen and Ed dropped me off. My parents told me to stay away from Southside because it was a bad section of town, but I just had to see you. I really missed you."

"I missed you too. I tried calling you several times today, and finally, when I called tonight from a friend's house, Miss Young picked up the phone. She told me you and Coleen stepped out, and then I called home. The rest is history, my princess," I said, handing her a hamburger.

"Well, how was your first day on the job?" she asked, biting into the hamburger.

"It was all right, nothing to brag about except working for Uncle Sam," I replied, taking a bite of my burger and a sip of Coke, not telling her that the job only lasted until the end of spring.

The night seemed especially calm and bright under the half-moon. When we got to Pine Grove, you could see most of the city, which was growing at an alarming rate. The city was lit up like a Christmas tree. The streetlights, coupled with house lights, highlighted Glen's beauty. I could just hold her and never let go.

Maybe I was getting too involved with her. I had seen what a one-sided love affair could do to a brother. It could ruin you for life, and mine had just started. I best not show too many emotions because I didn't think I could handle it if she dropped me.

"Oh, Tee! This hamburger is delicious," she said, speaking with a full mouth.

"Miss Dean makes a special sauce for her hamburgers. The sauce is also good on fries too," I said, stuffing the last piece in my mouth and washing it down with my drink.

"Now for dessert, let me introduce you to the pride of Southside—Miss Williams' sweet potato pie. These pies can calm the savage beast."

"Let me have a bite."

She took the miniature pie from me.

"Yes, that is good."

"Yeah, my princess, stick with me and I'll show you the world," I joked.

"Yes, and it's going to take a lifetime too," she teased.

"Why?"

"Because we walk everywhere we go," she chuckled, and we both laughed.

"Listen, Glen, things are going to get better. I promise you that," I said, pulling her to me and tasting her lips for the first time tonight.

"Well, since you put it that way, walking is not so bad," she said, returning my kiss.

"Are you finished with your drink?"

"Just about," she said, draining the bottle of its remaining liquid.

"Okay, then let me have it," I said, taking the bottles, putting them into the brown bag, and placing it beside a telephone post.

"I'll pick them up on the way back because Miss Williams charged me a ten-cent deposit on these bottles."

"And how about my potato pie?"

"Oh yeah, I forgot," I lied, reaching into the bag and pulling out the other pie.

"Your grandmother is so sweet. When I walked into your house tonight and introduced myself, I was so nervous and scared, but your grandmother said, 'Now come over here and give your Nannie some sugar.' And Little Daddy brought me some Kool-Aid and said he was glad he finally met the mystery lady. They made me feel so at home. I want you to thank them for me."

"Glen, you ain't going nowhere. You can tell them the next time you see them," I said, putting my arms around her shoulders.

"I don't know about that. I must have counted about ten pictures of different women all over the living room."

"You don't have to worry about those pictures. They belong to Daddy," I joked, and we both laughed.

"So why don't you practice with your church choir?"

"That's Connie and Cookie's junior choir. They belong to Tried Stone Baptist Church. The dude that was playing the piano is Connie's boyfriend, Cornell."

"Tee, what are you doing Wednesday evening at about seven?"

"I better be near you," I said, holding her tighter.

"Good, then we have a date."

"Wednesday at seven," I confirmed.

We walked in silence the rest of the way, staring at the starless sky until we reached Miss Young's house.

"Tee, I feel so secure when I'm in your arms," she whispered, kissing my neck.

"You know your prince will protect you unless there is a horse around. Then you are on your own," I chuckled, and she laughed.

"Anyway, you promised me that you wouldn't tell anyone about my encounter with the horse."

"My prince, I couldn't wait to tell someone," she teased.

"Yeah, but you didn't have to tell the whole damn hospital. Roy was the first one to come after me, imitating a horse. I was definitely the laughingstock of the hospital."

"Yes, but you are the first prince I know who is scared of horses," she teased. "There is no riding off into the sunset with you," she continued, bursting out in laughter.

"Well, just call me the walking prince," I said with a little irritation in my voice.

"You got that right. I've worn out two pairs of shoes dating you."

Glen was so tickled she almost dropped to her knees in laughter.

"Yeah, yeah, yeah," I said, feeling a little embarrassed.

"Baby, please don't take offense. You are the first man I've ever dated who didn't have a car, and that was always a prerequisite.

But baby, when I'm with you, I don't need one. No one has ever made me feel the way you do. When I look into those big beautiful brown eyes of yours, they tell me everything I need to know about you. You make me feel alive, and you make me feel like a woman. You make me laugh, and I pray to God that when you make me cry, it will not be soon, because I have fallen for you, my prince in shining armor," she said, pulling my head down to meet hers.

Then our lips met with the same eagerness as a starving baby sucking his mother's nipples.

I was in heaven.

CHAPTER 20

LITTLE RED
RIDING HOOD

It had rained earlier in the afternoon, so Daddy decided to pick me up from work. When we drove into the driveway, Robert Jr. had pulled up and parked on the side of the street in front of his house. Cousin Robert's car was the only one parked in his driveway, although there was enough room for both him and his son to tandem park. He had planted grass for the hundredth time and laid a blanket of straw over it. It was fenced off with string to keep the unwanted out.

When we were kids, we were the unwanted.

Cousin Robert's yard was the Congress Street Recreation Center. We played football, kickball, baseball, dodgeball, horseshoes, hide-and-seek, hopscotch, Cowboys and Indians, jacks, and marbles. We rode our bikes, tricycles, roller skates, scooters, wagons, and our personally constructed skate mobiles. It was our main entrance and exit to the Nasty Branch. I know Cousin Robert spent a small fortune trying to have grass like the rest of his neighbors, not counting the money spent on broken windows.

I guess Robert Jr. and I were the main culprits behind Cousin Robert's misfortune.

"Hi, Robert Jr. What's happening?" I asked, getting out of the car.

"D.C. is what's happening, Tee," Robert Jr. said, walking behind his car and onto the sidewalk.

He was wearing a black T-shirt that fit him like a second skin, displaying a huge mass of muscles.

"How you doing, Little Daddy?" he asked.

"The Lord's been good to me, Robert Jr. And how about yourself?" Daddy asked, standing by the gate.

"Couldn't be better, Little Daddy," he said, flexing his chest muscles and stopping at the driveway wall.

"Man, when are you leaving?" I asked, standing on the other side of the wall.

"I had a little setback, but it is only a matter of a couple of months," he said, flexing his biceps and stretching his T-shirt to the limit.

"Well, before you leave, you ought to give me that T-shirt. It's too small for you."

"For what? It's too big for you."

"I'm still growing. When I reach your age, that shirt should fit fine."

"Reach my age? Nigga, you crazy. I'm just four months older than you."

"Five months," I corrected with a smile.

"Hey, Tee, let's hit the streets this weekend," he suggested.

"Friday evening, about seven?"

"Make it eight."

"Eight it is," I confirmed, and then we shook on it.

I finished the last of the Old Spice cologne and inspected the growing peach fuzz under my nose in the bathroom. I grabbed my black pencil liner and went to work.

What men must go through to impress the ladies.

Then I removed my stocking cap, displaying wave after wave of sea-sickening hair. I used a soft hairbrush to remove the creases that the stocking cap had made. Satisfied with my reflection, I did a left face and high-stepped out of the bathroom, skinning and grinning. I was on a personal high until I got outside and looked at my transportation: a red bicycle, and it wasn't even mine. I pushed the bike through the gate. After pumping my bike ninety-five percent uphill, I parked it inside Miss Young's gate.

I reached for the doorbell, and before I could push it, the door sprang open, and my woman stood there dressed in red and smiling.

"You are right on time, not a minute too late or a minute too soon," Glen chuckled.

"Well, my lady, I camped here in waiting anticipation of the opening of this marvelous villa," I jested in my most Englishman's grammar.

We both laughed.

"Are you coming in, or do I have to come out there and get you?" she said in a deep and sexy voice.

"Is Grandma away, Little Red Riding Hood?"

I stuck my head in the door and suspiciously looked around the house.

"Yes, Grandma is away," she laughed, pulling me inside.

"Then the wolf is here to stay."

I growled, kissing her with the passion of a sailor coming home from the sea.

We must have kissed for ten minutes, which seemed like hours.

"Tee, I think my lips are numb," she said, biting on her lips.

"Girl, that was nice!" I said, feeling a little dizzy. "How about one more for the road?"

"That was a triple shot. I don't think I can handle another one," she laughed, closing the door.

"You look nice."

I backed Glen up against the door and kissed her nose.

"Hey, tiger, how about some iced tea?" she asked, gently pushing me away.

"No, my tigress, how about some hot you," I purred, looking down at her breasts.

"Well, hot me needs some cold tea to help cool off hot Tee."

She chuckled, pushing me away and walking toward the kitchen.

"Lord, have mercy, that must be jelly 'cause jam don't shake like that!"

I followed those tight-fitting red jeans into the kitchen.

"Tee, do you think my butt is too small?" she asked, pulling a tray of ice from the freezer.

"I don't know. I haven't seen your butt yet," I joked, grabbing her from behind and giving her a smooth body roll.

"I'm serious. Coleen is finally filling out, but I wish I could fit my jeans the way she fits hers."

Glen whined, moving her head back and forth on my chest and responding to my advances.

"My princess, there is nothing wrong with your butt, but a couple of pounds here or there wouldn't hurt none."

"What! I knew my butt was too small!"

She broke away from me and busted up my high.

"Glen, I didn't mean—"

"So where would I put a couple of pounds? Back here or on my sides?" she stormed, with her hands on her hips. "Where, Tee? Where?"

"Whoa! I'll take the two pounds back and put them right down here."

I shook my groin with both hands.

Her frown quickly turned into a smile as a tear rolled down her flawless face. The smile grew from a giggle into hearty laughter.

"You are my prince," she laughed, reaching for my hands, which were still locked on my groin.

"Listen, my princess, I find nothing wrong with you. You must believe that. I love you just the way you are. God couldn't have made a more perfect creature than the one I am holding in my arms this very minute."

Looking into her swollen eyes, I continued, "Now, what did you not understand about what I just said?" quoting my boss, Mr. Johnson.

There I went again, expressing my feelings to her. I am just one big fool when it comes to her. It seems I am out of control when I am around her, I thought.

"Tee, Coleen is so pretty, and I have seen you looking at her. I just want you to look at me the same way you look at her."

"Time out, sweetheart. Listen, if I am staring at your cousin, I am sorry. She does have a big, beautiful behind, and she was the talk of the party after you two left. But I was serious when I said that God couldn't have made a more perfect woman for me. He did make you for me, and I'll believe that until the day I die," I said, feeling her silky hair and blowing her face dry with my hot breath.

"Okay, my prince, I believe you. How about some tea?"

"Listen, from now on, when I see Coleen, even if it's on a train track and the train is bearing down on me, I'll close my eyes. I swear to God," I said, licking my index finger and raising it high in the air.

"Well, you don't have to do all that."

Glen brought two copper-colored glasses from the cabinet.

"It's just...I guess I've always been a little jealous of her. When we go out, she gets most of the attention, and she is so pretty. I remember when we used to go to a club called Gay 90s Night Club. My primary mission in life was to look just as good as Coleen. I used all kinds of makeup, and regardless of what I used or what clothes I wore—old, new, or borrowed—she still looked better," she said, removing the thawing cubes of ice from the aluminum ice tray, refilling it with water, and returning it to the freezer.

I could relate to her jealousy because I was always jealous of my cousins Butch and Robert Jr. too. Butch had always been the ladies' man, as far back as I could remember, because he had the hair, the looks, and definitely the money. He was older than me, which made him more mature, plus he had a couple of cars to choose from to ride his women around in. Now that's an unbeatable combination. Robert Jr., on the other hand, wasn't a threat until a couple of years ago, when he started lifting weights. I remember him putting bricks on each end of an iron bar and making his own bench press. Every day he would lift his homemade weights on the side of his house, right next to the horseshoe pits, which interfered with our horseshoe games. He had always been chubby, and of course, we teased him that he would always be fat. Then one day, after about six months of working out, he took off his shirt and the teasing stopped. He had transformed himself into the Incredible Hulk right in front of our eyes. He went from a sixteen-year-old to a twenty-six-year-old overnight. Now, he was tall, dark, handsome, and had a car.

It was all coming back to me now. I remember seeing Coleen at the Gay 90's Nite Club on Biltmore Avenue. Glen was the other girl. Coleen always wore a tight dress revealing her Coke-bottle-shaped figure with a butt too beautiful to describe. In fact, the last time I saw Coleen at the club, she was wearing a tight pink, shining dress. I know at least nine dudes intentionally bumped into her just to touch her. And of course, I did too, just to make it an even number. When I went with Robert Jr., most of the time I walked home, because he was always pulling someone, and most of the time it was a woman in her twenties. Occasionally I got lucky, and you could count them on two fingers, but girls were either my age or younger, never older. So now I could sympathize with Glen.

I took a drink of the ice-cold brew.

"I remember you now," I said, pointing my finger. "You used to wear your hair in a French roll, didn't you?" I continued. "Yeah, it was you, and I asked you to dance when Solomon Burke was at the club, and girl, you turned me down twice," I lied.

And it was a great lie because I could see the guilt on her face.

"Oh baby!" she said, looking at me and trying to remember back.

"I'm sorry, but I don't remember seeing you. I remember Robert Jr., but I don't remember you," she continued with her eyes apologizing.

"Oh, you remember Robert Jr. but don't remember me, is that it?"

"Well...uhh..yes," she said, dropping her eyes.

"I remember Coleen wearing a pink dress that night," I said.

"Yeah, and she wears it to death," she said sarcastically.

"What was I wearing?" she asked.

Oh boy, I think I just overplayed my hand. Think fast.

"Glen, you were so cold-hearted that night, that when I asked you to dance and it was a fast song, you didn't even look up at me...both times," I said, raising two fingers and bringing my voice up a notch.

"Come here," she said, motioning with her finger.

Like a puppy being called by his master, I obeyed.

I just love to make up, especially when it's not my fault or when they think it's theirs.

"Whatever you say, my princess," I said as our tongues met in a battle of dominance.

"I'll never say no to you again, I swear to it," she promised.

"They say, never say never."

"I'm not in the habit of repeating myself. I said... NEVER," she thundered, her voice echoing through the house and her eyes staring at me without blinking once.

"Okay, never," I conceded.

She motioned for more tea, and I declined. She took my glass and emptied both glasses of their contents into the sink, rinsing them off and placing them upside down on the draining board.

"Come here, my prince," she said, grabbing my hand and leading me back through the living room. She opened two multi-glass-framed doors and flicked on a light switch.

The room was spotless, with a dark blue sofa adorned with dark yellow pillows, two on each end. Directly behind the sofa were matching blue-and-yellow floor-length curtains that extended to each end of the rear wall. At each end of the wall were two long brass floor lamps that seemed to tower over everything except the drapes. Centered between the brass lamps was a stereo console, completely hidden from view from the main entrance.

The left wall held numerous awards and citations in 8 x 10 frames, showcasing the many achievements and accomplishments Miss Young had acquired over her impressively professional career. In the center was a well-used fireplace elevated two tiers up. It was protected by a bronze-colored screen, and to the right of it were matching fireplace tools, while to the left, a brass log basket held small, evenly cut logs, stacked neatly. The right wall, standing beside the lamp, featured a six-foot by seven-foot-wide dark-stained wood and glass book cabinet filled to capacity. I didn't much care about the titles of the books because I took to books like Dracula takes to the Crucifix.

Now, if you asked me about Superman, Batman and Robin, the Incredible Hulk, the Amazing Spider-Man, the Fantastic Four, the X-Men, or Wonder Woman and Supergirl, I could tell you, but that was the extent of my book reading. Cousin Lonnie always said if you don't want to see colored folks, go to the public library.

On the opposite end of the wall was a small, scratchless, polished antique desk with a four-wheeled, armed, flexible wooden chair. In the middle were two identical doors, like the main entrance doors, to the patio. Catty-cornered to the left wall by the main entrance was a black grand piano standing on a waxed wooden floor. If it wasn't for the used fireplace and the neatly stacked envelopes and papers on the desk, it would have been hard for me to believe people stayed here

Glen sat down at the piano and motioned me to sit down beside her.

"I like your playroom, but where's your TV?" I joked, looking down at the shining ebony and ivory keys that looked brand new.

I pressed a few keys, and the sound rang out.

"Tee, your fingernails are beautiful."

Glen lifted my hand for a closer inspection. "I've never seen a man with hands as pretty and soft as yours."

"Momma used to give me manicures until I learned how to do it myself. She said your hands reflect what's in your heart."

I proudly showed my other hand and extended my fingers, displaying a somewhat professionally done manicure.

"I'm jealous," she said, comparing her red-polished short nails to my much longer clear-polished nails. "I could go commercial with your nails, and no one would know they belong to a man."

"Thanks," I said, pressing a few more keys and watching my fingers through the reflection on the piano.

"Do you play?" she asked, playing a few notes that sounded familiar.

"I can play 'Jesus, Keep Me Near the Cross' pretty well, but nothing else."

"Tee, I had a dream last night that you left me for another woman, and I woke up crying. This song came to mind," she said, pressing the keys to a song I knew well: "Maybe" by The Chantels.

The lyrics echoed the pain of a young woman who lost the love of her life, and she yearned to get his affection back.

Glen had a beautiful voice, and the piano sounded like a Rolls-Royce compared to our piano, which sounded like a tractor.

As she was finishing, we harmonized the ending.

"My princess, that was beautiful," I said, giving her a standing ovation.

"Tee, I hope this is the last time I sing this song to you," she cried, with tears streaming down her rosy cheeks.

"That will never happen."

I pulled her up from the piano bench and held her in my arms.

"I remember someone telling me, 'Never say never,'" she chuckled, trying to hide her swollen eyes and runny nose.

"I'm not in the habit of repeating myself. I said NEVER," I bellowed, and we both laughed.

"Okay, never," she said, still holding her head down and patting my chest with the palms of her hands. "I have to go upstairs; be right back."

"Okay. May I help myself to some more tea?"

"Sure."

She walked out of the den and ran up the stairs.

After pouring myself a half glass of tea, I just couldn't get Glen's performance out of my mind. The Chantels couldn't have sounded any better, I thought, taking a sip of tea and returning the tea jug to the refrigerator.

"Hey, Tee!" Coleen said, as she walked into the kitchen with her hair in two shoulder-length braids.

"What's happening?" I asked, checking her behind out and reconfirming what Glen and I talked about.

Yes, it was big, and it looked good too, but I had no complaints about Glen's tush.

I turned away from Coleen as I drained the remaining cold beverage down my throat.

"I am starving," she said, reaching into the refrigerator and pulling out a glass bowl with aluminum foil around it.

"Have some cold chicken?" she asked, removing the foil and grabbing the fried breast of chicken.

"Thanks, but no thanks."

I placed the glass back on the draining board. I was a little amazed at Coleen and Glen's similarities.

"Tee, you have to excuse my hair. I just washed it, and you know what we have to go through to get it to act right," she said, removing a quarter loaf of bread out of the bread box.

"Well, I'm pretty sure you don't have to cuss your head out every morning before you can get a comb through it," I joked, and we both laughed.

"Well, I see you don't have a problem," she said, looking at my man-made waves.

"Yeah, but give me a couple of weeks after this stuff grows out, and I'll be praying to God for forgiveness for killing a hair comb," I joked.

"Tee, you know you are good for Glen because I've never seen her act this way before. You better treat her good or I'll give you one of these," she said, balling up her fist.

"Coleen, that's my princess and I'm her knight in shining armor."

"Okay, knight in shining armor," she joked. "I know you won't be riding up here on a white horse, my prince."

Coleen laughed so hard that she began choking on the piece of chicken she had in her mouth.

Is there anyone Glen didn't tell?

I felt humiliated, but it was rectified when Coleen started choking.

I took my time patting her back.

"Are you alright?" I asked.

"Yes, I'm fine, thank you," she said, taking a big drink of tea and wiping her mouth with a napkin.

Then she looked at me and burst into laughter again. I felt two inches tall.

Just choke again, I thought.

As I stood there trying to calm my irritation, Glen called out to me.

"Tee, Tee!"

"What?"

"Come here."

Coleen was still laughing and I was glad to have a reason to get away from her.

"Tee, I'm sorry, but it is so funny," Coleen said, coughing and wiping the tears from her eyes. Her face was as red as a beet.

"No problem, Coleen," I lied, hurrying out of the kitchen. I couldn't wait to give Glen a piece of my mind.

I walked into the den. "Glen?" I shouted.

"Baby, I'm upstairs. Come here for a minute."

I followed the sound of her voice. When I got to the top of the stairs, it was a different world. People definitely stay up here, I thought.

"Glen?"

"In here, baby."

I went down the hall and pushed the door open.

"Glen, I–"

It was like I was a born-again Christian, and all the arguments from being humiliated downstairs had miraculously disappeared when I gazed upon my angel lying in bed with a sheet over her. She obviously had no clothes on.

"Don't you want to join me?" she asked.

The room was dimly lit red, coming from a shaded lamp in the corner of the room. I could see just enough to figure out I was about to enter heaven. It took me less than a minute to change into my birthday suit. Clark Kent couldn't have changed into Superman any quicker. I knew this was going to be a good day.

I slipped under the sheet with her and said, "I thought you had gotten lost up here."

I wrapped my body around her like the red on a candy cane.

"Aren't you glad you found me?" she asked in a low, seductive voice.

I had no more to say, and the time for talking was over. You could have fried scrambled eggs on my back without any of it running off.

This was different. She was different. I was different.

I wanted to absorb myself through every pore in her skin. I could feel her rose garden against my stomach, and then the throbbing began as we locked our lips together, letting no air in or out. Then she touched me, and I exploded.

"Oh SHIT!... Oh baby! Ooooooh," I moaned.

"Tee, what have you done?!" she cried, still holding on.

"Ooooooh baby... ooh Jesus," I whispered, breathing heavily, then slowly catching my breath until my breathing had slowed down and I felt myself returning to normal.

Oh God! Let it stay heavy, if not hard, I prayed.

"I don't believe this is happening to me!" she shouted, finally releasing me, throwing back the sheets, and pushing me off her. I rolled over like a feather in a storm.

I had a funny feeling she was really, really mad at me. The next thing I heard was the door slamming shut. I grabbed myself and felt dead. Oh God, you raised Lazarus, so please do something for me, I prayed. I think I blew it this time—and all over her, to be exact. I just knew she was going to kick me out of here. Shit, I thought.

My breathing was back to normal when I heard the door reopen and shut again. Then I felt something warm between my legs.

"Don't worry about it, my prince," she said, her voice showing no contempt as before. She continued to wipe me clean.

I could see a dark red silhouette bending over me, but if I could turn the real lights on, just a quick glance at her heavenly body would make this night not a waste.

"Turn on the main light," I said, hoping she would follow my plea.

"No, I have no clothes on!" she whispered.

"Baby, just do... as... I..." I muttered.

"Oh, baby, yes," she said, jumping in bed.

Thank you, my Father, I owe you one, I prayed. With one swift move, I was on top of her and back in the driver's seat. My adrenaline was flowing, and I knew I couldn't blow it this time. Just take your time, I said to myself.

I began nibbling on her ear, and before I knew it, she had guided me inside her.

"Oh, yes!" I cried as our lips met.

Our kisses were more passionate and desirable than ever before. I could feel her walls tightening around me.

"Yes, my prince, oh yes!" she moaned.

Carla used to tell me that if I wanted staying power, I should think of food, so I started thinking about Nannie's fried chicken. I had always wondered why anyone would want to think about food at a time like this. I never wanted staying power until tonight.

Our bodies began to move in time to a silent beat. Her breathing started to increase rapidly as my thrusts became deeper and harder. Our body tempo moved up about three scales. The chicken thing was working because Glen was really enjoying this. Our bodies were soaked in perspiration, and her moans grew louder and louder.

"Baby, don't stop," she yelled, pushing my butt down with each thrust.

"Never, baby, never," I whispered, feeling her juicing up around me.

"Oh, Tee!" she screamed, locking her legs around my waist, thrusting upward. I met her thrust with an even greater one.

I think she blew out my eardrum, and I knew Coleen heard her. The next thing I knew, I was on the floor.

"What happened? Glen?"

I hope this is not another damn dream, I thought, still lying on the floor and holding myself.

"Coleen! Coleen!" she cried, running out of the room with a pillow shielding her breasts and womanhood.

I managed to crawl out of the room after her. She opened the door across the hall and went in.

Coleen was propped up in bed, pretending to be reading a Seventeen magazine.

"What's wrong?" she asked, dropping the magazine and spinning around in bed.

"Oh, Coleen, something happened to me in there!" she said, still breathing heavily.

"Yeah, I couldn't help but hear it," Coleen said, giving her a devilish smile.

"No, I mean something is wrong with me. I can't seem to find the words to explain it," Glen said, shaking with perspiration, her hair matted and clinging to the side of her face.

"Glen, are you in pain?"

Coleen pulled Glen down onto the bed and brushed her hair back.

"No, no, I'm not in pain. It's just that something happened inside me. I think he messed me up inside," she whined, peeping down at herself and then returning the pillow to its original position.

"Are you bleeding?" Coleen asked, trying to pull the pillow away.

"No, Coleen, I'm not bleeding."

Glen held the pillow tighter and flexed her legs in and out.

"Let me get this straight. You're not in pain, and you're not bleeding. Girl, you came," Coleen said, putting her arm around Glen's shoulders.

"What?"

"Fool, you had an orgasm!"

"You must be right. Oh, Coleen, yes, that's what I had. Oh, it felt sooo... good," she said, falling back on the bed. "Oh, Coleen—"

"Where's Tee?" Coleen interrupted.

I scrambled back to the other room.

I laid on the floor and closed my eyes. The thought of giving Glen so much pleasure excited me.

I could feel myself getting closer as I touched myself. Just a few more minutes, I thought, when all of a sudden, I was blinded by light.

When I finally began to focus, there Glen stood with a pillow in hand and revealed herself to me. She was magnificent, and for a moment I thought I had died and gone to heaven. Then I realized that she had caught me in the act of masturbation, and I was humiliated.

"Having fun without me, huh?" she chuckled, dropping the pillow and jumping on top of me.

The minute I felt her rose garden on my thigh, I exploded.

"Oh shit," I cried, wrapping my leg around hers and holding on for dear life.

"Tee!" she shouted.

"Ooooh, baby. I couldn't help it. Anyway, what happened a while ago? Why did you dump me on the floor? Did I do something wrong?" I asked, not giving away that I'd overheard her conversation with Coleen.

"I love you, baby," she said, moistening my lips with hers.

"Glen, it's ten o'clock!" Coleen yelled, interrupting our moment.

"Miss Young!" Glen said, rising up. "Tee, don't move," she continued, searching around the bed until she found the once-used face towel, and she raced out of the room.

Moments later she was back, wiping me off with the warmed-up cloth.

"What's his name?" she asked, wiping me clean.

"Junior," I said. "And what's her name?" I asked, looking at her rose garden.

"Well, ah, her name is... Kitty Cat," she said and burst out laughing.

"Well, Kitty Cat, I'm sorry I didn't get to christen you tonight, but there will be other nights," I beamed, glancing at my watch. It was a quarter till ten.

"I can say an amen to that, Reverend Tee Madden," she said, and we both laughed.

We dressed and went downstairs and poured ourselves some cold tea. I checked my watch, and it was ten after ten.

"I know you got school tomorrow and I got to see the man bright and early, so I better get out of here," I said, drinking the glass dry.

"What's your hurry? Wouldn't you rather be with me than the man?" she said, looking up at me with those dreamy eyes and wrapping her arms around me, gently kissing me on the lips.

"Well, since you put it that way, I can stay a little while longer," I said, returning her embrace and kiss.

"Glen, you and Tee come here for a minute!" Coleen yelled from the top of the stairs.

Glen led me back upstairs. Coleen was watching the Flip Wilson show with Gladys Knight and the Pips singing "I Heard

It Through the Grapevine." Glen grabbed my hand, and we raced into her room and turned on her smaller TV set. Then we propped ourselves up in her bed, popping our fingers and moving to the rhythm of the beat. After it was over, Geraldine came on.

"You know, Tee, I don't like the way Flip Wilson portrays us," she said.

"Baby, I don't think he is talking about all Black women. I just think it is an act."

"You don't think I act like that, do you?"

"No, her hair is a lot straighter than yours," I joked, climbing out of bed.

"Tee, where are you going?" she asked, grabbing my arm.

"Just stay till the show is over. Miss Young always comes in between a quarter to eleven and eleven," she said, tightening her grip on my arm.

After the show was over, I kissed her goodnight. When I got to the bottom of the steps, Miss Young was coming through the door. I raced back up the steps, almost running over Glen. I dove over her bed onto the floor and slid under. Glen ran in behind me and shut the door.

"Oh, Tee, if Miss Young finds you here, I am a goner, so please don't say anything," she whispered and sat up in bed, pretending to watch television.

Moments later, there was a light knock on the door.

"Glen?" Miss Young asked, pushing the door open.

"Oh, hello, Miss Young. How was your night?" Glen asked, not looking up from the television set.

"Is that Tee's bike outside in the yard?" she inquired, looking around and then at the closet door, which was about a couple of feet from the main entrance.

"Yes, ma'am, some of his friends dropped by, and he left with them. He said he would pick it up tomorrow morning. I hope his bike is not a problem."

I could see Miss Young's shoes. She dropped her keys on the floor, and I closed my eyes.

"No, it's not a problem," she said, picking up her keys. "Glen, do you have that umbrella I loaned you the other day? There's an eighty percent chance of rain tomorrow, and when it's that high, nine times out of ten it will rain."

"Yes, ma'am," Glen said, jumping up and opening the closet door, handing the black umbrella to its owner.

Glen took her time closing the closet door.

"Thank you, Miss Young, I really needed it the other night," she continued.

"Well, child, you are surely welcome. Good night."

Miss Young left the room, closing the door behind her.

Glen fell on the bed after locking the door, releasing the air she had held in when Miss Young first entered her room.

I finally got in bed with her, and we slept till five. I got up, kissed her goodbye, tipped down the stairs, and was gone.

CHAPTER 21

THE DECISION

Days at work seemed to get longer and longer. I couldn't get my mind off her. I started counting the hours and minutes before I would be back in her arms.

Mark and I were spending a lot of time together at work, and the more time we spent together, the more I tried to understand him. Mr. Johnson would come down and chit-chat every now and then, complimenting me on what a good worker I was. We talked about his wife, Debbie, and my girl, Glen. There was one thing we had in common: we were both in love with our ladies.

The weekend was here, and that meant she would be going back home. I needed a car for this weekend because I didn't think I could go three days without seeing her.

The eagle flies on Friday because the café was jumping with business. There was a couple dancing in the street as I was walking toward Robert Jr.'s house. I knocked on the brand-new screen door that our family friend Stringbean had installed. Cousin Betty yelled at me to come in. She was sitting at the card table with Stringbean playing nickel-quarter poker. He was over six feet and skinny—about a hundred and fifty pounds—like a string bean.

"Evening, Cousin Betty... Stringbean," I said, sitting down at the table.

"Evening, Tierron," Cousin Betty said, taking a long drag off her Pall Mall cigarette and exhaling.

"I'll take four cards." she said as she flipped over an ace of spades.

"Dealer takes one," Stringbean said, pulling the last Lucky Strike cigarette from his pack and crushing the pack before lighting up.

"A quarter...I don't think you hit," Cousin Betty said, blowing a smoke ring that seemed to encircle Stringbean's nose.

As long as I can remember, Cousin Betty always sat by the window facing the door 'cause that was her lucky seat.

Stringbean didn't look at his card, so nine times out of ten, he had two pairs. Cousin Betty knew that and must've hit a good hand, I thought as I looked on.

"So, you think I didn't hit?" he asked with the cigarette still in his mouth.

"A quarter better on your pair of aces," he continued, still not looking at his fifth card.

"Call!" Cousin Betty said.

Stringbean looked at me, and I returned his stare with a smile. He flipped his cards, queens and jacks.

Cousin Betty said, "Read 'em and weep," turning over two pair— black aces and black eights.

"Deadman's hand."

"Betty, you're the luckiest woman I know," Stringbean said. We all laughed.

"What's so funny?" Robert Jr. said, walking into the living room and buttoning up his shirt sleeve.

"My, my, do we look sharp. Got a date tonight?" Cousin Betty asked, admiring her son.

"I hope not. We're supposed to be going to the pool room tonight," I said, looking at him and wishing I had worn something else.

"Now, Momma, you know I always try to look my best when I go out. Because you never know what you might run into, right, Cuz?" he said, slapping my hands.

"Well, if you run into something, does that mean I have to walk home tonight?" I said, with a hint of disappointment in my voice.

"Now, Tee, when I run into something, I always take you home."

"Robert Jr., the last time we went to the Jade Club, I walked home," I reminded him.

"Tee, that was different. Maime was in town from college, and you know how I feel about her."

"Tee, what you need is a car," Stringbean said, drinking the last of his beer.

"Amen to that," I agreed.

"Well, before you two leave, one game of bid whist," Cousin Betty said.

"Okay, I'm with you," I said, grabbing the cards and looking for the jokers.

"One game, Momma, and we are out of here," Robert Jr. said, holding up one finger.

"Which one is the big joker?" Stringbean asked, pulling a cigarette from Cousin Betty's pack.

"The one with no writing on it," I said, showing him the card.

"Tee, let's show them how the game is played," Robert Jr. said, sitting down across from me.

In the first hand, Stringbean went set on a five special. The second hand, Robert Jr. bet a five no-trump, and Cousin Betty countered with a six no-trump, uptown. She and Stringbean turned all the tricks and won a Boston. Then the trash-talking started, which laughed us out the house.

Robert Jr. and I played about five games of pool, then decided to go to an after-hour joint in the mountains called Dolls. Our timing was perfect because in another hour or so, the place would be filled to capacity. Robert Jr. grabbed a corner booth, and I dropped a couple of quarters in the jukebox before the old folks started playing their down-home music. When I got to the table, Robert Jr. had ordered three half-fried chicken dinners and a couple of Cokes.

"Man, I could eat a horse," Robert Jr. said, popping his fingers to the beat of The Supremes' "Come See About Me."

"I know you're going to miss Asheville," I remarked, moving to the beat.

"Yeah, man! You know I'm going to miss Daddy and Momma and Nannie and them, but man, it's time to go. What are you going to do? Stay here, get married, have four or five kids, and live unhappily ever after? Man, that stuff isn't for me. There's got to be something else out there for me," Robert Jr. declared, lighting two cigarettes and passing one to me.

"Robert Jr., I don't know what I want to do. I know whatever it is, it's not in Asheville, North Carolina. The love bug has bitten me square in the behind, so that's why I am between a rock and a hard place. Glen's got my nose wide open, so wide you could drive an eighteen-wheeler through it," I admitted, inhaling and exhaling deeply.

"I've been reading about the Army, and they have some benefits. You can retire after twenty years with full medical care and draw half of your active retirement pay," I continued.

"Well, it's hard to retire when you are dead."

"What's that supposed to mean?"

"Tee, if you haven't heard, there's a war going on, and we are the first sent and first sent back in a pine box. Anyway, Cassius—ah, Muhammad Ali—said he doesn't have any problems with the Viet Cong because they've never called him a nigger," he explained, slapping my hand.

The waitress brought our orders, and we dug in. Robert Jr. finished his plate and started on the other. I managed to grab a chicken leg before he noticed. He still could eat chicken and make you hungry all over again.

The joint began to fill up, the air thick with conversation and smoke from cigarettes and cigars, so dense it felt like you could cut it with a knife. K.C. and Sandra joined our table, a couple who seemed to have been together since birth. They finished high school about six or seven years before we did. K.C., a cab driver who acted as though he owned the cab company, always mentioned a job opening whenever I saw him. It was an offer I always declined.

"Robert Jr., didn't I see you with Sister Baby down at Six Points the other night?" Sandra inquired, lighting up a cigarette.

"Could've been," Robert Jr. replied, not looking up from his plate.

"Damn, boy, don't you want to save the dogs some?" K.C. joked as Robert looked up with a chicken bone in his mouth, prompting laughter from us all.

"Man, leave me alone," Robert Jr. retorted, half his mouth hidden behind chicken bones.

"Robert Jr., you know Sister Baby is old enough to be your mom," Sandra teased, blowing smoke in his direction.

"Stop meddling, baby!" K.C. interjected.

"Sandra, Sister Baby is younger than you," Robert Jr. countered, giving us a smile and a wink.

"Oooooooh," K.C. and I sang in harmony, laughing as Fats Domino began singing, 'Whole Lotta Lovin'.

"Sister Baby is at least a couple of years older than me," Sandra protested, sticking her nose up at Robert Jr. then looking to K.C. for confirmation.

"Sandra, you look a lot better than she does," I commented, uncertain of whom I was discussing.

"That's right, baby. Why don't you listen to Tee?" K.C. said, pulling out a quart of Gordon's gin and a bottle of grapefruit juice.

"Where's that woman with the setup? She should have been here by now," he continued.

No sooner had the words left his mouth than the waitress set down a bucket of ice, two Cokes, four paper cups, and two quartered lemons.

"That will be five dollars."

"Hey! I don't need Cokes, just the ice and cups," K.C. countered, picking up the Cokes.

"Listen, Rockefeller, the price is five with or without the Cokes," the waitress retorted, hands on her hips and blowing a big bubble of gum.

"Daddy, just pay for it, 'cause I need a drink," Sandra interjected, glancing at Robert Jr.

"I'll take one of those off your hands," Robert Jr. chimed in, snatching a Coke from K.C.'s grasp.

"Thanks, man. Tee, you gonna finish the rest of those fries?" he asked, reaching for my plate.

"Help yourself. I can't eat another bite," I responded, picking some food out of my teeth with a pack of matches.

"Robert Jr., I would rather buy you a wardrobe than feed you," K.C. exclaimed, prompting laughter from the rest of us.

"I'm sure Robert Jr. can find a woman to both cook for him and buy his wardrobe," Sandra suggested in a deep, seductive voice, gently kicking him under the table. The kick was enough to make him flinch and glance at K.C., who was distracted by a woman in a red tight miniskirt at the jukebox.

"That's what I'm looking for, Sandra. Someone who will take care of me but isn't already taken care of by someone else, if you catch my drift," Robert Jr. replied sarcastically, his attention still partly on her.

"Hey Sandra, how about a dance?" I proposed, reaching across the table and moving to the rhythm of Marvin Gaye's "Stubborn Kind of Fellow." I pulled her up from the table before tensions could escalate.

I admired Robert Jr.'s attire: a light brown suit paired with a dark brown silky shirt, the top three buttons undone to reveal a gold cross nestled in his hairy chest—a detail he clearly wanted noticed, which seemed not to bother K.C. as he poured his second drink.

"Excuse me, Daddy," Sandra said, sidestepping past K.C.

"K.C., I promise I'll bring her back," I assured him, still holding onto her hand.

"You can keep her all night, but she's going home with me," K.C. chuckled.

We started swing dancing first, but as Sandra became the center of attention, she let go of my hand and did her own thing. Men called out her name, egging her on. Wearing a low-cut, tight, dark blue dress with red high heels and matching red moon-shaped earrings, Sandra shined. Then, realizing she was hogging the limelight, I launched into a boogaloo, followed by a James Brown spin and a series of hip rolls that had the crowd roaring. After the song, we hugged and laughed.

"Where did you learn to move like that?" she asked, still laughing, and placed a kiss on my cheek.

"Reverend Madden taught me those moves," I joked as we made our way back to the table.

"Sure, he did," she replied, patting my rear.

Upon returning, we found two beautiful newcomers had joined Robert Jr. "Sandra, Tee, this is Judy and Cindy from Brevard," Robert Jr. introduced, then whispered something to Judy that made them both laugh.

"Hey, what's happening!" I greeted.

Sandra offered them a quick, fake smile but remained silent.

"I see James Brown's got nothing on you," Cindy remarked, edging closer to Robert Jr., making space for Sandra.

Laughing, I said, "Like I just told my dancing partner, I learned it all from my grandfather, Reverend A.R. Madden."

"Reverend Madden is your granddad?" Judy asked, eyes wide with surprise.

"Yes, he's my grandfather," I replied, meeting her astonished gaze.

"Tyrone, right?"

"Tierron," I corrected gently, "but everyone calls me Tee."

"Yeah, now I remember you," Judy exclaimed, turning to Cindy. "He was the kid in the yellow Bermuda short suit, the one who got pecked in the head by one of our chickens, and that yellow suit turned blood red. Remember, Cindy?" she continued, laughter in her voice.

"Yes, I remember. There was blood everywhere."

"Yeah, that was me," I confessed with a grin.

I chuckled at the memory. "I remember it well; we were invited to dinner in Brevard that Sunday evening. The next-door neighbors had some chickens. I picked up a little chick, and then, all hell broke loose."

"I guess you don't remember us. It's been over ten years," Judy mused.

After a moment of reflection, it all clicked. "Yeah! I remember two snotty-nosed little girls who threw rocks at me," I said, faking a smile.

"That was me and Cindy," she admitted, smiling back.

"How about a drink?" K.C. interjected, offering a full cup to me.

"What's in it?"

I smelled the contents with a raised eyebrow.

"It's gin and grapefruit with a squeeze of lemon. It's do-it fluid, man. You might need it tonight," K.C. teased, sending a wink towards Judy and eliciting laughter around the table.

"You better behave yourself, Daddy," Sandra warned softly, tapping him on the arm.

"I don't think he'll be needing it on us," Judy retorted, shooting K.C. a stern look.

"Does it work on girls too?" Cindy inquired with a playful smile.

"Cindy!" Judy reprimanded.

"Don't be such a prude, Judy. I just want to taste it."

Cindy took the drink from my hand. She downed it all in one gulp, then handed me back the cup, now filled only with ice.

"No problem, there's more where that came from," K.C. assured, refilling my cup with gin.

"Tee, take a drink. It might put hair on your chest," Robert Jr. said in jest, sharing a knowing look with K.C.

The smell alone was terrible.

"I know you're not going to let a woman outdo you," K.C. challenged, with the rest of the table joining in to urge me on.

"Okay," I conceded, taking a sip.

The liquid felt like fire in my mouth. When I attempted to swallow, my throat seemed to burst into flames, and I accidentally sprayed everyone at the table, dousing K.C. the most.

"You're supposed to drink it, son, not spray it," K.C. managed between bursts of laughter.

"Next time, ask for some chaser. That was one hundred percent gin," he added, still laughing as everyone wiped themselves off.

The moment "It's A Man's World" by James Brown swelled through the speakers, Judy didn't hesitate. She pulled Robert Jr. out of his seat with a laugh, and K.C., seizing the moment, swept Sandra onto the dance floor.

"Tee, would you care to dance?" Cindy asked, her eyes sparkling with invitation.

"Sure," I replied, my heart heavy with thoughts of Glen, "but just so you know, I have a girl."

"I'm not asking for a ring, Tee. I just want to dance," she said with a playful smirk.

"Dance request accepted," I replied, standing and holding out my hand.

One of my biggest weaknesses was long hair, and Cindy had plenty of it.

Relax! Let go and let God, I prayed.

Cindy was Judy's younger sister by one year. Cindy and I were the same age. Both were going to Florida A&M. I still couldn't believe how much they had grown since the last time I saw them.

While dancing with Cindy, I kept thinking about Glen. I shared with Cindy all about my girlfriend, and she told me about a guy named Charley.

We finished our dance and returned to the table. I finally finished my gin and grapefruit after adding more water and grapefruit juice to an already diluted drink. I asked Judy whatever happened to the chicken. She recounted that the chicken attacked her grandmother about a week after it had attacked me, leading her grandmother to wring its neck and serve it with dumplings for dinner.

Robert Jr. and I left before closing time, and we left alone.

CHAPTER 22

THE

INTERROGATION

I talked Daddy into giving up the car after he took care of his business. It was Saturday, and Daddy had to get a haircut, his shoes shined, and pick up his suits from the cleaners. It was eleven o'clock before Daddy turned over the keys to me.

When I arrived at Glen's house in Canton, she was sitting in the front yard with her parents. She jumped up and ran to the car.

"Hi, my prince," she said, giving me a quick kiss on the lips when I got out of the car.

She grabbed my hand and pulled me toward her parents.

"Hi yourself, my princess. I missed you yesterday."

"You better have."

She squeezed my hand and gave me a smile that would put the Mona Lisa to shame.

Elizabeth Gibson Thompson
"Muv"

Glen's mother had thick, black semi-straight hair, with a round face identical to Glen's. Her cocoa-tan skin gave radiance to the yellow floral dress she wore, displaying her girlish figure. Glen's father was slightly bald, with light hawk-like brown eyes that seemed to watch your every move. He sat erect like he was king of his castle.

Glen's grandmother was a living doll and could have been easily taken for Glen's mother; their resemblance was uncanny. She had long black straight hair with streaks of gray and a smile that could soothe an angry beast.

"Mother, Daddy, and Momma, this is Tierron Lavon Madden, Tee for short."

I shook their hands and said, "I finally get to meet you. It's a pleasure."

"Have a seat and rest a spell. How about some lemonade?" Glen's grandmother asked.

Before I could answer her, Glen was entering the house.

"I don't mind if I do," I replied, watching the door close behind Glen.

"That's all Glen talks about is Tee this and Tee that. I think she really is fond of you, Tee," Glen's grandmother said, fanning herself with a church fan.

"Well, that's well and good, but how does he feel about her?" Mrs. Thompson asked, giving me a cold stare.

This was a direct question that needed a direct answer. I could have kicked my own tail for not foreseeing this moment.

Glen's father was sitting back in his chair, eyes probing, waiting for an answer. It felt as if he was a prosecutor and I was a defendant getting ready for cross-examination.

"I'm very fond of your daughter, Mrs. Thompson," I said, looking directly into her eyes.

"That's good to hear. But what I want to know is where is this relationship headed? Glen is a young, very intelligent, very pretty, and very desirable young woman. She is going to college and will soon be ready to settle down with someone. So, I'm asking again, what are your plans?"

She sat back in her chair with her arms folded across her lap.

My heart was pounding so hard that I swore I could see my chest vibrating with each beat.

"Mrs. Thompson, it is hard for me to explain in words what I feel about your daughter, but I have honorable intentions. I know those are just mere words, but if you could read my heart, you'd know I speak the truth," I said, swallowing a big dry lump in my throat.

"Those are mighty powerful words, but I believe you," she said, giving me a smile of approval.

Glen finally emerged from the house with a large glass of ice-cold lemonade wrapped in a napkin.

Was I ever glad to see her?

She handed me the lemonade and stood behind me with both hands resting on my shoulders.

"How long have you known our daughter?" Grandmother asked.

"Ma'am, the first time I laid eyes on her was about six or seven months ago," I said, taking half of the lemonade down before I removed it from my lips.

"What do your folks do?" Mr. Thompson asked.

"My grandfather is Reverend A. R. Madden," I said proudly.

"Who in the hell is Reverend A. R. Madden?"

He caught me by surprise; I was shocked for words. The ladies quickly placed their hands over their mouths to hold back their amusement.

"Daddy!" Glen shouted.

"Well, I don't know who the hell he is," he fired back, and the ladies burst out in laughter.

"Yes, sir, he's a...a...Preacher, and he's a—"

"Daddy," Glen interrupted, "he's a Baptist minister with churches in Fletcher and—"

"Brevard and Saluda, North Carolina," I finished, patting her on the hand.

"Well, the majority of the devils I know are in the church."

Mr. Thompson rose from his chair, and the laughter continued.

"Daddy!" Glen shouted.

"Well, Glen, I did say I didn't know him, so he's probably a good man," he said, reaching down beside his wife and grabbing a pack of cigarettes that was lying on the grass. He lit one up and placed the pack in his shirt pocket.

"Yes, sir, he is a good man," I retorted as Glen began massaging my neck and shoulders until I could feel the tension leaving my body.

"Well, all this talk has made me thirsty. Leal, I'm going on the hill. Want to go up there with me, Tee?" Mr. Thompson asked.

"No, Tee doesn't want to go up there on the hill with you, and you don't need to go either," Mrs. Thompson said, raising her voice a notch.

"Now, Leal, I'm a man and I go where I damn well please!"

He pulled a baseball cap from his rear pants pocket and mounted it on his head.

"Well, Tee, it's been a pleasure. Don't make yourself a stranger," he said, extending his hand.

"Yes, sir," I said, jumping up from the chair and firmly grabbing his hand. "You'll see a lot of me."

As I returned to my seat, Mrs. Thompson assured me, "Tee, we know your folks and they are good people. So don't get your dander up. He loves to talk foolishness."

"Yes, ma'am," I said.

"Yes, your mother had my picture on display in her shop for at least a year, right, Elizabeth?" Grandmother said, looking me in the eye.

"Yes, ma'am, I thought you looked mighty familiar," I lied, showing all teeth.

"Tee, I'm hungry. Let's go get something to eat," Glen said, pushing me up and out of the chair.

I handed Glen my empty glass and watched her disappear into the house as I said, "Well, it's nice meeting you all."

"We are glad we finally met you, and I hope it won't be the last time," Grandmother said, giving me a smile that I knew came from her heart.

"Wild horses can't keep me away," I said, which drew a giggle from both.

I should have known. Glen must have told everybody, including President Johnson, about the night of the famous horse introduction.

"Good day, ladies," I said with a little embarrassment when Glen walked out of the house.

"Momma, Mov, we're going over to Poor Boys. Do you want anything?" Glen asked, pulling me toward the car.

"Yes, you can bring me back a pack of cigarettes, Glen, 'cause your daddy just took mine," Mrs. Thompson said.

"I got a pack of Tareyton, Mrs. Thompson," I offered. "We would rather fight than switch," I quoted from the Tareytons cigarette commercial, holding up a newly opened pack.

"No, Lord, they are a little too strong for me. I smoke menthols. Glen knows what I smoke, but thank you anyway," Mrs. Thompson said, forcing a smile.

"How about you, Momma?" Glen asked.

"Nothing, honey, I have to be going. Gotta fix Homer something to eat," she said.

"Okay, Momma, I'll see you tomorrow then," Glen said, breaking away from me and giving her grandmother a hug and kiss.

As we were about to leave, one of the most beautiful creatures that I had ever seen was crossing the street. I tried not to stare, but that wasn't a possibility. She had flawless Hershey-chocolate skin with high cheekbones, and her lips seemed to be a shade darker. Her black hair was pulled back into a long, thick braid that fell between her lower narrow back and round buttocks. This rose of a lady wore a light blue blouse with short blue jean bib overalls and matching skin-colored sandals, and she wore no makeup. Her smile seemed to lighten up the already high-noon cloudless blue sky. Indeed, this was my first time seeing a chocolate Indian maiden. Hollywood always made them vanilla.

"This must be Tee," she said, coming closer and looking prettier with each step.

"Yes, this is my prince," Glen said, gently squeezing my arm. "Tee, this is my sister, Diana."

"Huh?" I muttered. "Yeah, that's me," I grinned.

"Glen has told me so much about you, I think I know you already," Diana said in a surprisingly sexy southern dialect.

Jesus, this is one beautiful girl. And that voice.

Still charmed by her exotic beauty and sultry voice, all I could say was, "I hope she said something good."

"All good, but if you hang around here long enough, we'll find something wrong," she joked, and we all laughed.

"Hey, listen, I'm a preacher's son. We don't do anything wrong, or should I say, get caught doing anything wrong," I joked back.

"Well, preacher's son, you better make sure you treat my sister right or else—" She shook a balled-up fist in front of my face and bit down on her lower lip. "I'm gonna give you one of these."

"I swear, I'll never do my princess wrong," I said, leaning backward with both palms facing outward.

Before we got to the top of the street, I was introduced to some of Glen's beautiful cousins coming out of a little snack bar and grill when we stopped to pick up a pack of cigarettes for Mrs. Thompson. I was pretty sure that there had to be some homely girls around here, but I failed to see one. Everyone she introduced me to, male or female, was kinfolk, except one. His name was Lenny, and he was Glen's ex. She had told me about their relationship, but I could not place him until now.

He and a couple of Glen's cousins, Paul and D.J., had just driven up beside us in his new yellow Pontiac LeMans. It looked like it had just been driven out of the showroom. Yes, it was a sight to behold.

I first met Lenny soon after his discharge from the Army because he used to date a couple of girls from the Saxton Apartments. I had always looked up to him because he was always clean, and our relationship had always been friendly.

Now that I knew who he was, I was jealous as all get-out, and I hoped it wasn't showing.

Glen quickly introduced us, and when Lenny tried to kiss her on the cheek, she pushed him away and rushed inside the snack bar.

"This is a small world, isn't it?" Lenny said, reaching for my hand.

"Yes, it is." I said, not responding to his hand.

"So, you are Tee," Paul said. "Glen has told us a lot about you," he continued, looking at Lenny and sipping on a beer.

"Well, I hope some of it was good," I said, giving him a smile.

"Son, you know you are a long way from home. Are you sure your folks know you're this far out?" D.J. joked, getting a little laughter from the others and slapping Lenny's hand.

"They won't lose any sleep over it, and I know Lenny's folks don't lose any sleep when he's in my neck of the woods."

I looked at D.J. and then at Lenny.

This was the first time I had used my home turf as a backup, and it felt good. I knew D.J. was ready to kick my butt, and Paul was there for the ride, but Lenny didn't want anything like this to happen because, like I said, he would be coming to my turf, and what goes around comes around.

"Well, I guess Glen has told you all about us," Lenny said, stepping in front of D.J.

"Yeah, she said she used to have a little crush on you before I came along."

I smirked, indicating the quantity of their affair with my index finger and thumb.

"She told you it was over between us... Man, we just had a lover's quarrel," he said, moving his head up and down and looking me in the eye.

"Hey, my prince, you ready?" Glen said, grabbing my arm.

"Yeah, I'm ready."

"Glen, come here for a minute," Lenny said.

"We have nothing to talk about."

Glen walked to the car and hopped in.

"It's been a pleasure," I said, looking at D.J. and Paul before getting into the car.

"Yeah, Tee, you take care," Paul said, with D.J. mumbling something.

Although I backed out of the parking lot with a victory smile on my face, I was still jealous as all get-out. Glen had told me about her affair with Lenny, but I never knew it was this dude. He definitely was a player, especially in my hometown, and nine times out of ten he had the same reputation out here. He had all the weapons: experience, maturity, a new car, money, and he wasn't a bad-looking dude; he was tall, dark, and handsome. Now after looking at my weapons, I scored him 8 to 3. This was like a poker game or a pool game: if you can't play a good game, talk one.

This dude had interrupted my heartbeat and was leading in points, but I knew that God had intended for Glen and me to be together. So now the score had changed to infinity plus 3 to 8, and it would remain that way unless I did something foolish, and Nannie and Daddy didn't raise a fool.

We dropped the cigarettes off at Glen's house, then we drove across town to a drive-in restaurant called Poor Boy's. Glen had recommended a chuck wagon sandwich, and I had no idea what one was.

"I really got the taste for a couple of chili dogs and some fries," I said, reading the large wooden outside menu that hung on the side of the building.

The waitress came out, and we ordered.

"Tee, you don't know what you are missing," Glen said, getting a little closer when this candy apple red 1950 Ford truck drove up.

The red and chromed exposed engine was spotless. The chromed wheels and oversized tires put it in a class by itself. Cinderella's chariot couldn't have been more impressive.

The driver had a curl dangling over his left eye with a cigarette in his mouth, and his blond ponytailed lady was bouncing to the loud beat of "Don't You Just Know It" by Huey "Piano" Smith and the Clowns.

"Glen, I know what I'm missing, but I can't indulge in it at this time," I said, putting my arms around her and patting my feet to the beat of my neighbor's music.

"You better be nice," she said, patting my thigh to the beat of the music and singing along with the Clowns and me along with Huey.

"I am nice; I still got my clothes on."

"I love you, Tee Madden, and my family loves you too. They think you are so well-mannered."

"Well, I don't know about your mother because of the way she looks at me. I think if looks could kill, I would have been dead a couple of hours ago."

"Oh, baby, Mother is blind in one eye; she was born that way. She means well."

"Baby, I'm sorry. I didn't know. And in case she doesn't like me, she is still going to see a lot of me."

I held Glen a little tighter and continued, "You know, your father is a character. I like him. I've never heard anyone express themselves like he does. And your grandmother is a living doll. You favor all three."

"OKAY. Here you are. Roll up your window a little," the freckled-faced redhead waitress said.

"How about this?" I asked, rolling my window up about three inches.

"That's fine," she said, hanging the tray of food on the car window. "Will there be anything else?"

After making an inventory of our order, "Some hot sauce and more salt, please," Glen said.

The food smelled so good, and I was dying to see what a chuckwagon sandwich would look and taste like. For some reason, I pictured it as some kind of barbecue sandwich. I took a bite of Glen's sandwich, and it was love at first bite.

"Get a Job" by the Silhouettes was blasting from the candy apple red truck, and the couple didn't lose a beat. It had me thinking about what I was going to do in about two months and days. Lenny had come into my life with a new car and money and a great possibility of regaining my woman back.

Where there is a will, there is a way, Nannie always says, I thought as I took a second bite of my hot dog.

The waitress dropped off some hot sauce wrapped in waxed paper and some extra salt.

"Thank you," I said, and she was gone.

"Tee, Mother told me one time when she and Daddy were out on a date, they had no money and they were approaching a hot dog stand, and she said, 'Honey, those hot dogs sure smell good.' Daddy replied, 'OK then, let's go down there and smell a while,'" she chuckled.

I roared with laughter. The hot dog I had in my mouth went all over the steering wheel and dashboard. I was laughing so hard that I started choking, and Glen began pounding my back. I just couldn't stop laughing. I could picture him saying that in his southern dialect.

"Okay, Glen," I said, catching my breath. Then I busted out laughing again, and this time I was laughing so hard that I expelled gas.

"Tee!" Glen yelled as she swiftly slid to the right door.

"Baby, I'm sorry," I said, still laughing.

After the air was cleared and we had cleaned up the mess, I knew I was in love. She made me laugh. She made me feel wanted. Now I was learning what love was all about.

We had so much in common. She was the oldest of three, and so was I. She stayed at 10 Schoolhouse Road, and I lived at 10 Congress Street. She was raised by her grandmother, and so was I. We were both born in the same year and in the same summer. She mostly favored her father, and so did I.

There was no way I was going to lose to Lenny. He had a better chance of getting through hell with gasoline drawers on than winning this one because this was my woman, I thought, as I looked at this woman who had changed my life.

CHAPTER 23

FINDING MY WAY

Daddy and I had just finished cutting the weeds and grass in the backyard and were resting under the apple tree with our straw hats over our eyes. The spring air was so refreshing, and the smell of the apple blossoms just made you want to sleep.

"Tee, how's that young lady of yours?" Daddy asked, speaking from under his tilted straw hat.

"She's fine, Daddy," I said. "But I just met one of her old boyfriends, and I am a little jealous," I continued, picking up a blade of grass and sticking it in my mouth.

"Well, did she give you a reason to be jealous?"

"No, it's just that I don't have a car, and she is so beautiful. I just sometimes feel I might lose her. I don't know what I want to do with my life, except spend it with Glen. She is going to be a nurse, and with my high school transcripts, I might be qualified enough to be the garbage man."

"I know this is not my son, feeling sorry for himself."

Daddy removed his hat and wiped the sweat from his forehead with his handkerchief.

"I mean I want to see the world and—"

"And you got a woman, and you don't know what to do," he interrupted.

"Something like that."

"Listen, son, you have got everything in front of you. Patience is a virtue, and that is an acquired quality that most of the time comes with age. Glen is a beautiful girl, and if she is meant for you, she is yours. Nothing and nobody in this whole wide world can stop you from keeping her. Now be a Madden and go out there and claim what's yours or leave it alone. And for God's sake, do what you got to do," Daddy preached, getting up and pulling me up with him.

***

Glen called me and said she had a surprise for me and to stay home. Momma and I were sitting on the porch when she drove up in a '55 brown Buick.

"Hey, whose car?" I asked, jumping in and giving her a kiss.

"I borrowed it for the rest of the week from my step-grandmother, Momma Florence. Do you want to drive?"

"Sure!"

"I'm hungry; let's get something to eat," she said, waving goodbye to Momma.

"I know the ideal place."

I drove to Rabbit's Tourist Court. It was one of the best fried food places in town. When we walked in, Jackie Wilson was finishing up "Woman, A Lover, A Friend." I took the booth beside the jukebox while Glen dropped some change in.

"Hey, my prince, what would you like to hear?"

"Play anything you want, as long as it reminds you of me," I said, looking at her slim figure.

"Well, that should be easy, sweet cakes, play 'Charlie Brown' cause he's a clown," Jake joked, as he and Sandy were walking toward the jukebox, with that same old dirty feathered hat on and showing all yellows and gold.

"Hi, Tee," Sandy said, looking at Glen in disgust.

"Hi, Sandy, I see you are still walking the dog. I thought he would be housebroken by now," I joked back.

"I know your momma taught you better. Introduce me, nigga," he said, looking at Glen and licking his balloon-inflated lips.

"Yeah, where are my manners? Sandy, this is my lady, Glenna Thompson," I said. "And this is... ay ...ay ...what's your father's name, Sandy? Jake, right?" I asked while popping my fingers and giving him a smile.

"Hi," Glen said, turning around with a smile and quickly dropping it when Sandy didn't return hers.

"I know damn well you know who I am, nigga!" Jake shouted. "I did have some good news for you, up until now, motherfucka. Since you don't remember me, I'll just keep what I got in my pocket, in my damn pocket, nigga!"

As soon as he said that, I knew either thirty-three or eighteen had fallen. Earlier today I played a quarter on thirty-three and on Momma's number eighteen, I thought, as the smile spread on my face like wildfire.

"Now, Jake, give up the cash," I demanded, jumping up and holding out my hand, trying not to show too much enthusiasm.

"Oh, now motherfucka, you know my name," Jake said, pulling out a large roll of bills and peeling out two twenty-dollar bills.

"Yeah, it's called selective memory," I chuckled, jerking them out of his hands, folding and sliding them in my pocket with one smooth motion, as "Tears on My Pillow" by Little Anthony and the Imperials rang out of the jukebox.

"Sweet cakes, if you need anything, I mean anything, just call on Jake, you hear," Jake said, giving my lady a thorough look-over.

"I thank you, but Tee gives me all I need," Glen said, wrapping her long slender arms around my neck as we began slow dancing provocatively to the song.

"In case he disappoints you, and he eventually will, sweet cakes, give big Jake a buzz, ya hear?" he said, while Sandy was pulling him toward the exit.

"Yeah, the only thing big about Jake is his lips and his belly," I whispered, and we both laughed.

We slow-dragged to a couple more songs and ordered fried chicken and fried catfish with all the trimmings. After stuffing ourselves, I got a room and a couple of Cokes. I practiced carrying her over the threshold as we entered the small room.

The mirror on the dresser had a diagonal crack running the length of it. It was nothing to brag about, but it was going to be our hideaway when we wanted to be alone, I thought.

The room cost eight bucks, and of course, I thought it was too much, but Glen split it with me. Although we always split our winnings, the forty dollars belonged to Momma.

I laid Glen down on the bed and furthered my inspection of the room. As I said, it was nothing to brag on.

"Have you been here before?" she asked, looking around the dimly lit room.

"No, this is my first time, but hopefully, it won't be my last," I chuckled, jumping in bed after taking my shoes off.

"The fish was so delicious, and those rolls just melted in my mouth. We are coming here again, aren't we?" she asked, all curled up in my arms.

"That depends on tonight's outcome," I joked, squeezing her a little tighter with my eyes closed.

"Well, if it is anything like the first night, we'll be back," she said, unfastening my belt, unsnapping my jeans, and sliding her warm hands down between my legs.

"Ooooooh, you better watch it; something might spit on you."

She quickly withdrew her hand. "I just wanted to know if you still love me," she giggled.

"Well, what's the answer? I don't remember giving you an answer,"

"Oh, you gave me the answer all right," she laughed and gently patted my genitals. "Let's just relax for a minute. I could lay here in your arms forever," she said, closing her eyes.

She had stayed up all night studying for a test on the skeleton and respiratory system, and I had moved twenty-five to thirty-pound boxes of files from one end of the federal building to the other. Before we knew it, we were both fast asleep. About an hour or so later, there was a hard knock on the door.

"Glenna! Glenna Aravia Thompson! Are you in there?" shouted a woman's voice.

We both raised up simultaneously, our hearts racing like they just finished the Kentucky Derby.

"Oh Tee, that's Momma Florence," she whispered.

"Who?"

"Glenna, I know you are in there. You better open this door, young lady," she demanded, but now the knocking was coming from the adjacent room on the right this time.

"Don't say nothing, Tee," she whispered, jumping up from the bed and tipping to the door, resting her ear against it.

"Glenna, I know you are in there. When we get back, you and my car had better be gone," the voice shouted, now about two doors down.

There were white gravel rocks leading from the courtyard to the parking lot next to the cafeteria and court lobby. We could hear departing footsteps and faint conversation. When we finally got enough nerve to peep out of the small window, we could see three women opening the doors to a black four-door Cadillac.

"Oh, Tee, I am in trouble," she said, as we watched the Cadillac drive out of the parking lot and onto McDowell. "Let's get out of here," she continued, jerking me through the door and running toward the car. By the time we reached the car, I was still trying to zip up my pants.

"Glen, take it easy, they haven't caught us yet," I said, getting into the car and driving out of the parking lot.

"Tee, I really am in some trouble, but Mother wasn't with her, because if she was, she would have been still knocking on those doors."

"I thought you said you had your step-grandmother's car?"

"Yes, I do, but she has two more cars."

"Everything is going to be alright. Let's get you to Miss Young," I said, taking a shortcut to her house.

"Tee, let's stop by the doughnut shop," Glen suggested.

"The doughnut shop?"

"Just do as I say, please, Tee."

We picked up two half-dozen bags of doughnuts, and she dropped me off at the house. Glen called me at about twelve and told me all was well. She used one bag of doughnuts to bribe Coleen into saying that we met them at Rabbit's to eat and we all jumped into Ed's car to go over to his friend's house to listen to the new Four Tops LP, leaving the Buick parked at Rabbit's.

When I asked about the other bag of doughnuts, she said Momma Florence dropped by with her friends after bingo.

She made coffee for the ladies, and they sat around drinking coffee and eating doughnuts. I could tell by her voice that she was out of trouble. I asked her where she came up with that perfect lie.

She said that she got it from me when we made love, and I was forced to spend the night with my bike in the front yard. I told her I hoped I wasn't teaching her bad habits. She said, good or bad, that I was her addiction. I must say, I liked the way she said that.

We decided that Rabbit's was a good place to eat, but for relaxing and being alone, it was too risky if we used her folks' car and especially my folks' car. We had one car, and Super Nannie wouldn't have just knocked, she would have knocked the doors down with one blow. I could see her pulling me by the ear and wearing my butt out with a tree—a large tree.

I had talked to Bae Bae, and we set up a date using his house for Saturday night. I had his place for about four hours while he took his lady out to the Jade Club and maybe to an after-hours joint. Anyway, we had to be respectable or presentable by two in the a.m. I bought some chips, dip, and 7-Up. I made some bologna and cheese sandwiches, quartered them, and wrapped them in foil. I had Bae Bae pick up a small bottle of Wild Irish Rose, and he placed it in the fridge to chill. I made sure that all the latest jams were in place before I left his house at about six that evening. Bae Bae had placed his house key under the doormat, and all was set for my date with Glen.

When we arrived at the house, I duplicated the threshold scene and gently sat her down on the sofa.

"Now don't you move, my princess. I am here to serve you and only you, my dear lady," I said, placing a wet kiss on her long slender fingers.

"Well, my prince, will you assist me in the removal of my slippers?" she giggled in a sophisticated tone of voice, pressing her hand to her lips to hold back the laughter, and raising and fully extending her legs.

"But of course, my princess," I said, mixing street slang and sophistication in my dialect.

Removing each slipper and holding both of her dainty arched feet in my hands, I could smell the scent of perfume as I gently kissed each red polished toe. Her feet were just as beautiful as her hands but a shade lighter. As I kissed the last big toe, I gave it a bath with my tongue. I had never, ever done anything like this before, but for some reason, it was a natural instinct, and it turned me on as much as it did her.

"Oh, yes, my prince, whatever you do, don't stop," she moaned, moving her head back and forth with her eyes closed.

Her cries of delight were really turning me on, and if I continued, I would explode, and the night was too young for any prematurity. After giving her right big toe the bath of its life, I gently blew it dry and softly placed both feet on the tiled floor.

"Now for a little music."

I stood erect and looked at this woman who was changing my life. Robert Jr. always said if a woman was making you do things that were not in your nature, you were inclined for a fall, and that's what fools were made of, I thought, turning toward the stereo console.

"Oh, Tee, that was so soothing. Who taught you that?" she asked, opening her eyes for the first time and spinning around with her head lying on the arm of the sofa and her toes wiggling wildly on the pillowed couch.

"Reverend Madden taught me that," I joked while I finger-searched through the LPs that were vertically stacked in the LP rack until I pulled out the Supremes' "I Hear a Symphony."

Glen was doing things to me that I had never imagined doing to anyone. I had always thought that feet were one of the foul places on the body besides the private parts. Now she got me tonguing her feet.

This woman got a big hold on me.

"Earth calling Tee...Tee!" she yelled.

"Yes, what's wrong?" I asked, snapping out of my daydream.

"There's nothing wrong with me. I was talking to you, and you were somewhere else."

"Sorry, what did you say?" I asked, giving her all my attention. She looked even better than the first day I laid eyes on her.

I better watch myself before she makes a pure fool out of me, I thought.

"Oh, nothing now, but you were serving me, and I want all of your attention," she said, opening up her arms.

"Just hold that thought while I get us something to drink." I raced toward the kitchen.

"Don't take all night," she said, dropping both arms in disgust.

I was back in a flash with a covered dish and a double shot of wine chased with 7-Up, with some cherries I found in the fridge.

"Tee, that looks delicious," she said when I handed her a half-filled glass of my concoction.

She smelled it, sipped, and then drank half of the brew. "This is good. What is it?" she asked, looking into the glass.

"Oh, it's my special drink for my special lady."

I turned my drink up and emptied its contents, then belched.

"Excuse me," I said, holding my hand over my mouth.

"Sure, what's on the platter?" she asked, looking at the dish I set on the coffee table.

"Food!" I shouted, removing the aluminum foil and placing one bite-sized sandwich in her mouth.

We ate everything on the platter and broke open the chips and dip. The special brew was doing its job of making us feel more relaxed, and the more I looked at her, the more she reminded me of Cousin Betty.

"Hey, do you know how to play cards?"

"I've played Old Maid before," she said, putting a dipped chip in my mouth.

"No problem. I'll teach you how to play bid whist," I proudly said.

"Let's dance."

She jumped up from the sofa and went over to the stereo and replayed the Supremes.

"Okay, but let me refill our glasses," I said, as I hiccupped going into the kitchen.

The wine was three-quarters gone and I was feeling no pain. I split it down the middle and added some cherry juice with the cherries and a couple of ice cubes to each glass.

When I got back to the living room, Glen was dancing and singing with the Supremes. I didn't disturb her because she was in her world, so I just sat on the arm of the sofa for a ringside seat. Now I know where the rhyme came from when they said, "Girls are made of sugar and spice and everything nice."

Glen epitomized beauty and class. She was my forever after. Now I know what Percy Sledge was talking about when he sang "When a Man Loves a Woman," because I was sucking on her toes, and the next thing she'll have me doing is sleeping out in the rain if she says that's the way it ought to be. Now that's power over someone, and I could feel myself slipping into her hypnotic charm, and it felt good.

If I was going on this trip, I might as well go first class, I thought.

As the song was ending, I started applauding and she lowered her head in acknowledgment.

"Thank you, my prince. I feel so good when I'm with you," she said, waltzing into my arms.

"Oh yeah, prove it then," I said, kissing her behind her earlobe.

"Oooooh!" she moaned. "I will, but I want to dedicate this song to you. It explains everything about me," she said, breaking our embrace.

Moments later, she was back in my arms, and we were dancing to Miss Aretha Franklin's "(You Make Me Feel Like) A Natural Woman."

She sang along with Aretha, and when she got to the chorus, she coiled her body around me, nibbling on my ear and telling me how much she loved me.

I wanted to tell her how much I loved her, but I kept my peace because if anyone could hurt me, it was her. I kissed her, hoping my silent response would answer all of her questions about my love for her. My desire for her was overwhelming, almost out of control, as I led her up the stairs into the guest bedroom. We quickly began removing each other's clothes when we heard a knock on the living room door.

"I am not answering that," I said, throwing my shirt down in the dark room.

"Roy! Roy! Open up," came a cry from a female voice.

"Tee, I think you better answer it. It might be an emergency for Roy," she said, turning my pants loose and they fell down to my knees.

"Shit!" I yelled, pulling my pants up and slamming the bedroom door behind me.

When I reached the front door, I had cooled down a bit, but the knocking and screaming had intensified on the other side of the door.

"Ma'am, Roy is not here. You have the wrong house," I said, trying to maintain my cool.

"Roy, just open the door," she said in a calmer tone.

That tone only enraged me.

"Lady, I told you there is no—"

My words stopped short as I unlocked and opened the door.

The next thing I saw was this short lady, with a light brown wig riding on the side of her head, with a straight razor against my throat.

"Who in the hell do you have in here? It better not be that white bitch Valarie," she yelled, pushing her way into the house, with nostrils flaring.

She had one hand holding my right upper arm and the other pushing the razor deeper against my throat.

"Ma'am, my name is not Roy," I whispered in a voice that was begging her not to cut me.

"Roy, goddamn it," she said. "Who in the hell do you have up in here?"

She guided me to the sofa and, with a little push, sat me down and then leaped into my lap.

"Tee, what's wrong?" Glen asked, rushing down the stairs.

"Glen, don't come down," I pleaded.

"Who in the hell is this bitch?" the woman yelled, now getting a full view of Glen.

Glen made an about-face and double-timed back up the steps in half the time she came down, slamming the door behind her.

"Miss, ma'am, ... I... ay..., don't know you and I know you don't know—"

"Roy, I'm going to cut your goddamn throat, you two-timing son-of-a-bitch."

She gave me a facial shower with her alcoholic breath.

I was thinking about what Spider-Man would do at a time like this. He would snatch the blade out of her hand and begin beating the shit out of her. Well, Spider-Man had better show up soon because I'd be damned if I was going to try it. I was getting a little mad because she thought I was Roy, and that was an insult in itself.

"Lady, my name is Tee, not Roy," I pleaded.

"Oh, now you are scared. I told you not to fuck with me," she yelled, then her eyes went from cold steel to a soft brown.

"Oh baby, I love your eyes," she said, kissing me with her big juicy wet pink lips, and that alcohol mixed with bad breath was sickening.

I almost threw up in her face, and of course, I gave it all I had just to bring it up. It just wouldn't come up all the way.

"Clara, that ain't Roy," came a familiar voice at the door.

"Girl, what are you talking about?" the woman asked, wiping her running nose with her free arm and hand, and sucking up snot.

"Clara, leave him alone," Mary Rose said, slapping the woman's armed hand away from my neck.

"Mary Rose, who is this crazy woman?" I shouted, clamping down on both her wrists, and spitting, trying to get that horrible taste out of my mouth, as I pushed, and Mary Rose pulled the little witch off me.

"Clara, this is not Roy, can't you see that? Girl, you better leave that moonshine alone."

"Tee, are you all right, baby?" Mary Rose asked.

"No, not until she drops this razor," I said, feeling something gooey and slimy in my other hand, then realizing that it was the product of Clara's running nose.

After she dropped the razor and it was secured in Mary Rose's pocketbook, which could have easily been mistaken for a suitcase, I released her.

"I'm sorry, I thought you were my Roy," she cried, pulling her blouse out of her skirt and blowing her nose on it.

"Girl, I told you that you were drinking too much. You are disgusting," Mary Rose said, handing her a handkerchief.

"Mary Rose, I got company, would you get her out of here?" I asked, turning my nose up at this little witch that had upset my night.

"Tee, she is really sorry," Mary Rose said, "and where is your shirt?" she continued, looking at my bare chest.

"Oh shit, Glen," I yelled, running up the stairs and twisting and pushing the doorknob, and bam! I bumped my head on the door because it was locked.

"Ouch!"

"Tee, is that you, baby?"

"Yeah, it's me," I said, rubbing my head when she opened the door.

"Tee, are you alright?"

Glen examined my neck and throat, and then held me close.

"Who was that lady, and why was she calling you Roy, and why–"

"It's over, just a case of mistaken identity," I calmly interrupted.

"Tee, I was so scared, I didn't know what to do. I first thought that you and that woman knew each other, I mean intimately," she said, looking up into my eyes, as tears rolled down her cheeks.

"No, like I said, it was a mistaken identity," I said, holding her in my arms as I felt the tension begin to leave her body.

I put on my shirt and washed my hands, and I made her do the same without telling her why. Then we walked down the stairs and into the living room, Clara and Mary Rose were about to leave. Clara had straightened up her wig, and Mary Rose was puffing on a cigarette.

"Oh, hi Glen," Mary Rose said, walking over to her and giving her a hug. "Clara is sorry about the mix-up."

I motioned for them to leave, and Mary Rose got the hint.

"Mary Rose, I'll see you later," I said, ushering them out of the house.

If I ever see Clara again, it will be too soon, I thought, as I shut the door and locked it.

CHAPTER 24

DECISIONS, DECISIONS

We both flopped down on the couch, breathing heavily like we just raced through hell. We said nothing for about ten minutes. I just wanted to be alone with Glen, and her with me. For some strange reason, we've always had interruptions. Maybe God was trying to tell me something, and I was too dumb to figure it out. I have always had problems reading and understanding the Bible with the "thou" and "thou nots." Nannie had preached to me numerous times about fornication, and according to her, I am sinning, and maybe I am. But what I got with Glen, I refused to believe that we were sinning.

Evidently, she will be my wife because I can't think of anyone more suitable for me than her, and I include Natalie Wood, Annette Funicello, and even Lena Horne.

"Tee, are you asleep?" she asked, turning toward me.

"No, just thinking about us," I answered, with my head against the top of the sofa and my eyes closed.

"A penny for your thoughts."

"Do you think we are committing a sin when we are together?" I asked, opening my eyes and turning my head toward her.

We were only a shoulder length apart, and I was looking at the most beautiful creature God had ever made.

She studied my eyes for a moment then she gently massaged my face with her long, graceful fingertips.

"I will begin by saying, I love you very, very much. To me, you're the light of my life, and without that light, my life would be surrounded by darkness. You are one of the sweetest, most darling, and serene persons I know. Always remember this: love is mental and physical attraction in the presence of emotional security. My prince, you are my love," she said, with her eyes wetting up, cupping my face with her soft and warm hands.

"I think that the greatest happiness in life is the conviction that we love each other. This love we have…We were made for each other. I was once told that 'love is a canvas furnished by nature and embroidered by imagination.' Obviously enough, we have furnished the constituents that have made our relationship just what it is and embroidered it with the happiness, faithfulness, truthfulness, and love that it needs to grow. Oh, Tee, my precious darling," she cried, with tears flowing like a downhill stream.

"When I look at you, I see good, and when I close my eyes, I see you. Don't you see? I see good in you. I see good in us. When we are together, this poem always comes to mind: 'How do I love thee? Let me count the ways: I love thee to the depth, breadth, and height of every mountain'… That is not an original," she smiled.

"That was written by one of my favorite poets, Elizabeth Barrett Browning. Tee, if what we have is a sin, then I'll die and go to hell loving you."

That sums it up, I thought, as our lips met with the fire and savage passion of two lovers starving for each other.

Yes, I wanted to make love to her on the couch or even take her upstairs to a bed like a civilized man would do. But at this moment, I was holding her in my arms. Knowing in my heart that our love for each other was more powerful than the Tigris and Euphrates Rivers combined and that our love was equally balanced, I wouldn't dare spoil this moment for anything else in this world.

The next time we make love, it'll be on our own terms, I thought, as I dried her tears with my lips.

"Glenna Aravia Thompson, what we have, God has given us. We are the Romeo and Juliet of the century and the King Solomon and Queen of Sheba of centuries past. What we have will last forever," I said as we embraced one another.

Then we fell asleep with a positive smile on our lips.

"Hi, Tee, Glen, it must have been some kind of party," Bae Bae said, smiling and holding his baby boy in his arms.

"Man, this has been one hell of a night," I sheepishly admitted, standing up and stretching, while Glen was awakening.

"What happened?" he asked, after he introduced his wife.

Glen and I went over our encounter with the witch from hell, which made a great conversation piece. While Glen was explaining her reaction when she first saw the razor at my throat, I couldn't help but think about how much she said she loved me just before we fell asleep on the couch. It is amazing how things work out. If the witch from hell hadn't shown up, I wouldn't have known how much I mean to this lovely God-sent creature.

***

Monday morning came, and it was raining cats and dogs. The weatherman said there was a thirty percent chance of rain, and normally with that forecast, you would get maybe a sprinkle, not a downpour.

By lunchtime, there was not a cloud in the sky. Nannie had made me a couple of lettuce and tomato sandwiches and packed me some Oreo cookies with a thick piece of sharp cheddar cheese. I could eat cheese and cookies all day until my belly dropped.

There were two long wooden tables with benches, a Pepsi soda machine, and a candy and cookie vending machine for the homemade lunches. Mark and I had arrived late because we had to dig up important files for eastern South Carolina, going back fifty years.

We normally sat with the boys in our department, which was about six including the boss, Mr. Johnson, who never ate with us. Jerry Erickson and Peter Van Pelt were discussing today's headline: "American Combat Deaths Exceed South Vietnamese."

"I tell you, Pete, we ought to drop the damn bomb and end that shit right now," Jerry said, making room for us at the table.

"Now, we can't just drop the bomb anytime we feel like it," Peter said, not looking up from the paper.

"Don't you guys ever get tired of arguing with each other?" Mark joked, removing a wrapped sandwich from his lunch box.

"Mark, our boys are getting killed over there, and these damn commie bastards are protesting against us over here. If it was left up to me, I'd send all of them to Russia and let them see what our boys are fighting for," Peter said, still hiding behind the paper.

"Well, if I was a little younger, like about Tee's age, I'd go over and fight for the good old U.S. of A.," Jerry said, taking a sip out of his Pepsi bottle.

"I don't know, we ought to go in there, kick some butt, and get our boys out of there before we lose more lives," Mark said, biting off too much meatloaf sandwich for his small mouth.

"Don't you think our experts at the Pentagon know what they are doing? It's just a matter of time, and those little yellow commies will be begging for peace," Peter said, finally looking up from his paper.

"I tell you what, we ought to send that Cassius Clay and the rest of those Communist assholes over there and let them see what freedom is like. Right, Tee?" Jerry said, with all attention on me.

"His name is Muhammad Ali," I said, putting some salt on my sandwich.

"What?" Peter said, now putting the paper down.

"You are talking about the World Heavyweight Boxing Champion, aren't you?" I asked, not waiting for a reply. "If you are, his name is Muhammad Ali," I continued, not dropping my eyes, but giving them a smile.

"His name is Cassius Clay, and someone is going to remind him of it one day soon. Now don't tell me you agree with him."

"No, I don't agree with Muhammad Ali, but I respect his decision. And anyway, we can win the war without him."

I bit into my second sandwich.

"You damn right we can, but it's the principle behind it. He's an American, and he's obligated to serve his country," Jerry said, pounding his fist on the table.

"Don't get so upset, Jerry. It is his right to fight for whatever he believes in," Mark said, bringing an apple out of his box and polishing it on his shirt.

Mark and I had this conversation before, and he sounded just like Peter and Jerry are sounding now. I thought it was amusing to hear Mark repeat what I had said to him.

"Mark, if every American thought like Clay in World War II, your family would still be in concentration camps," Jerry bellowed, and Peter let out a giggle.

"Muhammad Ali is a conscientious objector. I wouldn't want him beside me in a foxhole," I said, coming to Mark's defense.

"Clay ain't no conscientious objector; he fights for a living, for Christ's sake," Peter yelled, slamming his paper down on the table. His face was as red as a beet, and I thought I saw steam coming from his head.

"Well, Tee, what about you? Would you go and fight or would you be like Clay and run yellow?" Jerry said, patting Peter on the back to calm him down.

"First of all, his name is Muhammad Ali. Why are you constantly calling him Cassius Clay?" I asked, looking at Peter and then at Jerry.

"Because that's what his momma named him," Peter yelled, rising out of his seat and trying to incinerate me with his eyes.

"Peter, take it easy before your blood pressure climbs through the roof," Jerry said, now holding on to his arm.

I couldn't understand why they were so uptight about calling the Champ by his name. If he were here, I bet they would spell and pronounce his name in the same breath, I thought, as I took a sip of my Pepsi.

"Are you going to answer the question, or what?" Jerry said, removing his hand from Peter's arm.

"Why can't you say his name? His name is Muhammad Ali," I said, getting a little agitated myself but enjoying our debate.

"Okay, okay, Muhammad Ali," Jerry said, looking into the air.

"Peter?" I asked, giving him a smile and everyone, including the other table, started laughing.

"Alright, Muhammad Ali. Now answer the damn question, will ya?" Peter said, showing a little grin on his face.

"My grandfather said we all should serve at least two years in service, to show patriotism for our country," I said. "I would go in, but the Navy said I have a bad heart," I lied. "But if it was left up to me, I would join today and take Muhammad Ali's place."

It was silent for about a couple of minutes, then Peter yelled, "Bullshit!" and everyone laughed.

After work, I walked to the Army recruiter's office on Patton Avenue. I talked to Sergeant Finch, and he told me what I wanted to hear. I picked up a brochure and went home.

When I got home, Momma was doing an old customer's hair in the kitchen. She averaged about three to four heads a week, not counting the three heads in the house. This provided Momma with a little spending money and a little borrowing money for me.

"Hi, Man Boy, how was your day?" Momma said, blowing the pressing iron as she straightened a section of hair.

"Fine, Momma," I said, giving her a kiss on the jaw. "How you doing, Mrs. McCutcheon?"

"Boy, come around here and let me look at you," Mrs. McCutcheon said, grabbing my arm and guiding me around to her front, not moving her head, giving the hot comb a little respect. "Tee, you are just as handsome as your father. How have you been doing, child?"

"Working hard, every day," I bashfully said.

"I just know some girl is going to grab you up."

"Honey child, you are late, and she's got his nose wide open, too," Momma joked, and they both laughed.

I walked on into my room and just lay across the bed. I could still hear Momma and Mrs. McCutcheon talking about me. It was true, Glen had my nose wide open, but it was time to leave.

The recruiter had almost guaranteed my induction into the United States Army. I was between a rock and a hard place. I was definitely in love, and it wasn't lust this time. If I joined the Army, I was going to lose Glen, and if I stayed, my future looked awfully dim.

Oh, God my heavenly Father, show me which way I must go. I don't want to lose her, but if I stay here, I might lose myself. Please show me the way.

I prayed, with a tear rolling down my cheek as I drifted off into slumber land.

"Knock, knock," came the sound at the door.

"Man Boy, are you alright?" Momma asked, peeping her head through the door.

"Sure, Momma," I said. "I must have dozed off a spell."

"Oh, I just wanted to thank you again for the money. I was flat broke when you stuck that forty dollars in my purse. It couldn't have come at a better time."

She sat on the bed and laid her hand on mine.

"Momma, it's time for me to go. I know I am in love with Glen, but I am not ready for marriage yet. She's in school to become a nurse, and I am unskilled. If I don't leave now, I will never leave."

"Where are you going?"

She wet her fingertip and brushed my eyebrows.

"I am thinking about going into the Army," I said, resting my head on the headboard.

"How about your heart?" she asked.

"I had my heart checked out at the hospital before I left, and they gave me a go," I lied.

"Man Boy, can't you go in after that terrible war is over?"

"Momma, Daddy was in World War II, and Uncky was in World War I. If I get killed, I'll be worth fifty thousand dollars, and that could go a long way around here."

"Don't you ever let me hear you say that again. Fifty billion dollars is chicken feed when it comes to your life. I don't remember God putting a price tag on you when I had you. So that's telling me that you are priceless, and don't you ever believe any different. Do I make myself clear, young man?"

"Momma, I didn't mean it that way, but if I do get messed up over there, that money could finish paying off the house and the rest of the—"

Bam!

Momma almost slapped the taste out of my mouth.

"Listen, I must have stuttered, obviously I didn't make myself clear. No more talk about dying. Anyway, you owe me some grandkids, and you can't do that dead, so be a man and do what you gotta do. And if that young lady really loves you, she'll wait."

Momma gave me a kiss and slid me a folded twenty-dollar bill.

"Momma, that hurt!" I said, rubbing my jaw.

"It was supposed to hurt. Now do what you gotta do," she commanded, kissing me on my reddened jaw and walking out of the room.

I thought about what Momma had said about being a man and making decisions. I was having the time of my life with the girl of my dreams, but something was missing. Asheville had not been the same after graduation, and how I still missed my classmates, my school, and even my teachers.

I had a long talk with Daddy, and the next day I joined the United States Army.

CHAPTER 25

BREAKING THE NEWS

I called my friends and told them my decision. They thought I was crazy for even thinking about leaving Glen to the dogs. This was a decision I had to live with, regardless of how much I loved Glen; my heart was telling me it was time to go.

I had saved up over three hundred dollars, and with any luck, I could pick up some extra cash on the pool or card table to expand my cash flow. It was the middle of May, and my departure date to Fort Jackson, South Carolina, was the fifth of July. I had a lot of loose ends to tie up, most of which involved being with Glen. Going back to Rabbit's or Bae Bae's place was a no-go. I asked around and was told by one of Sandy's partners, who works as a maid at one of the motels on Tunnel Road, about the Mountaineer Motel.

As the days rolled by, I became more intrigued with the television series "Combat" starring Vic Morrow. Vic played Sergeant Saunders, who got shot every week, yet always came back kicking ass and taking names. It seemed the closer I got to the departure date, the more people were protesting the war.

A couple of months earlier, Ali had already made a statement, "I ain't got no quarrel with the Viet Cong." He had even made friends with the famous English philosopher Bertrand Russell, whom he never met. Although we were on opposite sides of the fence, I still loved the man. He was tall, dark, handsome and could talk more shit than a radio, and could beat your butt to boot. I didn't agree with his religion or his views on the military. I guess we just grew up in different places, but how I dug him.

Glen picked me up in the middle of the week after work, and we cruised the scene. I drove her all over town, showing her off. I even stopped people on the street asking for places that didn't exist just to show them my lady. We stopped by Six Points Drive-In restaurant for two minced barbecue dinners to go. When we arrived at the motel, it was dark.

After I paid for the room using an alias, I moved the car to the opposite end of the parking lot. Glen asked me to carry her over the threshold again. I hesitated because I had become a little superstitious since the last two times ended up ruining our night, but it was hard to say no to her. So, I crossed my fingers and wished for the best.

"So, how many times have you been out here?" she suspiciously asked after I had laid her and the food on the bed.

"This is my first time out here," I said, taking the two white boxes of food from her and looking around the clean room. The room cost me twenty-seven dollars plus a five-dollar allowance fee, which was for allowing eighteen-year-olds to pay for a room.

Interestingly enough, seventeen- and eighteen-year-olds were dying in Vietnam.

"Come here," she said, with legs crossed and her head propped on two pillows.

"I am going to get comfortable," I said, taking off my shoes and then my pants.

"Hey, I'm supposed to do that," she said, waving for me to come over.

"No, you can take these off," I joked, pulling the elastic on my briefs and sling-shooting it back to my stomach.

"Well, I am lazy, I need help with mine," she said, giving me a wink.

Before she could count to three, I was unzipping her blue and white dress. Smelling her sweet body mixed with a touch of perfume almost drove me crazy. I began kissing her neck until she jumped up.

"Let's eat first before the food gets cold," she said, dodging me with her bra and panties on.

"Well, suppose we get cold," I laughed, reaching out for her.

"Oh, now you're going to get cold on me?"

She locked us in a human embrace while her tongue searched for my tonsils.

"Glen, I love you," I moaned.

Before I knew it, I was inside her, feeling her warmth and closeness. When we had finished and I rolled over totally exhausted, she rolled on top of me, sucking on my lips like they were popsicles.

"Tee, don't you ever do me wrong or ever leave me because if you do, I'm taking this with me."

She grabbed my lifeless member and gave it a shake.

"Because he belongs to me," she continued, kissing my hairless chest and getting up.

"I am not moving, I am going to stay here forever," I moaned, looking at the body I was going to miss soon.

I must be a fool, giving all this up for the Army, I thought, when I heard the shower being turned on.

"Oh, baby!" she moaned in delight, "the water feels so soothing and invigorating. Get up, sleepyhead, and join me."

Her voice was hypnotic. I got up and walked into the bathroom like a zombie. I jumped in the shower with her, and she began lathering me down with soap, washing areas that had only been assigned to me to wash. I grabbed a face cloth, lathered it up, and began washing her. I was not going to miss a spot because before the night was over, I would know every inch of her lovely body.

Her hair was wet and had matted into long separate strings glued to her face. Her wet hairdo could have easily been mistaken for an exotic hairstyle from the Caribbean islands. I searched everywhere for one imperfection and, as I thought, she was personally made by God himself. There was no doubt in my mind.

I was going to turn her into a baby-making factory, I thought, as we dried ourselves off.

I quickly put my pants on, grabbed the empty bucket, and ran out the door. I filled the bucket with ice, bought two sodas from the machine, and was back before she was out of the bathroom. When she emerged, she had one towel wrapped around her breasts, falling mid-way to her thighs. The other was wrapped around her head like a turban. With her face washed clean of makeup, her skin was flawless, and her lips were a medium pink.

Then I wondered, does she ever get ugly? Even when she is sad and crying, she still turns me on, I thought, as I filled each glass with ice.

"I am starving," she said, grabbing pieces of barbecue and forcing some into my mouth after satisfying her hunger.

After we had cleared both boxes of any food, including breadcrumbs, we retired to the bed, where we made love with even more passion than the first night. Breaking our previous performance record by a huge margin, we won the gold medal this time by anyone's standards, I thought, with Glen nestled in my arms.

"My prince, I wish I could freeze this moment in time because I don't think it could get any better than this."

Glen snuggled closer while nesting herself on me. Her words seemed to stab at my heart and now was the time, if ever, to tell her what I had done.

"Glen, my love, I received a letter from Uncle Sam. I've just been drafted by the United States Army," I lied, rubbing her upper arm.

"What?"

She turned around in my arms and looked me in the face.

"I've been drafted by the Army, and my reporting day is the 5th of July," I said, looking down into her big brown eyes as they filled with tears.

"Do you want to go?" she asked, turning her face away from me.

I could feel her warm tears drop one by one on my chest and roll down the side. I don't know why I lied; it just seemed appropriate at the time. I hadn't planned for it to come out that way; it just did. Like Daddy always said, a man's got to do what a man's got to do.

"I've got to go, my princess."

"You come into my life one minute and you're gone the next," she said, placing her leg between mine.

"Listen, my princess, all is not lost. The question is, are you going to wait for me?"

I crossed my fingers and prayed for the yes word.

"Of course, I'll wait for you. Oh, Tee, I love you so much. I'll wait for you until hell freezes over."

"My princess, you don't have to wait that long," I said, as we drifted off to sleep.

I put in my two weeks' notice at work. It seemed like everyone thought I was some kind of hero. Then I started dreaming about going to Vietnam and me and Alvin York kicking some Viet Cong butt. I even dreamed up a hero's parade down Patton Avenue with all my family and friends fighting for my autograph. Everybody, from Daddy to my work buddies, became professional soldiers overnight, telling me the do's and don'ts of the Army. As the time for my induction came near, Glen and I spent every minute we could muster together, sometimes missing class and work.

***

It was a beautiful morning. Nannie had gotten up early to cook my favorite breakfast: ham and grits with red-eye gravy, homemade buttermilk biscuits, and coffee. Everyone got up to see me off. Daddy said one of his sermon prayers that took all of fifteen minutes. Nannie told me not to worry, that God had spoken to her in a vision, and that I was under the protection of the Almighty himself. Momma hugged me for a good five minutes, then whispered in my ear, "Keep God with you always, no matter what."

I kissed everyone goodbye, then jumped in the car. Daddy and I didn't say anything to each other on the way to the bus station. We arrived twenty minutes before departure.

"Daddy, I want you to know that I appreciate everything you have done for me. Without you and Nannie I wouldn't be who I am today. You have been really good to me, and I will always love you," I said with tears rolling down my cheeks.

Then we hugged each other, and I placed a kiss on top of his head.

CHAPTER 26

LEARNING THE GAME

When the mighty Greyhound bus rolled out of the station, I waved to Daddy, determined this time. It was either the service or I'd be on my own. I had close to four hundred dollars on me, so if I was going to be dealt a bad hand again, I could go anywhere in the U.S.A. with the little money I had. I just couldn't go home a failure again.

When I arrived, I was given a series of battery tests and completed a physical. Then we were housed and fed, even given a free haircut. I had no problems following orders this time. Although I picked up about twenty-five dollars playing pool at the recreation center, I was in bed by ten o'clock.

The next afternoon at thirteen hundred hours, I stood proudly with the rest of my brothers, my right hand held high and my left hand over my heart, pledging allegiance to the greatest country this world had ever seen, the United States of America.

After swearing in, personal clothes and basic equipment were issued. We were told that everything we needed was in our duffel bag, which weighed about eighty pounds. I weighed 145 pounds, so it was over half my weight. We were loaded up in the back of a deuce-and-a-half-ton truck. There were about twenty soldiers with twenty duffel bags. It was a covered canvas truck, and it had to be over 110 degrees inside.

When the truck finally stopped at our destination, suddenly about six to ten voices were screaming, hollering, cursing, and swearing, telling us to get our asses off the truck. It scared the shit out of everyone.

I grabbed my duffel bag with one hand and got out of the truck so fast it made my head spin. The drill instructors (DIs) had on their Smokey the Bear hats, and their fatigues fit them like the superheroes I grew up with. I was deeply impressed with how they motivated me—or scared the shit out of me—to lift that eighty-pound duffel bag without flinching. I thought I could go to war with them as my leaders.

After the third week of Basic, I began to learn how the game was played.

"Yes, Drill Sergeant" and "No, Drill Sergeant" became my second language. Physical training (PT) was never a real challenge, but I could have done better if I could have left the cigarettes alone. Listening became a priority.

I had to learn the hard way.

We were told not to talk in the mess hall after a grueling morning of PT. We were rushed into the mess hall for breakfast, and we had to eat everything on our plates. I asked a fellow trainee to pass the salt. Sergeant Cruz told me to place my plate on the floor, get down on all fours, and eat my breakfast like a dog. It was really hard to eat my biscuits because the food was very hot. After licking my plate clean, I was told to pick my plate up and stand. I stood up before I picked up my plate. Sergeant Cruz told me to drop back down, grab the plate with my mouth, and stand up without using my hands. With a little difficulty, I managed.

"Now remove the plate from your mouth," he commanded. "You're dismissed, Soldier."

I think Sergeant Cruz was pissed off at me for beating his ass at Ping-Pong ten straight times at a dollar a game. In the last game, I really embarrassed him in front of all the men, plus I was talking too much shit.

Lesson learned—never embarrass the boss and learn how to kiss ass without getting shit on your lips.

I saw no difference between Fort Jackson and the Navy Induction Center. I continued my hustles because it seemed like people would give up their money to avoid boredom. I sold a ten-cent candy bar for three to five dollars apiece. The Post Exchange (PX) was off-limits, so I was getting items with the help of a mailroom clerk, a specialist fourth class who had played for the Lee Edwards High School football team, the Hillbillies.

James Diggs, my homeboy who had played football before he busted his ACL in the tenth grade, said he'd always wanted to play the Stephens Lee Bears in football. Of course, I lied and said I was a tight end with three touchdowns to my credit. It seemed like every time we met, especially during mail calls, our high school rivalry would come up, or we'd talk about how great it was growing up in Asheville.

The guys in my company were all about the same age, eighteen to nineteen years old, it seemed. We came in all shapes and sizes. Some were in good shape and some not so good. After about six weeks, I knew this was going to be the next phase of my life. All the DIs were Vietnam returnees. They were all sharp as a tack. Sergeant Milton and Sergeant Cruz could have been Batman and Robin without the capes. I could picture all of the DIs belonging to the Justice League.

I could follow these guys to hell and back. I was learning what it meant to be a soldier.

Superman disguised as the President of the United States, my Commander-in-Chief, Lyndon B. Johnson without the cape. I could never see him leading a charge with his Clark Kent glasses on. He was fat and very old, but he was a Texan and a true cowboy. So, I guess he could ride a horse. He was my president, though he looked mighty suspicious after the death of President John F. Kennedy, which was the local gossip. On the positive side, he signed the Civil Rights Act of 1964 and the Voting Rights Act of 1965. He was a WWII veteran who served in the Pacific at the same time Daddy was there and was awarded the Navy Silver Star. He was definitely worthy of my loyalty and devotion, but I also pledged allegiance to the Constitution of the United States.

Yes, I was home; this is where I belong—the U.S. Army.

I must make it work.

My first check was eighty-seven dollars and fifty cents. I made more than that by selling candy bars alone. Plus, after receiving my pay, there must have been five or six charities like the Red Cross, Army Emergency Relief, and others. The DIs were there at each table to make sure we contributed to each one. My paycheck ended up being seventy-five dollars when I walked out.

I wrote to Glen once a week. It seemed like time was moving fast. My birthday was coming up, and I told Nannie not to send any food. I should have told Glen because she sent me a three-layer chocolate cake. There was a full-length mirror on the side of the orderly room where we inspected ourselves before entering. The cake was presented to me on my birthday in front of the entire company. The first sergeant had everyone sing "Happy Birthday" to me.

Then the cake was placed on a small table and chair in front of the mirror. I was commanded by the commanding officer to eat it without a knife or eating utensils.

The cake had "Happy Birthday, my Hero. Love, Glen" written on it. I was told to eat "Love, Glen" first, so I grabbed "Love, Glen" with my right hand and started eating. I finished about half the cake before my stomach said no more.

It took me about two days to recover from my upset stomach.

Here again, failure to communicate became an issue for me.

"Relax, let go, let God," I kept repeating to myself, remembering Big Sam and Sheba.

Every day it seemed I was learning or relearning lessons in this game called Army life. I was starting to think this Army thing was a bad idea.

One day, as we were training in the gas chamber, I had trouble adjusting my gas mask. Sergeant Milton came over to assist but adjusted it too tight, and I flinched with pain.

Sergeant Milton yelled in my ear. Then he pushed me inside. Once inside, I held my breath, removed my mask, and said my full name and service number. I tried putting my mask back on, but it wouldn't fit. My eyes were burning. I ran out about forty yards and collapsed. I was coughing and gasping for air.

After recovering, I found out what went wrong.

Sergeant Milton had adjusted my straps so tight that they were too small to be put back on. When I looked up, I saw the smile on Sergeant Milton's face. He gave me a wink. Now I thought he was trying to kill me.

I was still coughing and choking for air. Saliva was pouring out of my mouth, and I couldn't catch my breath. My throat was burning, and my eyes were watering.

Then there was laughter and giggling. When I looked up again, everyone was laughing and pointing at me.

Taylor from Knoxville, Tennessee, who could have been Kirk Douglas's twin brother, said, "Hey, Madden, there's a safer way of getting out of the Army."

More laughter.

I couldn't say anything because I was still trying to catch my breath and was still dizzy. I still thought Sergeant Milton was trying to kill me, so my only response to Taylor's remark was my middle finger.

At about nine-thirty that night, I slipped off campus to the nearest pay phone, which was about one hundred yards away. I called home. Nannie picked up the phone.

"Tierron, is that you?"

And before I could say yes, the whole family was on the phone. I had about eight dollars in quarters, nickels, and dimes.

When Momma got on the phone, the operator interrupted and said, "One dollar fifty cents, please."

I had my quarters, dimes, and nickels neatly stacked. I dropped six quarters in.

After talking to everyone in the house, Daddy finally got on the phone.

"How's my soldier boy?"

"I'm fine, Daddy. Can we talk in private?"

"Sure, son, give me a moment."

Then I heard, "This is man's talk."

Then I heard Nannie say, "Rev, is everything alright?"

"Liler, this is man's talk."

Then there was silence.

"Okay, son, what's wrong?" Daddy asked.

"Daddy, I think my sergeant is trying to kill me."

I explained what happened. Before I finished, the operator interrupted and said, "One dollar fifty cents, please."

"Did he draw blood?"

"No, Daddy."

"Are you injured?"

"No, Daddy."

"Are you dead?"

"What?"

"Did you die?" Daddy asked with a little more bass, just short of a yell.

"No, no, Daddy, I did not die, but—"

"Son, you're in training," Daddy yelled, sounding more like Sergeant Milton and not like Reverend Madden. "Did you learn anything from that?"

Yeah, that motherfucker tried to kill me, I thought.

"Yes, Daddy, I did," I responded.

"Well, son, God takes care of fools and babies."

"Be the baby," we both said in unison. We both laughed.

"Son, you are being trained by the best. It might help save your life. You know I was a medic running forward, reciting Psalms, tending to the wounded. I did my job. Your job is to become a soldier. Now, no more foolishness and get with the program."

"One dollar fifty cents, please."

"Are you going to finish what you started and keep up the Madden tradition? Remember you volunteered for this. Deal with it, soldier. I command you to be a man."

I done fucked around and called the wrong number. I'm talking to Sergeant Milton, I thought.

"Yes, Daddy, I am a man."

"One dollar fifty cents, please."

"I know you are, and next time call collect."

"There will not be a next time. I'll be home on the tenth of next month. Tell Nannie and Connie happy belated birthdays."

"I will, son. I love you."

"I love you, Daddy. Good night."

I stood there in the telephone booth trying to see Daddy's side of our conversation.

I am a soldier; I was born to be a soldier.

Satisfied with my thoughts, I recited the 23rd Psalm, which I'd known by heart before first grade. I slipped back on campus and into the barracks.

CHAPTER 27

BECOMING A GI

The next morning, I was still not 100%. Talking to the family, Daddy's inspirational speech, and my talk with God helped a lot. I was ready for anything.

Relax, let go, let God, I prayed as we assembled for roll call.

Taylor was still making jokes and talking shit about the gas chamber. I just went along with the bullshit. The more Taylor talked, the stronger I got.

After the roll call, the four-mile run was on. About two miles in, the soldier with the guide arm tripped over a rock in the road and twisted his ankle. The guide arm went one way, and Webster went the other way. Sergeant Milton looked at me then toward the guide arm. I ran over, picked the guide arm up, and dusted it off. I twirled the guide arm and looked at my company. I saw smiles of approval.

During the run with Sergeant Milton calling cadence, the more I fell in rhythm with his strong, deep baritone voice. For some reason, I thought Sergeant Milton was getting inspiration from me to continue my performance. I was thinking about

Momma as a majorette with her baton. I used to put on her knee-high white boots and would march, and she would give me pointers. That's how I learned how to twirl with mop handles, broomsticks, and branches.

We got back from the four-mile run, which seemed so quick. There were at least eight to ten trainees who said I should become the guide arm bearer.

Sergeant Milton didn't say anything to me, but his eyes and nod of approval said everything to me.

Webster had walked off his injury. He was about six feet four inches or six feet five inches and was perfect for a guide arm bearer. He was very inspiring, and he was very good at it. But I must say, I felt great, and so many trainees said I looked great. No one fell out of the run.

Normally, in a four-mile run, there would be at least four or five trainees who fell out. I had my day, and it felt great.

Yes, I am a soldier.

The Lord works in mysterious ways. "Thank you, my Father," I said, looking up and throwing a kiss heavenward.

Over the next few days, I started making adjustments. I needed to learn the game of becoming a soldier.

I started taking pride in my appearance. My boots started looking like Sergeant Milton's spit-shined boots.

I could disassemble and assemble my M-14 assault rifle in record time. I even disassembled and reassembled my weapon blindfolded. I won five dollars on that venture.

Webster started giving me pointers on the guide arm.

The PT test—I passed with flying colors.

I had grown up, or should I say matured.

My next assignment was Fort Rucker, Alabama, for the Aviation Repairmen's course (67A10). I remembered talking to the Army recruiter. I wanted to jump out of airplanes and shoot at people. Plus, fifty dollars a jump—twenty jumps a month—that's one thousand dollars I could send to Nannie.

Later, I found out that it was fifty dollars a month regardless of how many jumps, so the recruiter lied to me.

I was pretty good with my hands, Daddy always said. Aircraft Mechanic started sounding better than jumping out of planes as I made my final salute to boot camp.

I was now a bona fide GI (Government Issue).

CHAPTER 28

A Hero's Parade

Private Tierron LaVon Madden

"Ain't No Woman Like the One I Got" by the Four Tops was playing as the Greyhound bus left the bus station. I started thinking about my woman. I dozed off, and when I woke up, I was home.

When I stepped off the bus, Glen flew into my arms. I tried to stick my tongue so far down her throat that Glen gasped for air. One of the passengers on the bus said, "You two need to get a room."

Then I heard Nannie say, "They need to get married first."

Like always, Nannie slapped me back into reality. I was about to explode with desire, and if Nannie hadn't said anything, I would have messed up my Army-issued underwear.

After kissing and hugging everyone, Glen held onto my hands. I was really glad to see everyone, but I was really glad to be with my woman. Desire had consumed me.

Relax, let go, let God. Relax, let go, let God, I prayed.

Glen brought me back to reality. "Tee, I'll see you in a couple of days. I'm taking Mother to Bryson City. I'll be back on Monday or Tuesday, and we'll have all day to be together."

She was pulling me toward the parking lot where her mother was waiting.

"Good afternoon, Mrs. Thompson."

"Good afternoon, Tee. You look very handsome, soldier boy."

"Thank you."

"See you Monday or Tuesday at the latest," Glen said as she kissed me on the cheek.

Home was the same. At least it felt like it until I heard Nannie talking to Cookie.

"Young lady, when are you going to start ironing?"

"I already told you, tomorrow."

"You said that a day ago."

"I said tomorrow, and I have no more to say," Cookie snapped.

Now I was ready to watch Nannie get medieval and fly from the bedroom to the living room. There was silence and more silence, and I couldn't take it anymore.

"Nannie, you aren't going to let Cookie get away with that?"

With both my hands clamping my sides, I was still waiting for Nannie to bring out her weapons of mass destruction.

"Nannie!" I yelled.

"Tierron, lower your voice."

"Yes, ma'am, but—"

"Listen, baby, Nannie's getting old and—"

"You were getting old when you were beating the hell out of me!" I snapped back.

"Son, watch your mouth. Cookie, get the ironing board," Daddy commanded.

"Yes, Daddy," Cookie said in her most girlish voice, passing me with a bump and a grin.

I could tell Nannie wasn't the commanding officer in charge anymore. I could see a little defeat in her eyes. Daddy had become the commanding officer in charge.

I handed Nannie five hundred dollars from the money I had saved in case I didn't make it in the Army. I gave it to her as a peace offering, telling her how much I missed her and asked if she would teach me how to make her famous cornbread and red-eye gravy. I had a taste for some cornbread and milk.

"We are out of milk and country ham," Nannie said.

"No problem, I'll just run to Charlie's Market."

"Paul Cox has the best meats," Momma said, "and pick up a couple packs of cigarettes."

I remembered being sent to the store and buying three to six cigarettes for Momma and Cousin Betty at two cents apiece. How time flies.

I walked outside the house and smelled and felt the mountain air. It was totally different from Fort Jackson. I walked down to Cousin Betty's house. She was sitting on the porch with Big Mama, Cousin Betty's mom. I had my military fatigues on, and I was so proud of my uniform. My boots were shining like glass.

"Hey, Cousin Betty...Big Mama," I said with my best smile.

"Hi, Tierron," they both sang out like they were in a church choir.

"Tierron, you look more and more like your father," Big Mama said.

"I look a lot better than him," I said, sticking my chest out. We all laughed.

"Cousin Betty, I'm going to the store. Do you need anything?"

She smiled. "How time flies. My little boy has become a man."

"No, baby, we're fine."

I could tell she was proud of what she had helped raise. Oh, the joy she gave me knowing she approved of what I was becoming.

I went to Paul Cox first and picked up the meat and a carton of cigarettes for Momma and about four comic books. Then to Charlie's for milk and about three more comic books. I was gone for over two months. I hadn't read a comic book since I got caught reading The Amazing Spider-Man comic book during weapons cleaning, which cost me KP for a week. On top of that, I had to bury Spider-Man in a two-foot by two-foot by two-foot grave complete with prayer. I ran from Charlie's Market to home, giving Cousin Betty a treat by taking her back to memory lane.

On Sunday, I went to church in my Class A uniform. St. John Baptist Church in Fletcher, NC, looked a lot smaller. The outhouse still needed a paint job, and you still had to walk through the graveyard to relieve yourself. I always relieved myself behind the church, especially at night.

Everyone complimented me on my appearance. Deacon Thomas was there and made a special trip. He was one of my favorite deacons. I know Daddy must have invited him because he was a deacon at Brickton Baptist Church. I loved to hear Deacon Thomas pray because it was always the same, and you couldn't understand a word he was saying. I could mimic his entire prayer. I think Daddy got a kick out of it when we were alone. I could not talk about grownups. Nannie always said I needed to show some respect, so this was between Daddy and me.

Monday morning, I was up at the crack of dawn. Walking down to the bridge and sitting on its walls, oh how the memories started coming back—how we used to sing songs on the corner, how the streetlights were the spotlight and the bridge our stage. Robert Jr., Roach, Willie May and all her sisters, and I would harmonize. Sometimes people walking up and down Southside Avenue would join in. We sang "Money" by Barrett Strong and "The Great Pretender" by The Platters, with Willie May singing the lead. I especially loved "Stagger Lee" by Lloyd Price because I was the lead singer.

I know Mr. Berry Gordy would have given us a contract. The many times I played on and under this bridge! Something was different, and it was not the neighborhood, although everything seemed smaller.

I kept thinking about Nannie's dream, a traveler of many lands.

I had coffee and buttered toast with Connie, Cookie, and Anthony. Oh, how they have grown, especially Connie. I must confess I have some beautiful sisters.

After they had left for school, I got dressed in my Class A uniform. It was time for my final tour of my neighborhood. I caught the city bus in front of the Saxton Apartments. Going up Congress, I passed Mrs. Goodman's house, my fifth- and sixth-grade teacher. She threw class parties and served Kool-Aid, peanut butter and jelly sandwiches quartered, and cookies. I remember hearing the Five Satins singing "In the Still of the Night." Mrs. Goodman would make sure there was plenty of daylight between us.

Then she would play something fast, like "I Got a Woman" by Ray Charles. When this song came on, everybody was required to dance. There were no wallflowers; even Mr. Goodman danced.

I passed Barbara's house, my junior and senior prom date, another crush. Then I passed Katy's house, another crush.

At the top of Congress, Kat Miller's house was on the left; he ran the numbers game. Right across from his house was Rev. Posey's church, Tabernacle Baptist Church, where I was baptized.

We took a right on Livingston Street, down to Livingston Elementary School where I began my education. Right next to it was Mt. Olive Baptist Church, where I went to summer Bible school. Right across from the church was Sharon's house, another hottie. Taking a right on South French Broad, where Gail Sanders told me I had a sister and a brother.

Taking another right on Southside, there was the pool room where I picked up chump change.

By the time we turned to Southside, there were ten to fifteen passengers who all had questions. I answered them all, begging for more, which made me so proud to be a soldier.

I watched the rest of the neighborhood pass by until I got to Pack Square. I got off the bus and walked around to the Grover Arcade Federal Building where my old job was. Everyone greeted me and told me how good I looked. My main purpose was to see Peter, Jerry, and Mark, just to see their reaction. These white guys put me on cloud nine.

Mark asked me if I was ready to go to Vietnam. I told him that as soon as my training was complete at Fort Rucker, Alabama, I'd probably be there at the beginning of the year.

I walked back to Pack Square and passed the S&W Cafeteria where Uncle June used to work. I continued up Patton Avenue until I got to Newberry's Five and Dime. I remembered when Nannie and the ladies of St. John's were purchasing Christmas gifts but weren't allowed to use the bathrooms. Well, last year after gathering over thirty items, they had to relieve themselves. Nannie stopped at the exit, went back to the salesclerk, and demanded to talk to the manager. Talking to the manager,

Nannie said, "Young man, this requires a yes or no answer. We have over thirty items and need to use the bathrooms. We're not going to leave here until we do. I understand your store policy. If we can't use your bathrooms, you can help your clerk place all these items back on the shelf."

The answer was a quick and a loud yes. I remember telling Connie that if that was me, I would have said, "Either I shit here or leave the shit here." Connie thought that was funny.

The John Harding Shoe Store, where all the shoes were seven dollars and seventy cents, was next. I stopped by Kress's Department Store and picked up a few things.

The reality of it all was that I just wanted to show myself off. I walked down Biltmore between the Plaza movie theater and GI Outlet Store, which was the first place to give me credit and where I bought most of my clothes. Of course, I had to go into the GI Outlet to renew my acquaintance, and everyone was thrilled to see me and complimented me on how good I looked.

Once I got to the block, I dropped by the pool room, said my hellos, and then stepped into the Blue-Ribbon Café for a slaw dog. Sally was on the cash register, and I got a big hug and kiss from her. The slaw dog was delicious as always, and a free peach cobbler was a compliment from Sally. I had to stop by the YMI, and as expected, I was treated like a hero. The YMI was built by George Vanderbilt in honor of his Black employees. I just thought I was parading myself like I was a real-life hero. So, I decided to walk home.

I went down Biltmore Avenue, past the Fine Arts Theatre, and then past the Gay 90's Club. Down by the Jay Club that used to be the bowling alley, past the one-hour Martinizing Cleaners where Daddy would get his suits cleaned for Sunday, heading toward Uncle Jesse's Funeral Home. This building used to be the colored hospital where I was born. Then Uncle Jesse bought the building and turned it into a funeral home.

I was just about to go inside when Shumate, a long-time employee of Uncle Jesse and my neighbor, met me at the steps with more compliments. Then Uncle Jesse and Aunt Julia came down the steps, and you could tell they approved of their nephew.

Uncle Jesse said I was a spitting image of his baby brother C. Ray. Aunt Julia asked me if I wanted a ride, and I said no ma'am, I wanted to complete my mission of walking home.

I'd taken this route so many times, but this time as a U.S. Army soldier.

I walked down Southside past the Pepsi Bottling Company, then crossed Cox Avenue. I continued down Southside past the old bowling alley that was in the basement, where the balls were the size of cantaloupes. I used to set up bowling pins and clean up. Now it's a nightclub called the Owl's Lounge, where Connie's beau, Cornell, played the piano and organ.

Approaching Mary Ann Gilcrest's house, who was the greatest female athlete at Stephens-Lee High School, I couldn't help but recall her as a living legend.

Mary Ann scored forty-seven points in one game and was voted the most valuable player for three years. I remember her playing horseshoes; she threw nine ringers out of ten while I only managed six ringers out of ten. She shut me down.

I graduated with her younger sister, Ellen Gilcrest, who was one of the smartest in our class.

I stopped by Six Points and ordered Robert Jr.'s favorite dish, half a fried chicken dinner.

I continued my private parade down Southside until I got to Mr. Curry's Natural Herbs and Hair Product Shop. Mrs. Curry had to be one of the most beautiful women on Southside. When I walked in, she greeted me with a big smile.

"Tierron you have grown up and look so handsome," she said as she walked towards me with open arms. Of course, I met her with equal enthusiasm.

I bought a small jar of hair grease and explained my next tour in the Army, then told her how sorry I was to have missed Mr. Curry.

I then stopped by Mr. Haggins' Grocery Store. I remember before he opened up his store, he was selling fruits and vegetables out of the back of his truck. He greeted me and commented on how good I looked in the uniform. He told me he was proud of me and advised me not to be in such a hurry to go to war. He handed me a cold bottle of Coke, and I thanked him.

When I got to Southside Apartments, the city bus had dropped off a few passengers, and I knew most of them. They greeted me and gave me their blessings after we talked.

I crossed Southside to Paul Cox's store. Mr. Cox was a short, round Jewish man who always wore a white bib apron and could have been Santa's twin because of his white beard. We talked for a spell and he wished me luck. I shook his hand as I walked out the door.

Continuing my march home, I felt as though I had received a hero's welcome, even though I was the only one in the parade.

CHAPTER 29

How Do
I Love Thee

Time just seemed to fly as this was my last weekend. Monday morning, my bus was leaving for Fort Rucker, Alabama.

Since I'd been home, Glen and I had only been together a couple of times. But today was Saturday, and she told me she would be here to pick me up at about 10:30 this morning. She said she had a surprise for me.

She arrived at 11:30, knocked on the door, and Momma let her in. I was a little pissed off because 10:30 means 10:30. I had just finished reading an Archie's comic book and ran down the steps, hoping not to show my anger.

Nannie and Momma were smiling from ear to ear.

The minute I laid eyes on Glen, whatever was on my mind just vanished. She looked ravishing, and it seemed every time I saw her, she got more beautiful.

Thank you, God, for whatever I'm about to receive, I thought as our lips locked.

Nannie cleared her throat. "Alright, young man, be respectful."

Glen and I unlocked our embrace. "Yes, ma'am," we said simultaneously. We both grinned with our heads lowered, looking at each other.

"Tee, I'm sorry I'm late; it was unavoidable."

"No problem," I said, still mesmerized by her good looks. She was definitely worth the wait, I thought.

She grabbed my hand and told me to close my eyes as she pulled me towards the door. Once outside, she said, "Open your eyes."

Parked in front of our driveway was a 1964 burgundy Impala Super Sport two-door sedan.

We ran down the steps, and the next thing she said was, "You drive. This is my graduation present from Daddy June. Do you like it?"

"Baby, this car is fabulous."

I was looking at a black interior, bucket seats, hydro stick, and fender skirts, with a 283 V8 engine. This is a dream come true, I thought.

"Congratulations!" Nannie and Momma said, beaming with joy.

It seemed like as soon as I touched the key, it started up, and off we went. We picked up some fried chicken dinners, 7-Ups, cherries, and two Little Men, then headed to Tunnel Road.

We had the room for the rest of the weekend.

"Tee, it seems like you just got here, and now you're leaving me again."

"Yes, my princess, but now I can see the light at the end of the tunnel. I can see our future now. Baby, with you by my side, the world is ours."

I knew it was ours as we slid into each other's arms and made love until the pleasure consumed us and we drifted off into a deep coma.

That night, after we consumed a bottle of wine and I smoked half a pack of cigarettes, I got the courage to confess.

"Baby, I have something to say. I joined the Army. I wasn't drafted. I'm sorry for lying to you, but you've got your shit together. You are a nurse, have a nice ride, and your family truly loves you. I have nothing to offer you. The only thing I got is the Army until something better comes along."

"Well, my prince, I am your 'better comes along.' I really, truly love you. Do you love me? That's the sixty-four thousand dollar question," Glen said.

Then she continued, "Do you remember? My favorite poet is Elizabeth Barrett Browning? 'How do I love thee? Let me count the ways.'"

When she finished, I applauded but did not understand what she was reciting.

"Baby, those words are beautiful, but I don't understand after the first two sentences. They all sound the same. She sounds like a rich black woman."

"No, she was white, and her father was a rich slave owner."

"So let me get this straight," I said. "She owned slaves, and you like her because she can put some words together that sound pretty?" I asked with a little bitterness in my voice.

"She was an invalid and couldn't take care of herself. Her father owned a sugar plantation in Jamaica," she said.

"So, I guess she treated her slaves like human beings," I said sarcastically.

"No, baby, she didn't see any slaves. She and her siblings lived in London, England, and she was an abolitionist who cared about people. It was said her father's female slave had a baby with a white man, so she killed her baby because she didn't want the child to be born a slave, and the slave master ended up killing her," she explained.

"Okay, recite it again. This time, I'm going to listen to every word."

I hated literature. I couldn't understand why people liked poetry. I knew the 23rd Psalm and The Lord's Prayer by heart. I guess that's the only literature I know.

When Glen began this time, I watched and listened to every word she said. She blew my mind and was breathtaking. After she finished, she told me a short story about Elizabeth Barrett, who was an established poet and met Robert Browning, a poet in his own right, through correspondence. He began visiting her in London and exchanging poems. Elizabeth was always in bed during his visits, and during those visits, he fell in love with her. She resisted at first and finally fell in love with him. Her father never expected their love affair.

"Robert Browning encouraged her to walk, and with his help, she started walking on her own. They secretly got married in London with the help of her personal maid. They eloped to Italy, leaving a note to her father about what she had done. Her father never spoke to her again."

"Baby, you see that poem to her husband… anyone can recite that poem. A woman can speak it, a man can speak it. It's all spiritual."

Then she recited another poem. "Thou must love me, love me for love's sake. Don't love me for my smile or my hair or taking pity on me because if I should lose my smile or my hair would you still love me?" Glen said.

"Well, looks really count in a relationship. So, you are telling me if half my nose is missing you would still love me?" I asked.

She rolled on top of me.

"My prince, I'd love you with no nose. I will love you for eternity."

Then she kissed me, and for a minute, I started to believe her.

"So, you are telling me if my nose was missing you would love me? Baby, your nose is the best part of you."

"Oh, that's the first thing you noticed about me?"

I pulled her breasts to my face and slapped them against my cheeks, laughing each time.

"God loves me, and I love Glenna Aravia Thompson."

"You forgot something: My name is Glenna Aravia Thompson Madden."

For the rest of the weekend, we really got to know each other.

Monday morning, Glen took me to the bus station.

CHAPTER 30

YIELD NOT TO TEMPTATION

When I arrived in Fort Rucker, Alabama, it was raining cats and dogs. I was a soldier, and I could tell the difference between boot camp and AIT. We were treated like soldiers, not like trainees.

After processing, my training started in two weeks. I always wanted to know how a plane flies. Physics was a branch of science that really appealed to me. I remember a preacher man was talking to Daddy after Daddy told him I was going to be an aircraft mechanic.

"If God wanted man to fly, he would've given him wings," he'd said.

I guess that's why I love Superman—because he can fly. Watching Superman on television, bullets would bounce off of him, and when the bad guys ran out of bullets, they would throw their guns at Superman, and he would duck. That's why I like comic books; they're a lot better than the TV version. I had four Superman and Superboy comic books I hadn't read yet, and I saved my readings until I had nothing better to do.

Fort Rucker and Fort Jackson had one thing in common: GIs loved to gamble.

My pool games, ping pong, bowling, and card games kept money in my pocket. The enlisted club was for E-1s to E-4s. This is where we got more acquainted, and the beer kind of loosened our lips.

Hamp was from LA (Lower Alabama). Russell was from Georgia. Our friendship cost them five dollars apiece playing cut-throat. Of course, I introduced Cutthroat to them. They had a good game, but mine was better. So, I bought the beers, and we consumed about three each.

We walked back to the barracks and got to know each other. Both were draftees. I carried the company Guide Arm and became popular around the barracks. Taylor and a couple more were with me at boot camp, and of course, Taylor and I started talking about the gas chamber. We both got a kick out of my experience with Sergeant Milton.

After weeks of training, we finally got a break: a Friday night dance at the rec center. Hamp had the only car out of the three of us. He had family and friends in Ozark, Enterprise, and Dothan, Alabama. The plan was if it got too boring, we would go to the Elks Club in Dothan.

Wherever that was, I thought.

Russell had KP tomorrow, so his night was short. Hamp and I split the cost of a pint of corn whiskey, which cost me three dollars. There was only punch served at the rec center. There were two to three busloads of black girls from Ozark, Enterprise, and Daleville, Alabama. Hamp introduced his cousin Alma and her friends Phyllis and Lynette. Phyllis was short, petite, about five foot five, and almost an inch shorter than Hamp. You could tell they had some history. Lynette had to be over six feet tall with her short heels on. No doubt the tallest girl in the building.

Hamp and I drank about half a bottle of moonshine, and we were feeling no pain. I must have danced with seven or eight different girls, and they were all fast songs. I asked Lynette twice to dance, and she politely said no.

"Let's dance, Tee," Alma said.

I grabbed her hand, and we hit the floor to the beat of Martha and the Vandellas singing "Dancing in the Street" and then Mary Wells' "You Beat Me to the Punch."

When we got back to the table, everyone was laughing and talking about who was the better singer, Diana Ross or Aretha Franklin. My money was on the Queen of Soul, Aretha.

Lynette was now talking and laughing at everything. Alma asked Lynette how she felt and looked at Hamp suspiciously. Lynette held up a cup, singing along with the music.

"Hamp!" she screamed, "What did you give her? She can't drink alcohol."

"Hey, cuz, cool out. I just gave her a couple of shots. Look at her, she's fine and having a good time."

"I am having a good time," Lynette said while taking off her oversized sweater and removing her glasses.

Lynette was stunning.

We danced to "Fingertips" by Little Stevie Wonder. Then James Brown's "Try Me" came on. I politely grabbed her hand and headed back to the table.

She pulled me back and asked, "May we?" smiling and showing dimples for the first time.

Oh Lord, lead me not into temptation, I prayed.

It was like we were synchronizing. Two steps, and I fit her like the last piece of the puzzle. Her long arms were draped around my neck, and with my hands resting on her waist, we were close. You couldn't see daylight between us, but our clothes were barely touching each other. We didn't miss a step. Fred Astaire and Ginger Rogers couldn't have done any better.

When the song was over, we did the Cha Cha to the beat of "Hello Stranger" by Barbara Lewis, and people were checking us out like we had choreographed each movement. When we finally got back to the table, we got light applause.

"You sure you two haven't met before?" Phyllis asked, all cuddled up with Hamp.

"Lynette, are you okay?" Alma asked, touching her arm and handing her sweater and glasses to her.

"Hey, sister lady. I'm fine," Lynette said, giving me a light pinch.

"Just don't do too much. Take it easy," Alma said.

"It's been a long time since I've had this much fun. I'll be fine. Who's got a car?" she asked, looking at me.

I just shook my head. Hamp raised a finger.

"Let's go to Dothan. The Elks Club," she said, nodding her head up and down and looking at me.

I looked at Hamp, and we were all smiles. We dropped Alma off at her house.

A couple of hours later, we walked into the Elks Club. Of course, the moonshine was gone, so me and Hamp ordered two beers. Phyllis had two Sloe Gin Fizzes, and I ordered Lynette a Shirley Temple. Alma made me promise no more alcohol for Lynette.

"Please Mr. Postman" by the Marvelettes was playing. I taught her how to swing dance, and she told me a little about herself. She had to leave Baltimore because her husband of four months had put her in the hospital for two days. Her father, a preacher man, had put her husband in the hospital for more than a week. Lynette said her husband was charged with assault. Her husband never ratted on her father because they told him he was a dead man if he talked. She moved down here about six months ago.

We left the club around 2:30 in the morning.

I fell asleep and woke up with Lynette in my arms. Then I thought, what would C. Ray do, given the same circumstance? I already knew the answer.

I was thinking that she really had the hots for me, and C. Ray would be proud. The breathing got louder, and she was shaking. I opened my eyes, and she was foaming at the mouth. I could only see the whites in her eyes.

"Oh shit! Hamp! What the fuck?" I screamed.

Phyllis woke up.

"Oh my God, she's having a fit," she screamed.

Hamp was yelling about demons and shit. I was scared as hell and pinned in my seat. Her left leg was over my right leg, and I couldn't move.

Hamp finally stopped the car and opened my door. I fell out. Phyllis straightened Lynette out and laid her on her side while Hamp wiped her mouth with his handkerchief.

In about a minute or so, Lynette sat up as if nothing had happened. It was blacker than a cypress swamp outside, but the Buick Electra 225 was lit up inside. I was still shaking and praying to God to forgive me for almost cheating on Glen.

"It happened, didn't it?" a surprisingly soft voice asked.

"Yes, it did, sister girl," Phyllis said.

"I'm so sorry," Lynette cried out. "Tee, where is Tee?"

Looking around, I was about to get in the front seat. I cursed myself for being an asshole, so I took my time going around the car.

"I'm here. How are you?" I asked in my most humble voice.

"I'm fine, I just don't remember anything."

Well, I'm glad she didn't remember because she almost scared the shit out of me. I know she scared the piss out of me.

Hamp was still talking about demons and shit.

This time I wasn't C. Ray. I smiled to myself.

Hamp started talking about exorcists, and Phyllis and I said together, "Shut up, Hamp!"

I felt guilty for last night's events. Was I my father's son? Was I really like him? I know I like women. I like being around them. I love to smell them—not the man-made scent or the sweet-smelling oils, but the natural fragrance that God has placed in His natural recipe to make woman.

Why was I so attracted to Lynette?

When we danced, we fit like a glove. Was it her flawless skin or those long legs that seemed to wrap around me when we slow danced? King David was married to many women and had a harem of young women but was drawn to Bathsheba.

YIELD NOT TO TEMPTATION

She was a married woman, and he made their child heir to his throne.

Lynette had physical beauty, and that was undeniable, but Glen was my lady, and she was all I needed. Oh, my Lord, was that a test last night? Please don't test me again; I am not that strong. This guilt that I feel... is this a God thing or a Satan thing? I don't think King David had a problem with his extramarital affairs like I am having at this moment.

I need to call Glen.

Hamp had to return his uncle's Electra 225 to Mobile, Alabama, but while we had it, we took the ladies out a couple of times. I told Lynette about Glen and how I loved and missed her. She said that she and her husband were on speaking terms. He had stopped drinking, but getting back together was a NO with both letters capitalized

Lynette said she had an epileptic seizure that night and that was the second time. The first was before the last beating. She was on medication but forgot to take her last two doses.

"What I had is what the old folks call a grand mal seizure, which is one of the worst ones. I'm so embarrassed, and I'm so sorry I put you through that, but you took it like a man," Lynette said.

Not looking her in the eyes, I responded, "No problem, I said.

Then we departed.

CHAPTER 31

THE SURPRISE VISIT

I was doing fine in school and maintaining an eighty-six average, which is about a B. I would have been doing better if I could concentrate. Most days, I would be daydreaming, and when the instructor called on me with questions or to read a certain paragraph, I was lost.

Tex, from Dallas, Texas, teased me every time he caught me daydreaming. "Jody's got your girl and gone," he would say. He was about my height but roughly twenty pounds heavier, with cue ball eyes that I half-expected to pop out.

Bernstein was the smartest one in class. He had been drafted out of college for not maintaining his grades. Then there was Givens, whose red hair perfectly matched his equally red nose. He had no eyebrows. Despite our differences, we had more in common than most soldiers in the barracks. We played a multitude of card games together.

Bernstein asked me to be his pinochle partner at a penny a point, a dollar a set, and two dollars a game, playing against Tex and Givens. He handed me two new decks of pinochle cards. I think he was testing me to see if I could play.

"Is Tex your name?" Bernstein asked.

"Yes, I was named after Tex Ritter."

"Who the hell is Tex Ritter?"

"One of the pioneers of country music."

"Who is your favorite cowboy?" I asked Tex, still shuffling the cards.

"Don Meredith is the greatest Cowboy," Tex said.

"Well, if you know so much, then what was his horse's name?" I asked jokingly.

"How in the world would I know his horse's name?" Tex shouted.

"Then he is not a real cowboy if he doesn't know the horse's name," I shouted back, almost bursting into laughter.

"Madden, Tex is talking about the Dallas Cowboys football team. Don Meredith is the quarterback," Givens said.

"I know who Don Meredith is. I'm talking about real cowboys like Roy Rogers. His horse is named Trigger," I said, showing all my pearly whites.

"So, you know about cowboys, do you?" asked Tex.

"Well, Roy Rogers happens to be my favorite cowboy and yes, his horse is named Trigger. Who is your favorite cowboy?" Tex continued.

"Hopalong Cassidy, better known as Hoppy, and his white horse is Topper."

Bernstein's mouth almost dropped to the floor. "I thought you were from South Carolina somewhere," he said.

"No, I'm from North Carolina. So, if Roy Rogers is your favorite cowboy, what is his wife's horse's name?"

"I... I... ah... ah," Tex mumbled.

"Dale Evans is her name," I replied.

Bernstein and Givens started laughing.

"I know his freaking wife's name," Tex responded. He gathered his cards and suited them up.

"Well, if you know his wife's name," I said, "then you should know what her horse's name is."

There was more laughter.

"Madden, go to hell," Tex said. Givens doubled over in laughter.

"Okay, Tex, your bid," I said.

"I pass," Tex said.

"I save," Bernstein said.

"Well, New York, I'm going to save your ass. 51," Givens said.

"59," I said, looking at Bernstein lighting a cigar.

"Pass," he said, blowing out the match without looking up.

I looked up, surprised.

Givens was smiling at me. "Well, I'm not saving your ass, Madden. Pass," he said.

"New York, why did you pass on me? I do not have a marriage but I have a thousand aces," I said.

"My bad, I just got two marriages, both in hearts, and that's all the hearts I got," Bernstein said, laying down his hand. "My bad, partner, I should have saved you," he apologized again.

About halfway into the game, we were about twenty-two points up when Bernstein bid 150. My eyes went up. I had aces and a double pinochle. That hand ended the game.

Bernstein shouted out, "You owe us nine dollars and forty-seven cents."

"By the way, Madden, what's the horse's name?" Tex asked.

"Buttermilk," I said.

"Whoa! I knew that, man. You're right, it's Buttermilk. I can't believe I didn't get that. So, you are a cowboy," Tex said.

"No, but I watch a lot of cowboy flicks on TV," I said.

We both smiled. Bernstein handed me my split. I told him he could have the difference.

"Thanks for the tip."

"Later, gents," I said while walking out.

When I got back to the barracks, I received a telegram stating that my wife would be at the Fort Rucker bus station at 9:30 p.m.

Whoa! Shit, what the fuck, grabbing my head.

My mind was running a hundred miles per hour. Since I've been in Alabama, I've heard nothing but bad things happening to Black people. I knew I had to get to the station on time so she wouldn't be alone for a single second.

Think, Tee, think.

Bus station…where is the bus station?

No bus station, only a bus stop outside the main gate. I can run to the main gate in twenty minutes.

I had ninety-six dollars and some change, including my winnings.

I was ready for my woman. I repeated the 23rd Psalm over and over again. Take care of my woman, Father, please, I prayed.

About nine o'clock, I got a call from Glen, masquerading as my wife. I ran to the orderly room and picked up the phone.

Breathe, Tee, breathe.

"Glen?" I questioned.

"Hey, my prince. Surprise!"

"Glen, where are you?"

"I've checked in at the guesthouse."

Before the words had left her mouth, I was out the door. It took me less than fifteen minutes to get to the guest house. Glen was standing at the soda machine with two Cokes in her hand. Now I'm thinking, who is this beautiful mature woman that looks like Glen?

We got to the room. I must have stuck my tongue halfway down her throat. After we had calmed down, I said, "Okay, baby, first of all, you look incredible."

I just couldn't get over how good she looked. Glen had about five chicken sandwiches wrapped in foil in her big pocketbook. We finished eating and got comfortable.

"Now baby, talk to me. What's going on?" I asked.

"I'm pregnant, and I don't know what to do," she said abruptly, searching my eyes for an answer.

"Okay," I said. "What is the problem?"

"Do you love me?"

"Yes," I said after a long pause.

"Will you marry me?"

"Yes," I said, and we both fell into bed and went into a deep sleep.

I woke up at about seven in the morning. I still had my clothes on, and as soon as I walked into the bathroom, Glen walked in with two cups of coffee and a couple of Danish rolls.

"They think you're an officer and I'm your wife," she said.

Oh great. Having been in the Army for only a few months, I'm going to jail for impersonating an officer.

"Okay, baby, how much money do you have?" I asked.

"About one hundred fifty dollars."

"Let's party!" I shouted.

Everything was closed for business on the weekend, so I showed her around the camp. I called Hamp and Russell, and told them to meet us at the EM Club tonight, my treat. Glen had packed two suitcases of clothes, not including that big pocketbook she carried. I went back to the barracks to get ready for tonight. I walked back into the guesthouse at 8:00, and when I opened our room, Glen was more stunning than before.

I used Glenna's eyebrow pencil to enhance my mustache. We got to the club at 8:30, and Hamp, Russell, Phyllis, and Lynnette were seated at a table. Two empty chairs were between Hamp and Lynnette.

I'm fucked, I thought.

"Hey, everybody," I said, sitting next to Lynnette. When everyone got acquainted, Glen asked the ladies to accompany her to the powder room. After they had left, Hamp and Russell burst out laughing.

"Okay, you guys, you got me, but don't roll on me tonight. I can show you what a crazy guy can do," I said in my most commanding voice.

"Hey, man, we're cool. If you could have seen the look on your face when you first came in and saw us. Man, I'd give you twenty dollars right now if you can give me that look again," Hamp said.

"I got twenty dollars more for that same replay," Russell added, and they both couldn't stop laughing when the women got back.

"What's so funny?" Phyllis asked.

"It's time to order!" I shouted.

After everyone had ordered, except me and Glen, I asked, "Glen, what would you like?"

"Something delicious!"

"She'll have a Shirley Temple with extra cherries and a Screwdriver with cherries for me," I ordered.

"I Love You 1000 Times" by The Platters came on, and Glen and I reached for each other. When we got up, it seemed like everyone in the club focused on Glen. We finished dancing, I held her close, and said, "I hope you're not disappointed in your drink because there is nothing more delicious than you."

"So, you really did miss me," she said. My smile answered her question.

Hamp and Phyllis were still dancing to "Night Train" by James Brown. When we got to the table, our drinks were there along with Russell and Lynette.

"You two look good together," Russell said.

"Yes, they do. You two look like brother and sister—older sister," Lynette said.

Oh, shit.

"Whoa, how old are you, Lynette?" Glen asked.

"She's twenty-six," I said, drinking my drink.

"Well, one day I hope I make it to twenty-six," Glen said.

Lynette corrected her, "Twenty-four, I just turned twenty-four."

"That's nice," Glen said.

The rest of the night went fast. I covered all the drinks. It was about twenty-five dollars. We left before closing, with two fish sandwiches and fries.

"The Shirley Temple was good, but tomorrow I want a Screwdriver with cherries," Glen said, walking back to the guest house.

"I don't think you can handle a man's drink," I said.

"I tasted both of your drinks. I can handle it if you can."

We talked, made love, talked some more, and made love again. The next thing I knew, it was morning and Glen was gone. As soon as I got up, Glen walked in with two cups of coffee.

"Good morning, my man."

"Good morning, my woman."

"What's on the agenda today?"

"Well, there's not much we can do on Sunday. I need to talk to my First Sergeant. He'll be at the recreational center playing 9-ball with the Sergeant Major. They always play on Sunday around noon for a little wager."

After breakfast, we strolled over to the rec center. I spoke to the First Sergeant, and he gave me the information I needed. Vietnam was the answer. Graduation was less than a month away. Advanced training started directly after graduation. If I put in for Vietnam, he'd make sure I'd be there before Christmas with a guaranteed leave.

Tex, Givens, Bernstein, and a cute blonde girl with two long braids and a cowboy hat identical to Tex's were playing cards.

"Afternoon, everyone," I said. "Glen, these are my card partners: Tex, Givens, Bernstein…" I paused, holding my hand out, waiting for someone to introduce the blonde.

"I'm Geraldine," she said, shaking my hand.

"We were playing spades. I hate spades," Givens said, pulling out two bucks and handing them to Tex.

"Oh, stop being a sore loser," Geraldine said, getting up from the table. "Come on, Babe, we've got to pick up the meat. Daddy wants it on the grill before 1:30. Babe, you know I don't want to hear Daddy cussing you out for being late."

"Okay, okay, Geraldine," Tex said, putting on his boots.

"I told you those boots were too small," Geraldine said. "Okay, Babe…Ms. Glen, nice meeting you," she added while pulling him away.

Glen and I both sat down at the table.

"I must be blind or something; I can't see what you see in Madden," Bernstein said, smiling at Glen. "Or maybe she is blind," and they both laughed.

"Let's play some cards," I said.

"I don't want to play spades," Givens said.

"How about pinochle?" I asked, and they both started laughing and stared at Glen.

"She knows how to play pinochle?" Bernstein asked.

"Yes, she does," Glen replied, bringing out pinochle cards.

"You know we don't play pinochle for fun," Givens said.

"No problem. The game is to 300," I said, shuffling the cards. "I'll shuffle the cards, and Glen can deal."

"Glen, what are you? I mean, are you a Latina?" Bernstein mumbled.

"Do you mean, what is my ethnicity?" Glen said, now looking up from her cards.

Glen's remark seemed to stun Bernstein.

"As far as I know, there are no Latinos in my family. I'm Black, and I am a Tar Heel."

"What is a Tar Heel?" Bernstein asked.

"Jesus Christ, Bernstein, she's from North Carolina, a Tar Heel. Didn't they teach you that in college? Shit, man, I knew that before I got my GED," Givens said.

Glen put the deck down on the table and placed both hands over her mouth to stifle her laughter. Naturally, I bellowed out in laughter too.

Then Glen dealt the cards. Bernstein bid 50, I bid 51, Givens bid 52, Glen bid 58, Bernstein bid 60, I bid 65, Givens passed, Glen passed, Bernstein passed. I laid down a run in hearts and aces. Glen had 60 Queens; we melded 85 points. The game lasted less than an hour. We won 300 to 245.

"You guys owe me a couple of beers," I said.

"Good game, Glen," Bernstein said.

Glen responded, "My prince taught me well."

"Nice meeting you, Glen, and have a safe trip back home," Givens said.

Glen's bus was leaving tomorrow for Canton, North Carolina, at 0900 hours. I couldn't see her off because I had duty. I promised her I'd be home before Christmas.

CHAPTER 32

I DO

Before graduation, I made sure my military attire was perfect. I carried the company guide arm like it was my third arm. I got compliments from the battalion commander. I talked to the chaplain almost every day and helped clean up the chapel after services. Three days after graduation, I had my walking papers. I'd be home before Christmas.

I called Glen using the chaplain's phone. She had told her parents that we got married at Fort Rucker.

Her mother asked her, "Where is your wedding ring?" She said I was bringing the ring with me.

I told Glen I bought ten boxes of Cracker Jacks and couldn't find a ring. She didn't think that was funny. I must confess, the thought did cross my mind, but I eventually got a real wedding ring.

Daddy married us at 10 Congress Street. I could tell Nannie, Momma, and the rest of the family were happy for us. I felt a little guilty for Glen. I had come into Glen's life and interrupted her parents' dream of her becoming a professional woman. I think Glen felt the same way Momma did just before she had me.

Nannie insisted we stay the night in their bedroom. After the house was cleared of family and friends, Momma and Glen went out for a little shopping. Nannie sat me down to talk about my responsibilities as a husband and a father. She began by telling me that my wife comes before everything except God. She started quoting the Bible and had me read Proverbs 18:22, which says, "Whosoever finds a wife finds a good thing and obtains favor from the Lord." She had me repeat this about five times.

"Nannie," I said, "I love Glen. We will be fine," kissing her on the cheek.

"Nannie, where are my pictures of my classmates?" I asked.

"You don't need them. You are married," she said in a stronger voice.

"Yes, but they are my pictures," I pleaded.

"What do you need them for?" she demanded.

I could tell this was getting too serious, so to break the ice, I said, "Well, in case our marriage doesn't work out, I can go back to my ladies," I said jokingly.

She slapped my cheek and said, "Tierron, you don't need those tempting Jezebels. You are married and have made a vow and oath to God."

"Nannie, I was just kidding around," I cried.

"There is no kidding around when it comes to the glory of God."

At that moment, I knew I'd never see those pictures again.

That night, Glen and I were lying in each other's arms.

"Glen, how do you feel being a married woman?" I asked.

"I feel no different than yesterday."

"I loved you yesterday as much as I love you tonight," she said, kissing me on the forehead.

I just couldn't believe Nannie had gotten rid of my pictures. How dare she!

I started kissing Glen, and desire and rage took over me. The bed was making noise, and Glen reminded me that Daddy and Nannie were in the next room. Glen was telling me to quiet down. I just made the bed cry out more. Even after we finished, I made sure the bed was still moving and making noise.

I can't believe Nannie threw away my pictures, I thought as I was still bouncing on the bed.

The next morning, Nannie couldn't look me in the eye, and that felt pretty good. Daddy patted me on the back for my performance.

After we ate breakfast, Daddy had to give his sermon on the dos and don'ts of marriage. Daddy was seated in front of us on the couch, talking to the ceiling. I knew this was going to be a long talk, so I whispered to Glen to give Daddy a little peep. Her dress was just above her knees.

"No," she whispered back.

Daddy was still preaching to the ceiling.

"Daddy could use a little thrill," I persisted.

"No, Tee," Glen almost screamed as I was tickling her sides.

Daddy finished and told us how proud he was of me.

"Daddy, didn't you say something about obeying your husband?"

"Yes, your wife should honor and obey her husband," Daddy said.

"Well, Glen is going to hell because she disobeyed me."

"What didn't she do?"

"Glen, tell my father why you disobeyed his son."

I knew she wasn't going to say anything.

At that moment, Glen said, "Rev. Madden, this is a girl thing," now looking at Nannie and Momma. "Ladies, can we talk?" she asked, moving towards them.

"Whoa, whoa," I said, stepping in front of Glen. "I was just funning around, baby."

"Behave yourself," Daddy said.

Later that day, on the way to Canton to visit Glen's family, I asked her if she was going to tell Nannie about my little prank.

"Oh, wouldn't you like to know," Glen said. "But I do know one thing about my husband—you are scared of your grandmother," she said, bursting out in laughter.

When we got to my in-laws' house, we noticed something on the trunk of the car. "Just Married" was sprayed on the trunk, and balloons were attached to the rear bumper.

Busted again, we thought.

Arthur Glendon and Elizabeth Thompson
"Papaw and Muv"

It took me the rest of the day to clean the car. I also got to know Glen's father, Papaw, a little better. My father-in-law took me up the hill to some of his watering holes. We drank corn liquor and sipped beer. Coming home, we sang, "She'll Be Coming Around the Mountain When She Comes," and of course, the ladies were mad at Papaw for getting his young son-in-law drunk.

I disagreed, stating I was high and madly in love with his daughter. Papaw had told me he had a steel plate in his head from the war and drinking eased some of the pains. He told me not to be a hero, just do my job and come home to his daughter and grandchild.

Mary Conley Forney
"Granny"

We spent the last days at Granny's house. We picked up a six-pack of Dr. Pepper and Sara Lee's pound cake with icing. The cake would be our wedding cake to be cut on my departure night. Glen's eyes were swollen from weeping. The closer I got to my departure, the more she wept.

Our last night was our honeymoon. We had Granny's tuna fish sandwiches surrounded by large stuffed olives and cold Dr. Peppers. I frosted the cake using chocolate, strawberry, and white icing with three birthday candles. Each one represented me, Glen, and the baby. I did not want to know the gender. If we have a boy, he would be a junior, and if it's a girl, her name would be Tammi, spelled with an "i."

I love the song "Tammy," so I named her after Debbie Reynolds' number one hit. Elizabeth would be her middle name after Glen's mother.

I put a fresh log in the fireplace and slipped under the covers nude, waiting for my bride to enter the bedroom. It took her about thirty minutes before she entered. I had drunk two bottles of Dr. Pepper and eaten six quarters of finger sandwiches.

When she finally entered the room, she was wearing a white see-through negligée with white fur, not showing her motherhood. She was absolutely stunning—all the words that describe the most beautiful woman that God has ever made.

After lighting the three candles and putting them on a stack of 45 records, the only light in the room was from the fireplace, three candles, and a small lamp on the nightstand. I pulled back the covers, and she slid right in. We had that negligée off so quick, it had to be magic—now you see it, now you don't.

I explored every inch of her body with my tongue. I was smelling my woman the way God had made her. Now I'm thinking, I must be a damn fool, leaving my woman to go off and fight a war. I can still hear Tex saying, "Jody's got your girl and gone."

Glen's body was screaming for my entrée. My tongue was coming up to her navel, but I smelled something that was not Glen.

Glen screamed.

The little lamp with Glen's see-through negligée was up in flames, and we were extinguishing the flames with Dr. Peppers. Then Granny was knocking on the door, shouting she smelled something burning.

"We had a small mishap, but it's under control, Momma," Glen said.

"Tee, are you alright?" Granny asked.

"Yes, ma'am, everything is under control," I confirmed.

The lampshade and see-through negligée were unrecognizable.

After finishing the sandwiches with the remaining Dr. Peppers, we cut the cake and exchanged "I love yous," then we both blew out the candles.

We cuddled in bed while singing along with "Ruby and the Romantics" – "Our Day Will Come," and we'll have everything. Then Glen said, "The baby just kicked."

She grabbed my hand and placed it on her swollen stomach. I felt the baby kick, and for the first time, I felt like a father.

"Oh, my God, look what I have made," I said, smiling from ear to ear.

"You did not do this alone," Glen snickered. "My prince, you're going to have a daughter."

"A daughter? Are you sure?" I asked. "But it kicks like a boy."

"No, my love, it's a girl," she said, rubbing her stomach. "Tammi Elizabeth Madden," and she responded with a couple of kicks.

We listened to "With a Child's Heart" by Stevie Wonder. Then Glen recited "If—" by Rudyard Kipling. Her recital became a song of passion.

I, in turn, started questioning the reason for my departure.

Why am I leaving my lovely wife to fight someone in their own country?

Why am I so willing to kill someone?

Oh, my Heavenly Father, help me understand my current mission, I prayed.

I focused back on my wife's recital.

"If you can fill the unforgiving minute with sixty seconds' worth of distance run, yours is the Earth and everything that's in it, and—which is more—you'll be a Man, my son," Glen concluded.

I thought of the 91st Psalm.

Then I kissed her, and the song "For Once in My Life" by Stevie Wonder was playing.

I had everything I could ever need right here in this room, and I realized I have "THE GIFT".

I knew, at that moment, I was coming back to be with my new family.

* 9 7 8 1 9 5 0 6 8 1 7 0 9 *